HOW TO
RESEARCH
& WRITE A
SUCCESSFUL
PhD

PEARSON

At Pearson, we take learning personally. Our courses and resources are available as books, online and via multi-lingual packages, helping people learn whatever, wherever and however they choose.

We work with leading authors to develop the strongest learning experiences, bringing cutting-edge thinking and best learning practice to a global market. We craft our print and digital resources to do more to help learners not only understand their content, but to see it in action and apply what they learn, whether studying or at work.

Pearson is the world's leading learning company. Our portfolio includes Penguin, Dorling Kindersley, the Financial Times and our educational business, Pearson International. We are also a leading provider of electronic learning programmes and of test development, processing and scoring services to educational institutions, corporations and professional bodies around the world.

Every day our work helps learning flourish, and wherever learning flourishes, so do people.

To learn more please visit us at: www.pearson.com/uk

HOW TO
RESEARCH
& WRITE A
SUCCESSFUL
PhD

KATHLEEN McMILLAN &
JONATHAN WEYERS

PEARSON

Harlow, England • London • New York • Boston • San Francisco • Toronto • Sydney
Auckland • Singapore • Hong Kong • Tokyo • Seoul • Taipei • New Delhi
Cape Town • São Paulo • Mexico City • Madrid • Amsterdam • Munich • Paris • Milan

Pearson Education Limited
Edinburgh Gate
Harlow CM20 2JE
United Kingdom
Tel: +44 (0)1279 623623
Web: www.pearson.com/uk

First published 2013 (print and electronic)

ISBN: 978-0-273-77391-7 (print)
         978-0-273-77406-8 (eText)

British Library Cataloguing-in-Publication Data
A catalogue record for the print edition is available from the British Library

Library of Congress Cataloging-in-Publication Data
A catalog record for the print edition is available from the Library of Congress

10 9 8 7 6 5 4 3 2 1
17 16 15 14 13

Print edition typeset in 9.5/13pt Helvetica Neue Pro Roman by 3
Print edition printed in Malaysia (CTP-PPSB)

SMARTER STUDY SKILLS

Instant answers to your most pressing university skills problems and queries

Are there any secrets to successful study?

The simple answer is 'yes' – there are some essential skills, tips and techniques that can help you to improve your performance and success in all areas of your university studies.

These handy, easy-to-use guides to the most common areas where most students need help, provide accessible, straightforward practical tips and instant solutions that provide you with the tools and techniques that will enable you to improve your performance and get better results – and better grades!

Each book in the series allows you to assess and address a particular set of skills and strategies, in crucial areas of your studies. Each book then delivers practical, no-nonsense tips, techniques and strategies that will enable you to significantly improve your abilities and performance in time to make a difference.

The books in the series are:

- *How to Write Essays & Assignments*
- *How to Write Dissertations & Project Reports*
- *How to Argue*
- *How to Improve your Maths Skills*
- *How to Use Statistics*
- *How to Succeed in Exams & Assessments*
- *How to Cite, Reference & Avoid Plagiarism at University*
- *How to Improve Your Critical Thinking & Reflective Skills*
- *How to Improve Your Memory for Study*

For a complete handbook covering all of these study skills and more:

- *The Study Skills Book*

Get smart, get a head start!

CONTENTS

RESEARCH METHODS

WRITING UP YOUR RESEARCH

EXAMINATION AND BEYOND

ABOUT THE AUTHORS

Dr Kathleen McMillan was formerly Academic Skills Advisor and Senior Lecturer, University of Dundee.

Dr Jonathan Weyers was formerly Director of Quality Assurance, University of Dundee.

Both are now freelance authors specialising in books on skills development in Higher Education.

This book represents a synthesis based on over 60 years of combined administrative, teaching and advisory experience, much of it devoted to postgraduate level. We have supervised and supported numerous PhD students, conducted postgraduate induction events and led skills workshops covering such diverse topics as thesis writing and personal development planning. Our backgrounds in the Arts and Humanities and Life Sciences respectively mean that our support has covered a wide range of subjects – from biology to orthopaedic surgery; information and communication technology to law, as well as English as a foreign language.

Above all, we have spoken to countless students, both individually and in focus groups, and have consulted with fellow academics about research skills that underpin a wide range of disciplines. As well as gaining PhD qualifications ourselves, we have also observed at close quarters our own children taking on postgraduate study and training.

Our former responsibilities involved drawing up regulations for PhD study, responding to research student feedback and a range of postgraduate committee work. We have carried out a number of relevant projects, most notably the writing and editing of an extensive Website providing guidance for postgraduates studying at the University of Dundee. Our collaborative writing has produced eight books on diverse aspects of learning and writing at university level. Most of these have appeared in several editions and they have been translated into a total of seven other languages.

In short, we have read widely, thought deeply about relevant issues and tested many ideas related to the postgraduate research experience. This book is a distillation of all the best tips and techniques we've come across or have developed ourselves.

PREFACE

We're delighted that you've chosen *How to Research and Write a Successful PhD* and we'd like to think it's because this book promises insight into the postgraduate experience and gives you plenty of useful tips to help you take on the challenge of a research degree.

We recognise that adjusting to this level of study is not always easy. There are challenges related to the necessary depth and originality of research work, but also to organising one's activities over three or more years to culminate in what is possibly the longest and most complex piece of writing you will ever produce – the PhD thesis.

Of course, you will already have developed some essential skills from undergraduate days, especially if this involved an honours year in which a dissertation or research project was an important outcome. Nevertheless, there is a step change in the quality of work required for postgraduate research, which effectively must meet the full publication criteria of the academic world.

We start the book, therefore, with chapters that identify and discuss the essence of postgraduate work. We then move on to the identification of a topic for your research and how this can be framed as a formal research proposal. The next section deals with the essential skills of a postgraduate, especially those related to information literacy. The focus here is on taking responsibility for your own skills development as a trainee 'professional researcher'. Following this, we move on to discuss the interactions you will have with others during your PhD research and how to make the most of these relationships, whether they be discussions with your supervisor(s) or progress committee, working within a research team or with the audience when presenting a seminar or poster.

Research methods are, of course, an essential component of postgraduate work. Whilst we cannot give specific advice here, we are able to focus on some essential generic skills, including those related to critical thinking, ethical research, citation, referencing, data acquisition and data analysis. The thesis write-up is the most difficult stage for many students, and here our emphasis is on generic guidance for becoming an autonomous writer. Along the way, we discuss how good writing is planned and constructed and how to structure and present your thesis. Finally, we deal with the PhD *viva* and the follow-up in terms of publishing your research and moving on to the next stage of your career.

We've tried to remain faithful to the idea that this book is one that you can dip into when you feel you need friendly advice and assistance. We had many types of students in mind when we decided to write this text and we hope that it will meet your own specific needs. Of course, research approaches vary across the wide spectrum of subjects studied at universities. These diverse discipline contexts have been accommodated by focusing on generic guidance but differentiating advice where appropriate, and particularly where research practice differs across the science and non-science divide.

We hope you will enjoy your years as a postgraduate researcher – certainly, you will find it a time of significant personal development, and eventually, with your contribution to knowledge and understanding placed in the public domain via your thesis and other publications, highly satisfying. We'd be pleased to hear your opinion of the book, any suggestions you have for additions and improvements, and especially if you feel that it has made a positive difference to the way you study and approach postgraduate research.

Kathleen McMillan and Jonathan Weyers

ACKNOWLEDGEMENTS

As PhD students ourselves as well as supervisors, trainers and examiners of PhD students, we have gained much from interactions with colleagues and students. Much of our accumulated wisdom from these exchanges is expressed in this book. Some of this material was developed during the construction of the postgraduate section of the website Advance@Dundee (internal to the University of Dundee). We thank all of our colleagues and friends who helped us with that project, especially Margaret Adamson. We have also contributed to the training of PhD students, especially in the area of writing up, and we thank colleagues for the opportunity to develop our ideas and contribute in that area.

Many others have influenced us and contributed in one way or another to the production of this book, including: Rami Abboud, Richard A'Brook, Michael Allardice, John Berridge, Richard Campbell, Cathy Caudwell, Louisa Cross, Stuart Cross, Margaret Forrest, Martin Glover, John Hillman, Andy Jackson, Allan Jones, Rod Jones, Peter McEleavy, Janet McLean, Christine Milburn, Kirsty Millar, Dave Murie, Fiona O'Donnell, Richard Parsons, Neil Paterson, Jane Prior, Colin Reid, Mhairi Robb, Dorothy Smith, Eric Smith, Gordon Spark, David Walker, Lorraine Walsh and David Wishart. We are indebted to the support and interest of the Royal Literary Fund and particularly the RLF Writing Fellows in our university, distinguished authors in their own right, who have given wise words of counsel: Bill Kirton, Brian Callison, Jonathan Falla and Gordon Meade. Also, we acknowledge those at other universities who have helped frame our thoughts, especially our good friends Rob Reed, Nicki Hedge and Esther Daborn, as well as the membership of the Scottish Effective Learning Advisors who work so energetically to help students to develop many of the key skills that are addressed in this book.

We owe a special debt to the senior colleagues who encouraged various projects that contributed to this book, and who allowed us the freedom to pursue various avenues of related scholarship, especially Robin Adamson, James Calderhead, Chris Carter, Alan Davidson, Ian Francis, Rod Herbert, Eric Monaghan, Graham Nicholson and David Swinfen.

At Pearson Education, we have had excellent support and advice, especially from Steve Temblett, Simon Lake, Rob Cottee, Tim Parker, Ros Woodward and David Hemsley.

Finally, we would like to say thanks to our long-suffering but nevertheless enthusiastic families: Derek, Keith, Nolwenn, Fiona, Tom and Eilidh; and Mary, Paul and James, all of whom helped in various capacities.

PUBLISHER'S ACKNOWLEDGEMENTS

The sections 'Designing experiments' and 'Sampling' in Chapter 24 are partly derived from material in Jones, Reed and Weyers (2012), with permission. Table 2.1 is reproduced courtesy of the SCQF Partnership. Table 20.1 is reproduced courtesy of Dr Eugene Garfield.

In some instances we have been unable to trace the owners of copyright material, and we would appreciate any information that would enable us to do so.

HOW TO USE THIS BOOK

Each chapter in *How to Research & Write a Successful PhD* has been organised and designed to be as clear and simple as possible. The chapters are self-contained and deal with particular aspects of the subject matter so that you can read the book through from beginning to end, or in sections, or dip into specific chapters as you need them.

At the start of each chapter you'll find a brief paragraph and a **Key topics** list that let you know what is included. There is also a list of **Key terms** at this point that highlights words that may be new to you or may be used in a particular way in the chapter. Should you be uncertain about the meaning of these words, you will find definitions in the **Glossary** at the end of the book.

Within each chapter, the text is laid out to help you absorb the key concepts easily, using headings and bulleted lists to enable you to find what you need. Relevant examples are contained in figures, tables and boxes which complement the text. The inset boxes are of three types:

Smart tip boxes emphasise key advice that we think will be particularly useful to you.

Information boxes provide additional information that will broaden your understanding by giving examples and definitions.

Query boxes raise questions for you to consider about your personal approach to the topic.

Finally, the **Action Points** section provides three suggestions for possible follow-up action as you consider ideas further.

INTRODUCTION

TAKING ON POSTGRADUATE STUDIES
Preliminary considerations

Studying for a PhD will involve the exploration of uncharted territory not only in your research project, but also in your personal development. Making the right choices for project, supervisor and department are important. This chapter introduces the issues to be considered when applying for a studentship and outlines the milestones of a typical PhD.

KEY TOPICS

→ Being realistic about postgraduate research

→ Deciding what to study, where to study and with whom

→ The application process

→ Approaching postgraduate study in the right frame of mind

This book starts from the assumption that you have already made the fundamental decision to carry out postgraduate research. There are many potential reasons why you might wish to take this direction, including:

- a desire to contribute to the sum of human knowledge and understanding;
- the wish to stretch your intellect to its limits;
- a deep interest in a particular subject area or topic;
- the chance to learn alongside an acknowledged expert;
- the hope of making a difference to the world and its people;
- the need to gain a qualification that will prepare you for a desired career path;
- an attempt to delay the time when you must leave the university environment.

Whatever your motive(s), you will have a significant personal stake in this project – your time, money, family and future career may all be affected by your decision. It makes sense to approach this undertaking with a clear view of what you need to do to accomplish the goal of gaining a doctoral degree.

BEING REALISTIC ABOUT POSTGRADUATE RESEARCH

Many of the initial feelings of becoming a postgraduate research student will mirror those you may have felt as a new undergraduate student. You will possibly move to another location, adopt different patterns of working, form relationships with new people and have to come to terms with a higher level of study. Yet, in other ways, becoming a new postgraduate will be very different from that undergraduate experience because:

- there is no 'road map' in terms of a syllabus and course/module structure;
- there will be far fewer students studying for the same degree and, in all probability, no one carrying out exactly the same research;
- to a far greater extent, you will be expected to direct your own activities and create your own goals.

Understandably, this might cause some apprehension. However, you should take confidence from the fact that that you have demonstrated the ability to cope through your earlier experiences and qualification(s). Dealing with the challenges of postgraduate research will, nevertheless, require a proactive approach. To channel your effort effectively, it is vital that you comprehend the nature and requirements of work at this new level.

One key way in which a postgraduate's life differs from that of an undergraduate is in work-rate. Usually, PhD students are expected to work a normal 9–5 day, just as if you were in regular employment. Some types of study are particularly demanding, requiring lengthy sequences of reading or inconveniently timed procedures. Supervisors often lead by example, putting in long shifts from very early starts to their days, and may expect you to do the same. Bear in mind too that you will not have normal student holidays. Your leave entitlement will be determined by your studentship. Most state a 6–8 weeks' allowance per year, and you should expect to plan ahead and inform your supervisor when you would like to take leave.

What will postgraduate study be like?

Here are some questions to ponder before you start:

- **Will it be easy?** No, because that's not really the point. The aim is to stretch your knowledge and understanding to its limits. That's a tough experience.

- **Will it be enjoyable?** Not always – you can expect up and downs. Sometimes, you may experience extreme elation, for example, when you make a research breakthrough. At other times, it may seem like a slow grind.

- **Will I be able to cope?** Very probably. Your undergraduate honours degree classification (almost certainly an upper second or first) demonstrates that you have the ability to adapt to this more independent, self-directed style of learning.

- **Will it expand my mind?** Almost certainly, yes. It has the potential to take you to intellectual places you cannot imagine when you start.

- **Will it develop my skills?** Definitely. As well as project-specific skills, you can expect to develop many generic skills and especially those relating to expressing yourself in writing.

- **Will it be rewarding?** Not necessarily in monetary terms (at least, not in the short term). Rather, you can legitimately expect fulfilment at a deeper personal level.

- **Will it help me to get a job?** Don't bank on it. A postgraduate research qualification can act like a double-edged sword. It might allow a brilliant fit with a job specification; on the other hand, you may end up seeming to be over-qualified.

- **Will it be worth the effort?** Absolutely. The points above represent a reality check – because life often isn't as straightforward and smooth as we'd like. By the time you finish your PhD and are walking across that graduation platform you will be a very different person: enriched, fulfilled and on top of your world.

Most PhD research projects are allocated three years of funding and are expected to be completed within this time, although some stretch beyond this. The UK research councils (**Ch 5**) monitor completion rates and penalise universities whose students tend not to submit on time, so expect keen interest in your progress as a result. Universities are also required to meet certain quality standards in relation to the postgraduate research experience, and may be reviewed periodically by external bodies. The relevant codes of practice, which apply throughout the UK, set standards for such matters as admission, supervision, ethics and treatment of appeals and complaints.

Influences on your PhD performance

Examples of stimuli from different sources:

- **Yourself** – you set your own agenda and work-rate; provide project ideas; establish the standard and efficiency of your work; and supply the impetus to complete on time.
- **Supervisor** – imposes standards and work ethic; provides project ideas and working environment; and gives feedback.
- **Department and University** – provide a regulatory framework for supervision and facilities; an agenda for monitoring progress; administer progress monitoring schemes; set up examinations; and award your qualification.
- **External agencies, such as the Quality Assurance Agency and the Higher Education Academy** – create benchmarks for University regulation; publish codes of practice; audit how these are implemented; and monitor student satisfaction.

Table 1.1 provides a sequence of the key events and milestones for a typical research project, together with an indication of standard work activities and how these will be associated with different thought processes and writing skills. Looking at relevant sections of this table from time to time should assist you to gauge your progress and assess your training requirements. You may find that progress monitoring meetings will prompt such evaluation, but should understand that, at this level, the onus is on you to set a personal agenda.

You will find that you will be more productive in your research if you set aside time to socialise, relax and pursue your hobbies and interests. Research students in certain subjects may find research in libraries and archives somewhat lonely. Meeting other postgraduates socially can make all the difference. Sharing accommodation could be one way. Also, postgraduates can join any University society that interests them, including the postgraduate society.

Table 1.1 **A timeline for postgraduate study and the activities and academic development associated with this level.** This is necessarily a generic model and so events and research work will differ according to individual contexts, disciplines and institutions. In particular, where a postgraduate is studying part-time or does not have a continued physical presence in a department, some of the following points will be slightly different or even irrelevant. Personal development in thinking and writing will depend on the individual.

Sequence	Events and milestones	Focus of work activities	Development of thinking and writing
Pre-registration	Identifying research field, institution, supervisor	Scoping possible areas of research	Decision making
	Writing and submitting a research proposal	Writing the proposal	Basic review of research area and potential topics
	Registration for study	Completing forms	Mental preparedness
	Administration	Gaining access to IT and library facilities	
Year 1	Initial supervisor meeting	Setting up work space; discussing departmental and supervisor's policies for postgraduate study	Recognising probationary context
	Regular meetings with supervisor	Research planning	Learning to plan
	Literature search	Identifying literature	Learning to manage time
	Standardising information collected on source material	Organising records of sources; learning how to use referencing software if appropriate	Grouping resources thematically; thinking critically about content
	Literature review	Initial assessment of literature	Analytical and critical thinking
	Postgraduate training	Training in research or other practical techniques; safety induction as appropriate	Development of skills

Continued overleaf

Sequence	Events and milestones	Focus of work activities	Development of thinking and writing
	Research planning	Designing research strategy including methodological approach and equipment if appropriate	Clarification of research topic and related thinking
	Leading undergraduate tutorials or demonstrating	Tutorial, lab or field work (sometimes lecturing)	Planning ahead; thinking through assessment and feedback matters
	Seeking ethical approval	Writing application for ethical approval	Considering ethical aspects of your research
	Experimental work (if relevant)	Pilot work	Designing experiments; planning the necessary resourcing; analysing data
	Reading of literature and attendance at seminars and meetings	Note-making, listening and note-taking	Growing awareness of work in the field
	On-going literature searching and reading; critical appraisal of existing work	Maintaining a research diary/log/notebook as record of work	Deeper thinking about the research field; beginnings of original thought
	1st year report submission for evaluation and examination	Responding to feedback from supervisor's weekly reports/meetings	Submitting weekly reports to supervisor
	Progress Monitoring Committee	Writing about and defending research ideas	Thinking more deeply about the research field
Year 2	Transfer to PhD regulation	Agreeing action plan for research and completion with supervisor	Developing experimental techniques
	Regular meetings with supervisor	Experimentation/study	Writing up draft results and conclusions
	Working within the research team	Contributions to group research projects	Thinking beyond personal research topic; expanding knowledge the field
	Continuing observational or experimental work (where relevant)	Carrying out work of high quality that might appear in the thesis	Collecting and analysing data

	Scheduled meetings with supervisor	Assessment of significance of data	Writing up draft results and conclusions
	Continuing observational or experimental work (where relevant)	Follow-up data collection	'Completing the story' by adding missing data or redesigning approach
	Departmental presentations	Preparation of presentations	Receiving appraisal and feedback from knowledgeable peers
	Progress Monitoring Committee	Submission of progress reports and evaluation of achievements thus far	Preparing draft material for thesis
Year 3 (and possibly 4)	Literature review	Return to literature for confirmation; refining and/or expanding ideas and carrying out further reading	Drafting of Introduction; contextualising your approach
	Final observational or experimental work (where relevant)	Data collection	Collecting and analysing data; drafting of notes for materials and methods; results; early conclusions
	Thesis writing proper	Attempting to write a near-final version, possibly using notes and early draughts as source	Writing first draft; thinking anew about approaches and results and their context
	Submission of draughts to supervisor	Writing to deadlines and attending meetings	Considering feedback on your work
	Final editing and proofing	Writing to deadlines	Checking for consistency and completeness; creating reference list
	Arranging for soft binding of thesis and submitting thesis	Printing 'final' version of thesis	Finding last-minute errors
	Viva voce examination	Defending your thesis and the work behind it	Making required corrections
	Publicising your ideas and findings	Writing poster presentation; conference paper; article for publication	Adapting to new or different styles of writing; responding to feedback from referees
	Graduation	Applying for jobs; revision of CV	Thinking about a future career

Developing your social life as a postgraduate

Here are some tips for getting involved:

- Find out about the postgraduate society and the events it organises.
- Locate the postgraduate common room within the department – or perhaps the room used jointly by postgraduates and staff – and visit it regularly to meet up with your peers.
- Discover whether there are any university facilities for postgraduates (some institutions have a postgraduate study area and/or a postgraduate club/bar) – and check these out.
- Explore the opportunities for sport and exercise.
- Join clubs that interest you.
- Take part in student union activities, including representation.
- Enquire about becoming an assistant warden of a hall of residence (with the possible bonus of living rent-free).

As a postgraduate, your financial situation will depend on what sort of funding underpins the project. In some disciplines, particularly science, the research group leader will already have applied for a studentship or negotiated a quota studentship from a funding body or research council. These studentships normally include a full financial package intended to cover university fees, materials, some travel funding for conferences, and a stipend (payment) to cover living expenses for the student. Research council grants are standardised (with London weighting, if applicable), but some industry- or university-funded positions may pay better. You may be able to balance your budget by carrying out teaching duties (**Ch 13**) or minimising accommodation costs by acting as a hall warden. Having a job in the evenings is technically possible but usually is frowned upon as it will limit significantly both your study time and energy reserves.

DECIDING WHAT TO STUDY, WHERE TO STUDY AND WITH WHOM

In essence, there are two types of postgraduate project:

1 Those where the research aims have been defined in some detail as part of the process of gaining funding for the studentship.

2 Those where personal or external funding is available for a studentship, but the precise project has not been defined, or only a general subject area is suggested.

Both types may be advertised in relevant academic publications or online. In addition, many departments will accept independently funded postgraduates who apply autonomously.

The first 'closed' kind of project is more common in science-related disciplines. Choosing which of these positions to apply for will depend on factors such as:

- the attractiveness of the project;
- the reputation of the supervisor (who is often specified);
- the reputation of the institution;
- the stipend and other financial issues;
- personal desires, such as a wish to move (or not to move) to a specific location.

In many cases, the topic may seem rather esoteric and possibly narrow. You may need to carry out some research to find out what it might involve and where it might lead. You should be encouraged, however, by the fact that the proposal is likely to have been through a rigorous peer review process where its relevance, topicality and chances of success will have been assessed.

The second 'open' type of project occurs more frequently in arts-orientated PhD programmes. Here, you would be required to identify a specific topic and possibly frame a research proposal (**Ch 3**). Sometimes finding a supervisor and/or a source of funding are tasks that fall to the student, sometimes the supervisor and/or funding are allocated by the host department. The supervisor is generally conducting research into a similar or related field.

In many ways the student–supervisor relationship is one of the most important aspects of postgraduate study. You may need to assess whether you feel compatible with a potential supervisor, and *vice versa*. This is necessarily a personal matter. **Chapter 10** details the nature of this partnership and if you need to select a supervisor, this may help you develop a personal set of criteria. One of the best ways to find out about supervisors is to seek the opinion of those already studying in the department if possible.

Factors to take into account when framing a project or deciding on the suitability of a project

Make sure you are making an informed choice by doing background reading, speaking to a range of staff and students, and asking the right questions when you have the opportunity.

You may wish to consider the following:

- **Your personal level of interest in the topic.** This will help to motivate you through three or more years of study and when things aren't going well.

- **The underlying problem that the research aims to tackle.** This needs to satisfy any inclination you have for 'applicability', or convince you that the topic is interesting in its own right.

- **The research approach.** This may seem easy or hard; up-to-date or established-but-uninteresting; risky or secure in providing results; innovative or tried-and-tested. Decide which options best match your personality and ambition.

- **Availability of resources or experimental material.** To make good progress, you will need ready access to research sources or experimental data, or both.

- **Feasibility.** A highly interesting project might be thwarted by time constraints, sheer difficulty or methodological problems.

- **Depth.** You will develop more advanced skills by tackling a more difficult subject.

- **Quality of support and supervision.** You will need to get on with your supervisor, but this presupposes that they will be available to meet you. A noted authority may lack the time to see you as frequently as you might wish.

- **Impact on your CV and career options.** This may not be obvious at the outset, although it should be possible to assess the types of 'sellable' skills you will be able to develop.

Having multiple supervisors

There are a number of scenarios where you might have more than one supervisor. They might have complementary expertise relevant to your project, or one may be performing a mentoring act for another who does not yet fulfil the university regulations for solo supervision, which usually requires experience in the role as a co-supervisor. **Throughout this book we will use the term 'supervisor', while acknowledging that on occasion, this might properly be 'supervisors'.**

THE APPLICATION PROCESS

The application process for 'closed' projects is very similar to applying for a job: the PhD post is advertised by the university in the appropriate publications. These announcements are frequently released between January and the summer period for the forthcoming academic year, so start looking early. Research council funding for postgraduate study is awarded to individual institutions and students seeking funded places must apply through their chosen institution and not directly to the relevant research council. Further information is available on the websites of each of the research councils. In general, the minimum stipulated requirement for a higher degree course is a 'good honours degree'. This usually means an upper second or better – although criteria may vary with different admissions tutors, and the popularity of the project area. Normally you will be asked to submit your CV including your expected degree classification if you have not already graduated. You may then be short-listed for an interview. The format of this will vary with institution but generally consists of an initial, formal interview before a postgraduate committee, frequently a panel of three academics.

What might they ask me at interview?

Be prepared to answer questions of the following types:

- Why do you want to do a PhD?
- What are your future career goals?
- What is your understanding of the general subject area?
- Why do you want to pursue this particular topic?
- Can you outline your current research (Honours project) or previous research projects?
- What do you see as the key research questions?
- How would you approach this research?
- Would you enjoy living in the area for the following three or more years?
- What are your hobbies/interests outside of your academic studies?

Whatever procedure is required, you can assume that you will be asked for a reference giving an account of your suitability to become a research student. This should be written by someone who knows you well and can testify to your performance academically and your level of interest in the area of work you wish to pursue. It would be wise, therefore, to ask a member of the academic staff in your most recent university or college if they would be willing to do this for you. If the institution you are applying to has a special form for references then be sure to give that to your referee as soon as possible to allow them time to complete it. Otherwise, just ask for either a sealed or an open reference and include it with your application letter as noted above.

As well as a formal interview you will normally have a more informal chat with your potential supervisor. This is an ideal opportunity for you to ask questions and for you both to get a feel for whether or not you can get along together, both professionally, and on a personal level. After all, you are about to embark on at least three years of work together, so it is very important that you get along. You should then be informed shortly after the interview(s) whether or not you have been successful in gaining the position. If you are unsuccessful, do not be disheartened, as competition for studentships is often high – instead, view the interview experience positively as a way of gaining confidence in answering questions about yourself.

APPROACHING POSTGRADUATE STUDY IN THE RIGHT FRAME OF MIND

The competition in research is fierce. You should be in no doubt that working for a doctoral degree requires immense commitment and the time requirements are very demanding. You will be stretched intellectually and as well as strong perseverance and determination, you will need to be organised and efficient. Aspects of your non-working life will probably change.

At the same time, it is a privilege to be allowed to enter the world of research. You will already have demonstrated that you have the necessary ability, but this sheltered environment will provide you with opportunities for contact with like-minded and similarly qualified individuals; the chance to work with and learn from noted authorities, some of whom will be authentic geniuses; and the space, time and working conditions to test your own mind to its limits.

To be successful, and in particular to complete your studies on time, you will need to be clear about your overall aims and the routes required to achieve them. It will not be possible to map out all your work accurately and in detail, otherwise it would not be worth doing. Nevertheless, you should try to anticipate your training and skills needs; you should be proactive in arranging the necessary meetings, visits and in gaining access to research materials and facilities; and possibly most important of all, you will need to understand the need for 'closure' (most research is, after all, open-ended) and willing to accept the compromises required for completion in terms of a written thesis.

Most PhD students experience highs and lows as they progress through what is necessarily uncharted territory. It will be important to remain upbeat during episodes of apparent frustration or disappointment (**Ch 11**). Recognising this aspect of research life and remaining well-motivated is a vital key to successful postgraduate study.

ACTION POINTS

1.1 Consider your strengths and weaknesses in relation to the challenges of PhD research. Showing awareness of these at interview might be beneficial to your cause. This self-knowledge may also help you to take anticipatory action, for example, by signing up for additional training (**Ch 5**).

1.2 Review the timeline for postgraduate study (Table 1.1) and create a set of targets for yourself. Think about where you would like to be in your research at different times. The majority of PhDs are completed in a hurry at the end of the studentship period, and sometimes beyond (often, importantly, once the funding has ended). Although research work is necessarily unpredictable, resolve to be among the minority who have planned their work carefully and given themselves the best possible chance of completing on time, avoiding a last-minute rush.

1.3 Get yourself organised. Regarding the points made in 1.2 above, one of the keys to meeting targets is being organised in your work, so ensure your filing (both computer and hard copy) is in good order right from the start – and periodically review its status, giving it an overhaul from time to time. Ensure that you always keep a back-up of all your files.

2

PRINCIPLES OF POSTGRADUATENESS

How to approach study at this new level

How does research at PhD level differ from that carried out for an undergraduate degree? Gaining an understanding of your new level of study is important to ensure your efforts meet your supervisor's and examiners' expectations. This chapter provides insights into your new study environment; your role and those of others; and the challenges of being a researcher.

KEY TOPICS

→ Recognising the challenges and expectations of postgraduate study

→ Understanding the criteria for the award of a PhD

→ Joining the academic community

Making the step up to doctoral study may have been an easy decision, or it may have been one that required prolonged thought. You may have been confident that you were ready for this level, or you may have thought anxiously about whether you were ready for the inevitable academic challenges. Even if you haven't thought deeply about this matter at all, there is merit in considering what lies ahead and what will be required of you. Several different sources will exert an influence, including:

● The academic community, as represented by the University and your examiner(s) – for example, what will they require of you in terms of standard of work and the presentation and examination of your thesis?

● Your supervisor – for example, what would he or she like you to achieve, perhaps as a contribution to a wider research theme?

- Yourself – for example, what are your personal goals in terms of expanding your understanding and developing skills?

This chapter deals primarily with the requirements of the academic community – arguably the most universally significant; expectations in the other areas will depend on your circumstances; they are covered particularly in **Chapters 1, 5, 10** and **33**.

Gaining expertise

One way of describing your achievement at the end of a postgraduate degree is that you will have carried out a sufficiently extensive and deep investigation to have become one of the world experts in your particular subject area. The subject may be narrow, and in fast moving-topics, the expertise temporary, but this description provides an excellent overarching goal for your studies.

RECOGNISING THE CHALLENGES AND EXPECTATIONS OF POSTGRADUATE STUDY

The challenges of postgraduate research will differ depending on your field and topic within it. Most people who have successfully completed a doctorate would acknowledge that they had to develop old skills as well as acquire new ones, especially in the earlier stages of postgraduate studies (**Ch 5**). Your research may lead you into new fields where you have to adopt new approaches or techniques (**Chs 17–24**). You may need to learn how to use sophisticated specialist software to help with data analysis (**Ch 23**). You will certainly need to develop the scholarly writing expertise expected at postgraduate level (**Chs 26–30**).

Your institution will require certain things from you, including:

- the dedication of time and energy to complete your project on time;
- the application of intellectual integrity to your research task so you conduct your research honestly and ethically;
- a contribution to the collegiate environment of your institution, possibly through the teaching activities involved in tutoring or demonstrating or participating concurrently in other research projects.

Your supervisor will anticipate, in addition, that you can:

- organise your time to meet the demands of the research;
- participate in purposeful meetings to review the work in progress;
- approach your studies with a questioning and open mind;
- analyse and critique work in your field;
- analyse and critique your own work;
- demonstrate original thinking;
- be productive in the conduct of your research and related writing.

In return, your own commitment to the research process will lead to some expectations of your chosen institution, for instance, that:

- you will be able to work under an expert in the field, who will provide suitable supervision;
- you will be allowed (within reason) to do your research in your own way but under the tutelage of your supervisor;
- you will be provided with opportunities to consult with your supervisor on a regular basis; and that
- you will have access to the facilities to enable you to conduct the research professionally and thoroughly.

As a graduate, you may have carried out a research project or dissertation at undergraduate honours level; moreover, having been accepted for postgraduate studies, it is likely that you will have performed well in that exercise. The experience will certainly have given you a flavour of what to expect in a PhD. However, the criteria for postgraduate work are generally more rigorous than work at undergraduate level. Details are naturally discipline-dependent, but in general, your research will be expected to be:

- More extensive. You will have a longer period to carry out your investigation, so both your investigation and its write-up can and should be wide-ranging, encompassing all relevant aspects of your field and possibly beyond.
- Deeper. In one to three full-time years of study (or more), you will have the time and resources to look into your topic in greater detail and to investigate each element fully.
- Original. You will have the opportunity to display innovation in the way you tackle the project, whereas at honours level you might been on safer ground, perhaps following the approach of a previous study.

- More rigorous. Essentially, the outcome of your research needs to be of publishable standard. It must have a theoretical underpinning and use appropriate research methodologies. This means that the methods must be reliable, the results repeatable (in the sciences), the analysis wholly appropriate and the conclusions valid. A judgement on this will be carried out by an authority in the area (the external examiner) or, if you submit parts of your thesis to a journal, by academics with knowledge of your subject (see **Chs 31** and **32**).

Another way of approaching this matter is to consider the different aspects of study, including the relevant skills that are required. Table 2.1 provides an example listing of expectations under five relevant headings of this type. This should provide a benchmark with which you can judge both your present status and later progress.

UNDERSTANDING THE CRITERIA FOR THE AWARD OF A PhD

As an undergraduate, you will probably have been familiar with 'learning outcomes' and 'marking criteria' related to your courses. These are normally published in the course handbook and would have defined what the academic staff expected you to be able to achieve, and, consequently, their benchmarks for assessing your assignments and exam papers.

Due to the widely differing nature of each PhD project, and the necessarily 'unexpected' outcomes of this type of research activity, there can be no similar detailed information at this level. However, your completed work will be assessed by an experienced external examiner and, normally following an oral exam (often referred to as the '*viva*' which is short for the Latin '*viva voce*', meaning 'by the living voice'), they will use their professional judgement on whether to recommend the award of the relevant degree (**Ch 31**).

Universities differ, but the broad criteria used in this judgement essentially follow the expectation that your thesis should be 'novel, reliable and personally owned', that is, showing original research, be of publishable quality and be all your own work unless the contribution of others is acknowledged. The different sections of the thesis (**Ch 28**) provide opportunities to verify that you have satisfied these criteria, as summarised in Table 2.2.

Table 2.1 A description of the level of study expected in postgraduate research. Taken from the 'level descriptors' published by the Scottish Credit and Qualifications Framework (***www.scqf.org.uk***, accessed 16 June 2012). In that system, doctoral studies are placed at Level 12, with Level 11 covering Masters and Level 10 undergraduate honours. This source allows further direct comparisons to be made between expectations for undergraduate and postgraduate work, should you wish to make them.

Aspect	Postgraduate (doctoral level) descriptors
1 Knowledge and understanding	Demonstrate and/or work with: • A critical overview of a subject/discipline, including critical understanding of the principal theories, principles and concepts. • A critical, detailed and often leading knowledge and understanding at the forefront of one or more specialisms. • Knowledge and understanding that is generated through personal research or equivalent work that makes a significant contribution to the development of the subject/discipline.
2 Practice: applied knowledge and understanding	• Use a significant range of the principal skills, techniques, practices and materials associated with a subject/discipline. • Use and enhance a range of complex skills, techniques, practices and materials at the forefront of one or more specialisms. • Apply a range of standard and specialised research/equivalent instruments and techniques of enquiry. • Design and execute research, investigative or development projects to deal with new problems and issues. • Demonstrate originality and creativity in the development and application of new knowledge, understanding and practices. • Practise in the context of new problems and circumstances.
3 Generic cognitive skills	• Apply a constant and integrated approach to critical analysis, evaluation and synthesis of new and complex ideas, information and issues. • Identify, conceptualise and offer original and creative insights into new, complex and abstract ideas, information and issues. • Develop creative and original responses to problems and issues. • Deal with very complex and/or new issues and make informed judgements in the absence of complete or consistent data/information.

4 Communication, ICT and numeracy skills	Use a significant range of advanced and specialised skills as appropriate to a subject/discipline, for example: • Communicate at an appropriate level to a range of audiences and adapt communication to the context and purpose. • Communicate at the standard of published academic work and/or critical dialogue and review with peers and experts in other specialisms. • Use a range of software to support and enhance work at this level and specify software requirements to enhance work. • Critically evaluate numerical and graphical data.
5 Autonomy, accountability and working with others	• Exercise a high level of autonomy and initiative in professional and equivalent activities. • Take full responsibility for own work and/or significant responsibility for the work of others. • Demonstrate leadership and/or originality in tackling and solving problems and issues. • Work in ways which are reflective, self-critical and based on research/evidence. • Deal with complex ethical and professional issues. • Make informed judgements on new and emerging issues not addressed by current professional and/or ethical codes or practices.

Table 2.2 **A mapping of basic thesis components to the criteria of novelty, reliability and ownership.** Ticks indicate parts of the thesis where you will have an opportunity to demonstrate that you have satisfied the criteria. Not every thesis will incorporate all these components (**Ch 28**).

Thesis component (where present)	Criteria for successful postgraduate work		
	Novelty	Reliability	Ownership
Declaration			✓
Acknowledgements			✓
Introduction	✓		
Materials and methods		✓	
Results		✓	
Discussion		✓	
Conclusions	✓	✓	
References			✓

What does 'publishable' mean?

This means that if you submitted your work in the relevant format and writing style for a typical academic journal in your subject area, it would be likely to satisfy the criteria for publication if space allowed. Each journal publishes its expectations for submitted work covering both format and quality of work and it is worth studying some of these outlines for your subject area.

- The requirement for novelty. This ties in with the expectation that the work is publishable due to its originality. Your thesis needs to present a new contribution to the literature in your field, advancing the academic community's knowledge and understanding. You will have opportunities to establish this in the Introduction and Conclusions parts of the thesis, where, amongst other things, you should place your work in its academic context and explain why it is novel.

- The need for reliability. Here, definitions differ slightly among disciplines. In the sciences, a key meaning is that, potentially, your work must be capable of repetition by a 'competent technician', that is, someone with similar skills to you. This explains the emphasis on detail in the Materials and Methods section, and for information on replication and statistical analysis to be provided in the Results section. In many non-sciences, the emphasis is rather that the 'position' you arrive at must derive from verifiable sources and follow a logical argument.

Valuing and overcoming perfectionism in research

An inherent paradox in research is the fact that it requires and rewards perfectionism, yet this very quality is an obstacle to completion and closure of a research project. For example, perfectionism and rigour are required in the accuracy of reporting and language (**Ch 26**); in conducting experiments or making accurate observations (**Chs 22–24**); and in tracking down and acknowledging all possible sources (**Chs 7, 8, 20, 21**). Anything else will be heavily criticised. However, almost by definition, research is never complete: there are rarely definitive 'answers', and there is always the need for further study. Where you draw a line under your work is often dictated by time pressures rather than a natural end point. Compromise will be required in terms of imprecise methods, incomplete data, missing information and uncertain conclusions, and that cuts against the grain of perfectionism. The mistake is in thinking that it can possibly be otherwise.

- Demonstrable ownership. Partly due to its specialised nature, research degree work is vulnerable to plagiarism and the possibility of unacknowledged outside help. A thesis is not written under exam conditions, and others may have helped you significantly. Further, the examination committee may not always know in detail about other work carried out in your field and be unable to judge unerringly whether ideas or data have been copied from others. For this reason, you will be asked to write and sign a declaration (**Ch 30**) and be expected to follow the academic conventions of citation and referencing to acknowledge the influence of other authors (**Ch 20**). In part, the purpose of the *viva voce* exam (**Ch 31**) is to allow you to demonstrate that you understand and can explain your thesis as an indication that it was indeed your own labour.

'All my own work' – the thesis declaration

Most university regulations for postgraduate degrees state that there should be signed declaration at or near the start of a thesis (**Ch 28**), affirming that, unless otherwise stated:

- the candidate is the sole author of the thesis;
- all references cited have been consulted by the candidate;
- all the work in the thesis has been done by the candidate;
- the work has not been previously accepted for a higher degree.

If the thesis is based upon joint research (sometimes the case in the sciences), it is also expected that the nature and extent of the candidate's individual contribution is defined.

There is also a technical requirement to submit your thesis in the expected format and binding (**Ch 30**) – it might have to be resubmitted if the examination committee decides that it fails to meet these conventions.

JOINING THE ACADEMIC COMMUNITY

As you progress in your postgraduate studies, you will sense that you are gradually becoming a part of an academic community. People will be interested in your work and thoughts. They may wish to collaborate, to ask for your help or to debate issues with you. Some may influence your thoughts hugely. Some will become life-long friends.

However, as with any other community or society, becoming integrated is a two-way process. You will need to reach out in similar ways to your peers, perceived superiors and external authorities. Your initial shyness will soon disappear when you realise that your fellow students probably have the same apprehensive feelings as yourself and that even crusty old professors have a soft human side (sometimes).

Ideas for linking with other researchers

- **Show an interest.** Ask about their work and read up a little about it if necessary.
- **Find out others' views.** Ask what they think about the main issues in your own work.
- **Share your own views.** Be willing to reveal your own thoughts and/or results.
- **Read others' papers.** Become informed about their interests and ideas.
- **Attend seminars and ask questions.** Find links to your own studies.
- **Research alongside others when you can.** You might pick up useful tips.
- **Spend time in the common-room.** Take part in the intellectual and not so intellectual banter.
- **Attend social events.** Get to know your colleagues' personalities.
- **Email or write to the authorities in your subject.** Seek out their views.
- **Attend training programmes.** See if you can learn from the approach others are taking.
- **Attend conferences.** Present your own work; meet other like-minded people.
- **Explore opportunities for collaboration.** Try to work with others and use their facilities.
- **Create a research blog or social media site.** This might help you to make and maintain contacts.

One important aspect of postgraduate study is that it offers you a 'taster' of what it might be like to follow an academic career. For example, it will allow you the chance to find out whether you might be suited to university-level teaching (**Ch 13**). It might also provide a springboard to launch a professional research career.

As a novice member of an academic community, you will be able to observe other academics in action; gain a sense of how competitive the academic life can be; and see from the inside how an academic department actually works. If it does seem to suit you, then you can try to enter academia, either directly or, more likely, by applying for a postdoctoral position (**Ch 33**). On other hand, you may decide that working in a university, research institute or the development section of a company is not for you. If this is the case, you can make a break and move on elsewhere after the postgraduate study period.

What is a post-doc?

Post-doctoral (post-doc) positions occupy a place between a PhD studentship and a lectureship (or full-time research post). They are generally untenured, and based on a three-year salaried contract. Post-doc positions offer a chance to use or extend your expertise, build a publication base and make new contacts. They are often regarded a staging post on the way to a research or lecturing career.

ACTION POINTS

2.1 Construct realistic aims for your research and discuss these with your supervisor. This may indeed be a requirement of your university's progress monitoring system or a required aspect of a research proposal. Such research aims, however, should always be flexible. They should be modified in the light of experience. They need to become more realistic and achievable the further into your studies you go.

2.2 Review your university's requirements for achieving a postgraduate research degree. Do this at the outset. Do not be under any illusions about what you need to accomplish.

2.3 Try to become more aware of your personality traits. How might these affect your research progress? Often, personality tests are offered as part of the postgraduate training programme, but they are also available online or via your careers centre. The results should not be considered definitive, but they may give cause for reflection.

GETTING STARTED

3

IDENTIFYING AND FRAMING RESEARCH QUESTIONS

How to set targets and formulate hypotheses

Having a level-headed view of how you will approach your PhD research is an essential starting point. This involves framing the research questions or hypotheses you will seek to answer. Setting provisional goals and milestones is an important way to get your studies off to a good start even though your ideas and plans will be tested and refined as time goes on.

KEY TOPICS

→ Generating ideas

→ Exploring the literature

→ Narrowing your options

→ Creating goals and framing research questions

→ Setting up explanations and hypotheses to test

Depending on the type of research project you have signed up for (**Ch 1**), you will have different levels of decision to make regarding the direction of your work. If the project area is relatively open, you will self-evidently have a relatively high freedom to select a precise topic and targets. If the project area is well defined, your choices will be narrower, but there will still be some need to select between options and decide upon an initial approach to the study.

Both are reasons why some universities or departments ask their postgraduate students to complete a research proposal at an early stage, so that the scoping part of the research process is well documented and can be checked by the relevant progress monitoring group. This requirement recognises the importance of having a strong starting point and clear aims right from the beginning, and also allows

Importance of making the right choices for your research

Finding suitable research questions to ask and the best methods to answer them. Your task is therefore to find a path between straightforward research with a high chance of obtaining useful results and complex or difficult research with a high 'tariff' for its uncertain outcomes.

such matters as ethics approval to be monitored. The structure and content of a formal proposal is examined in **Chapter 4**.

GENERATING IDEAS

Generating new ideas for research requires a certain amount of relevant knowledge. You will therefore need to carry out some background reading. This might build on knowledge from your undergraduate days or the studies you did when selecting your research position (**Ch 1**). It may require a completely new literature search or one that is in greater depth, perhaps requiring assistance from a subject librarian (**Ch 7**). **Chapter 8** provides tips for reading and analysing the research literature.

This phase of your project can consume valuable time. While surveying the literature you should maintain a balance between a focused consideration of options and the width and depth of your reading. Because of the appeal of the topic, you may find yourself easily distracted into areas of marginal value. Take a note of this interesting material, but move on swiftly at this stage. Most topics are multi-faceted and there is often the temptation to try to address too many issues. You may have to be selective in narrowing down the research topic.

Getting to grips with jargon and difficult ideas

Having to comprehend the terminology and complex concepts of a new topic can initially result in a hazy understanding of the foundations of your work and, hence, difficulty in framing suitable questions. One way around this is to go back to basics, possibly by reading a general textbook of the area. You may also wish to create a personal glossary of terms to help you learn the specialised terms involved.

EXPLORING THE LITERATURE

Your initial literature trawl might involve:

- An analysis of up-to-date reviews of your subject area. The aim would be to explore the current state of knowledge, seek out potentially productive research directions and find areas with unanswered questions.

- A thorough read of key papers. These might be identified with the help of your supervisor and might indeed have been mentioned in a grant application, if relevant. Otherwise, you may find them highlighted in subject reviews. You should read these sources for clues about evidence, methods and suggestions for future work, either written up in the paper, or that arise from your own thoughts while reading about the subject.

- Reading relevant publications from your supervisor's portfolio. This will not only give you an appreciation of his or her work in the area, but may also provide you with useful sources for further reading.

- A study of the research methods used in your area. In the sciences this might be highly technical in nature, while in the non-sciences, it might involve broad-brush approaches to the topic. You should be aware of the possibility of using methods from one subject or discipline in another, as these cross-disciplinary lines of enquiry can often be very productive. This is a reason for consulting a wide range of sources.

A brainstorm (**Ch 9**) could be a good way of encapsulating the main themes on a single sheet of paper, allowing you to see connections and themes in the literature at a glance.

In the light of your early reading, and after thinking through the options, you should construct a short-list of ideas to discuss with your allocated supervisor or, in some cases, a potential supervisor. Ahead of time, you should consider the pros and cons of each so you are in a position to debate the viability of each choice.

NARROWING YOUR OPTIONS

One way of narrowing your research options is to try to answer the following questions:

- What really interests me? A topic that holds your attention and motivates you will keep you going through any tough patches. Learning for learning's sake simply because a subject appeals to you is a noble aim in itself and one that guides much research effort. The answer to what attracts you lies somewhere in your personality and in the way in which past lecturers or readings have fired your interest. However, you should be aware that a superficial appeal may pale when you have to deal with the complexity at the heart of some topics when these are studied at doctoral level.

- What do others view as the unanswered research questions? These may have been signposted in up-to-date textbooks and in the discussion/conclusions sections of recent publications. Working on one of these areas will ensure your work is relevant and 'newsworthy', but these questions will probably be unanswered for a reason – they are probably difficult to solve.

- What am I equipped to do? This question refers both to your personal abilities and to the availability of equipment and other resources. For example, you may not wish to tackle a topic that requires advanced mathematics if this is not your forte; on the other hand, you might be able to capitalise on the availability nearby of a new scientific instrument that will allow you to gain interesting and novel results very quickly.

- What is the competition? Trying to beat the challenge of another research group can provide great motivation, although being sucked into someone else's battle (perhaps on your supervisor's behalf) might not serve you well. Not all areas are highly competitive, but joining one is a high-risk strategy because it could mean you will be beaten in the race to get results or face fierce objections to your specific methods or conclusions. Conversely, competition is probably an indicator of the academic or economic worth of any outcomes that can be expected.

- What barriers are there to studying a specific topic? These could prevent you making good progress. As examples, you might need to obtain permissions (perhaps to study a site of special scientific interest); you may need to make a complex ethics committee submission (**Ch 19**); you may require to be trained in a specific technique; or you may require a very expensive piece of equipment. However, the mere fact that there are obstacles to overcome should not put you off and it may narrow the competition.

A quick read around a new subject – what should you be looking for?

When establishing your knowledge-base around a new research area, you should attempt to find out:

- the past authorities in the area, that is, those researchers who established the foundations of the topic;
- the major schools of thought in the area;
- the key research findings and relevant publications;
- the researchers and research groups currently active;
- the areas currently being worked on and any trends in focus or findings;
- the jargon of the subject, and what the terms mean;
- the research methods in use, both in the past and currently;
- sources of research materials and evidence;
- pointers to productive new areas of work.

All in the detail

In some cases, and especially in the sciences, you will be interested in the minutiae of methods. Bear in mind that although published Materials and Methods are supposed to allow a competent worker to repeat research (Ch 28), this is not always the case in practice. The text may assume readers know about certain details that could make a difference to the success of the technique or subtly affect results. There are benefits from carrying out a very simple experiment as a pilot to familiarise yourself with the precise methods, check that these work and ensure your designs for future experiments are practical. Ideally, this might include a copycat treatment to see whether you can obtain a similar result to your source.

CREATING GOALS AND FRAMING RESEARCH QUESTIONS

When moving from this 'options appraisal' to a goal-setting stage, the watch-word is 'practicality'. There is no point in having unrealistic goals such as 'solving world hunger', even though that potential outcome might be driving your interest. You need to set yourself realistic targets for what will probably be, at best, a two-year phase of intensive research, assuming that the preliminary phases of research and writing up consume a normal amount of time. Part-time students are more likely to have to set their research topic within a longer time-span. This should be taken into consideration in identifying research targets that will endure and be achievable.

This phase involves framing a research question that you will be seeking to address. A generalised approach that might be adopted is shown in Figure 3.1. The word 'address' is used deliberately here rather than 'answer', because a clear-cut answer or conclusion is rarely possible, and, in fact, you will gain credit by considering the evidence from all sides of an argument or case, arriving at a clearly stated viewpoint, and giving reasons for adopting this position.

A primary requirement is to frame research questions so that you can obtain *some* outcome from your work that you will be able to describe and then discuss in your thesis. Of course, you would also like this to be of interest to the research community and thereby provide you with the status to move perhaps to your next research position or a job. Hence, a subtle mix of easily obtained results and more tricky outcomes is desirable.

Your research goals should be:

- Detailed. They should include specifics about outcomes, as opposed to vague wishes or a title encompassing a diffuse area of study.
- Measurable. They should be quantifiable, so that you and others can decide that you have achieved the targets you have set. There should be concrete intermediate and final outcomes that will allow you to evaluate your progress.
- Realistic. They should be attainable, given the resources at your disposal (including personal abilities, time, equipment, availability of research materials, permissions).

Time as an important resource

Any student who has just completed a PhD will tell you – time is the one thing they wish they'd had in greater abundance. It is all too easy to underestimate the time it takes to achieve your research goals. Things nearly always proceed at a slower pace than you imagine, either due to unexpected delays or problems along the way. Therefore, always take care not to be too ambitious in your plans and leave plenty of time for dealing with contingencies.

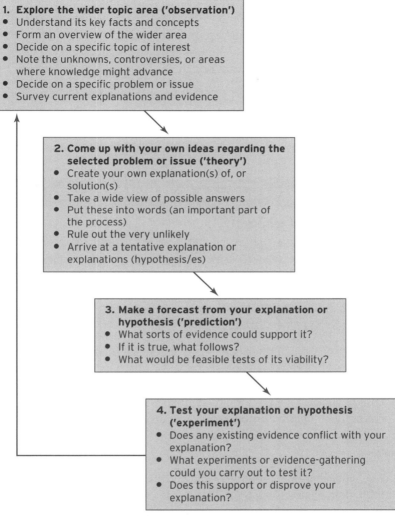

1. Explore the wider topic area ('observation')
- Understand its key facts and concepts
- Form an overview of the wider area
- Decide on a specific topic of interest
- Note the unknowns, controversies, or areas where knowledge might advance
- Decide on a specific problem or issue
- Survey current explanations and evidence

2. Come up with your own ideas regarding the selected problem or issue ('theory')
- Create your own explanation(s) of, or solution(s)
- Take a wide view of possible answers
- Put these into words (an important part of the process)
- Rule out the very unlikely
- Arrive at a tentative explanation or explanations (hypothesis/es)

3. Make a forecast from your explanation or hypothesis ('prediction')
- What sorts of evidence could support it?
- If it is true, what follows?
- What would be feasible tests of its viability?

4. Test your explanation or hypothesis ('experiment')
- Does any existing evidence conflict with your explanation?
- What experiments or evidence-gathering could you carry out to test it?
- Does this support or disprove your explanation?

Figure 3.1 The four-stage process of forming and testing a research question or hypothesis. This is a commonly accepted description of the route for formulating or refining a research question or hypothesis and then testing it. The process can be cyclical, as indicated, with the results of tests being fed back to the start as new observations.

These research goals will lead naturally to research questions. A general approach to the framing of research questions might be to write down your goals as a series of statements that you would like your research to answer. An example could be 'I would like to find out whether children from lower socio-economic backgrounds are more or less likely to fail if they come to University'. This might lead you to a series of narrower research avenues. For instance, in the above example, you would probably need to look into definitions of socio-economic backgrounds and set criteria for the notion of 'failure'.

This thinking might even lead you to think of a tentative title for your thesis and possibly the potential titles for the different chapters within it. Even though you may change these at a later date, they may help to make the nature of your researches more concrete and outcome-led.

SETTING UP EXPLANATIONS AND HYPOTHESES TO TEST

Science-related research

In the sciences, the research questions for PhD studies can simply be the hypotheses you would like to test by seeking out relevant evidence and comparing with the theoretical expectation. This notion fits with the framework of understanding described in Table 3.1. However, many who study the philosophy of science feel that there may be more human intuition in 'real' research than is indicated by this analysis.

Each hypothesis is normally cast as a simple statement, such as 'the reason obesity reduces lifespan is because of the risk of diabetes and the consequent debilitating conditions'. The next stage is a statement along the lines of 'if that is the case, then we would predict that...' (for example, 'if so, we would expect mortality assigned to specific diabetes-related conditions to be correlated with the weight of the patient').

Nearly all science deals with the testing of small-scale hypotheses. Each hypothesis involves a prediction and its testing via an experiment (Figure 3.1). An experiment is a test under controlled conditions that reduces the number of changing variables (often called 'factors' or 'treatments'), ideally to a single factor of interest in the context of the hypothesis (**Ch 24**). No hypothesis can be rejected with absolute certainty, especially when there is variability in the results of the experimental test (which there nearly always is). The field of statistics for a large part deals with assigning probabilities to the results of hypothesis-testing (**Ch 23**).

Someone who proposes a new theory will probably become quite famous in their research area and will be much quoted. These people

Table 3.1 **A hierarchical view of the theory underpinning any particular research area.** This model applies best for scientific areas of research.

Paradigm
At the top of the hierarchy is the paradigm, a theoretical framework of understanding that is so successful and well-confirmed that most research in the area is carried out within its context. By definition, such notions are rarely challenged by the results of research, and, even if they were, workers in the field would require reasonably extensive corroboration before they would shelve the framework. • *An example of a paradigm might be: 'Physiological systems are capable of being controlled via the concentrations of chemical messengers called 'hormones'.*
Theory
Next in the hierarchy is the theory, a collection of hypotheses. This is more tentative in nature than a paradigm, and might be overturned if evidence justifies this; it is differentiated from a hypothesis by being applicable to a wider range of natural situations. • *An example of a theory could be that the hormone ghrelin acts to increase hunger in mammals by acting on the hypothalamus.* Related to a theory is the notion of a scientific law, a theoretical understanding that can be encapsulated in a mathematical equation. These are more prevalent in the physical sciences. • *A familiar example of a law might be $e = mc^2$.*
Hypothesis
The hypothesis is, in effect, the 'unit' of understanding. It is an explanation that can be tested by experiment and can essentially be found to be untrue if the evidence suggests so. This property of hypothesis is known as falsifiability. If confirmed, a hypothesis will be retained with greater confidence, but if falsified, it may be rejected outright or it might be modified and retested. • *An example of a hypothesis could be that the hormone abscisic acid works by stimulating potassium efflux from stomatal guard cells.*

may become the standing 'authorities' of the subject – but perhaps this is something to aspire to in your overall research career rather than in a three-year research project.

Researchers who try to overturn a paradigm will meet a lot of resistance from the academic community (many of whom may have a vested interest in its continuance). Their ideas are often met with incredulity and it may take time and the accumulation of new evidence to persuade others to change their views. Such events are rare and understandably those whose radical views are later accepted are feted for their impact on a subject area. An example might be the concept of continental drift (later, plate tectonics), as originally

Where do the ideas for new hypotheses come from?

This may be a question that exercises you if you are new to research. Generally speaking, they are said to arise from observations or the results of previous experiments. They normally require one or more of the following thought processes:

- analogy with other systems;
- recognition of a pattern;
- recognition of departure from a pattern;
- invention of new methods for research;
- development of a mathematical model;
- intuition;
- imagination.

championed by Alfred Wegener and others, which initially met great resistance from established geological scientists. As a PhD student, attempting to overturn a paradigm may not be a constructive strategy to adopt.

The concept of repeatability

This is vital to the rationale of the Scientific Method. The essential result from an experiment should be reproducible, providing all aspects remain equal (not always easy). Acceptable non-consequential differences should be within the bounds of error predicted by statistical analysis. An accepted hypothesis should therefore be testable again and again, with the same result, except for the occasional 'blip' where, considering statistical variation, the error data suggest that there is finite but small (usually less than 1 in 20) chance of a different result (Ch 23). This predictability underpins the utility of most scientific disciplines.

Non-science research

In the non-sciences, investigative approaches in many areas are less rigid than within experimental methodologies. This means that the tactics that researchers adopt are diverse and rely very much on the contexts of individual studies as well as on the philosophical underpinning and the research objectives. In short, there is no 'right way' to conduct research in many non-scientific areas. Hence, it may be that there is no clear hypothesis set as a preliminary to undertaking the research and that the research questions may arise from the circumstances, for example, from dialogue with subjects.

ACTION POINTS

3.1 Make contact with the relevant subject librarian in your university library. They may be able to assist with your initial research enquiries, either by showing you collections or by framing search queries for databases.

3.2 Identify the key paradigms and theories that underpin your preferred research area. In sciences, what hypotheses have been tested in recent research papers? Which might be important for your own project? In non-sciences, what philosophical approaches lie behind recent research publications?

3.3 Think of three goals for your research. Assess their quality using the three criteria given earlier in the chapter.

WRITING A PROPOSAL OR RESEARCH PLAN

How to outline your approach to postgraduate study

Depending on individual contexts, you may be required to submit a thesis proposal. You should regard your proposal as much more than an administrative exercise; it can help you to organise your preliminary thoughts, plan your approach and complete your work on time.

KEY TOPICS

→ Benefits of writing a proposal

→ What will be taken into account in assessing your proposal?

→ Writing your proposal

A proposal or research plan may be required before you are accepted for PhD study, or it may form part of the induction or progress monitoring scheme. Either way, the proposal is generally submitted before you start studying in depth or writing seriously. In some cases, your choice of topic may influence the selection or allocation of the person who will act as your supervisor.

This proposal or plan will outline the scope and methods of the research you intend to carry out and, in some cases, will indicate how you plan to organise your writing. Depending on the practices in your institution, your proposal will be considered by either a Research Committee or by your potential supervisor. You may be offered feedback and advice on how to proceed. Once approval is given for your proposal, you will be given the formal go-ahead to proceed with your studies under the guidance of your supervisor.

Administrative uses for research proposals

The proposal document may be used:

- to help allocate a supervisor for your research (**Ch 10**);
- to evaluate safety needs for your research;
- to consider ethical dimensions of your research (**Ch 19**);
- as a reference point for considering your later progress (**Ch 16**).

BENEFITS OF WRITING A PROPOSAL

The discipline of composing a proposal is a valuable exercise and you should approach this task in a positive frame of mind. The benefits include:

- ensuring your research has aims and objectives that are achievable in the time allocated;
- compelling you to read and review some of the relevant background material to orientate your thoughts;
- checking that you have a realistic notion of the research methods you could and should use;
- making sure you think about resources you may require at an early stage;
- ensuring that resources whether in terms of material or access to information will be reliably and realistically available to support your research;
- verifying that you have considered safety and ethical issues relating to your research;
- assisting you to create an outline structure for your dissertation or report;
- helping you to create a viable timetable for your work;
- matching your interests and needs to an appropriate supervisor (where relevant).

In some cases, acceptance of the research proposal may be a condition of being admitted to a course of doctoral study, especially where the applicant is self-funding or where competition for research places is significant. You may, for example, have nurtured an interest in a topic within your field where the area and method of study seem clear to you. Nevertheless, it is necessary to undertake this scoping exercise so others can ensure that what you seek to do is viable in practical terms as well as being profound enough for study at doctoral level.

WHAT WILL BE TAKEN INTO ACCOUNT IN ASSESSING YOUR PROPOSAL?

The person or group reading your proposal will be considering it from several viewpoints. They would expect you to be able to answer 'yes' to the questions in the checklist below:

❏ Have you carried out appropriate background reading?

❏ Do you have an up-to-date and accurate view of the research field?

❏ Have you outlined the focus of your studies in sufficient detail? (In some disciplines, this means the hypothesis you intend to test.)

❏ Is the scope of your proposed study realistic in the time allocated?

❏ Is your proposed research study sufficiently original?

❏ Is your proposed research sufficiently challenging?

❏ Will the research allow you to demonstrate your academic ability?

❏ Will the research give you the opportunity to develop and refine your skills?

❏ Are the proposed methods appropriate and are you aware of their limitations?

❏ Are you likely to gain access to all the resources you need?

❏ Have you considered the cost implications that uniquely apply to this research?

❏ Are you planning to deal with safety and ethical issues appropriately?

❏ Is the proposed structure of your dissertation or project and the underlying research evident?

❏ Will your proposed dissertation and the underlying scholarship meet the requirements of the department or university regulations?

❏ Is the project likely to make a contribution to knowledge in your field?

Finally, and in summary:

❏ Are your project and the resulting thesis likely to meet the required standard?

A key element that will be assessed is the research question, 'core hypothesis' or main idea underlying your project (**Ch 3**), so you should try to express this clearly.

Topics that will be looked on favourably are those that are novel, take an unusual perspective on a research area, and are relevant within the research field as it stands at the time of writing. A mistake commonly made is to try to cover too 'large' a problem or too wide an area of discussion, rather than one capable of adequate analysis given the resources likely to be at hand.

WRITING YOUR PROPOSAL

In many cases, an official form may be provided for your thesis or project proposal. This will normally include some or all of the components shown in Table 4.1, so that the person or committee evaluating your proposal can answer the questions noted in the previous section. Where no official form is provided, then using selected items in the 'Component' column in Table 4.1 will provide a framework for creating your own research proposal document.

Arriving at a position to write a proposal will require that you carry out an appropriate amount of background reading (**Chs 3** and **8**). At an early stage, try to arrange an appointment with a staff member for a brief discussion about possible directions. If you have been allocated a supervisor, then consult them; if not, think about who you would like to be a supervisor and ask them. Prior to this you could discuss your proposal informally with others to 'rehearse' points for discussion so that you can identify weaknesses in logic in your plan.

Choosing a title

The point at which you write your proposal may be the first time you have concrete thoughts about your title. Consider adopting a two-part title – an attention-grabbing statement, followed by a colon or a dash and a secondary title that defines the content more closely. Note that the title given at the proposal stage should be seen as provisional, for the nature of the study and the outcomes may dictate a change at the end of the process.

Table 4.1 **Typical components of a thesis or project proposal.** The choice of elements used will depend on the discipline and level of study.

Component	Content and aspects to consider
Personal details	Preferred name and contact details
Details of your degree course or programme	There may be subtle differences according to your precise degree
Proposed title (it may alter as the work evolves)	This should be relatively short; a two-part title style can be useful
Description of the subject area/ Summary/Background/Brief review/ Statement of the problem or issue to be addressed/Research question	A brief outline that provides context such as: a synopsis of past work; a description of the 'gap' to be filled or new area to be explored; a summary of current ideas and, where relevant, hypothesis/hypotheses
Aim of research	General description of the overall purpose; a statement of intent
Objectives	Listing of specific outcomes you expect to fulfil in order to achieve the aim
Literature to be examined	The sources you intend to consult
Research methods or critical approach	How you propose to carry out your investigation
Preliminary bibliography	Details (in appropriate format) of the key sources you have already consulted
(Special) resources required	Information sources, samples, instruments, people (subjects), and other requirements
Outline plan of the dissertation or project report	For example, the likely section or chapter headings and subheadings
Indication of whether discussions have already been held with a nominated supervisor/indication of a potential supervisor	Valid only in cases where there is an element of choice of supervisor
Indication of whether discussions have already been held with the programme or course director in case of a project report	Valid only in cases where this is an administrative requirement
Names of possible supervisors	Your chance to influence this aspect, where relevant
Timetable/plan	A realistic breakdown of the stages of your dissertation, ideally with milestones
Statement or declaration that you understand and will comply with safety and/or ethical rules	The committee's guarantee that you have considered these; details may be required in certain cases (see **Ch 19**)

Example of refining a subject area

Where the area of study is 'open', you may need to consider various aspects of a potential research area before refining this to a more specific topic. Let's say you are interested in bicameral systems of government. Clearly you cannot expect to write a PhD thesis on this topic in its generality. Suppose you had been enthused by a past lecturer (a potential supervisor?) who talked about the checks and balances that arise from having two chambers of government. The issue has become more topical in recent times and your interest in contrasting the idea of an elected second chamber with one that is dependent on patronage and selection seems to resonate with proposals to reform the UK House of Lords. You feel that the debate has not covered some implications arising from these reform proposals. Potential areas for scrutiny might include:

- examining the current composition of the House of Lords and the levels of participation and contribution to the governmental process made by life and hereditary peers respectively;
- contrasting these with similar inputs by elected Members of the Commons;
- considering how peers might be elected and what period of service might apply;
- reviewing the pros and cons of party-political affiliations in the second chamber;
- evaluating an electoral college approach to composition of a second chamber;
- appraising the potential powers of a second elected chamber and the role that such a chamber might fulfil in a modern political system and the legislative process in particular;
- exploring the need for and implications of ensuring checks and balances on the powers of both Houses.

These issues collectively might become the framework of a thesis project. However, an alternative approach might mean that the thesis would focus on only one or two of these aspects. Scoping potential issues in this way is a way of helping to define your topic, in this case, within an appraisal of election rather than selection as a means of creating a bicameral system. This might translate into a provisional thesis title such as: 'Representative Second Chambers: the United Kingdom House of Lords as a case study.'

Present your proposal neatly. It should be word-processed and should stick very closely to any recommended word limits. Regardless of any length constraints, try to make your proposal succinct and to the point. There will be ample time to expand your thoughts when writing the real dissertation or project report. The proposal committee will be trying to arrive at a quick decision and this will be made easier if your proposal is 'short and sweet'.

The language in your proposal should be clear to the non-specialist, but must include appropriate terminology to show that you understand key concepts and jargon. Set yourself realistic aims and objectives, bearing in mind the need for originality in your work. The group considering your proposal will be aware that a major reason for students having problems with dissertations and project choices is that they were over-ambitious at the start.

Try not to prepare your proposal in a rush. If possible, write out a near-final draft and leave it for a few days before coming back to it again with a critical mind, then make suitable modifications before your final submission.

The difference between aims and objectives or goals

A statement of both 'aims' and 'objectives' for your research may be required in your proposal form – and the distinction between these can be confusing. Widely accepted definitions generally suggest that aims are statements of intent or purpose that are broad in nature, and hence defined in general terms perhaps relating to an overall outcome, while objectives (goals) are outlined in more specific terms and tend to relate to individual, achievable outcomes that are required to fulfil the ultimate aim. For example, the aim of a dissertation might be to 'summarise viewpoints within a particular research field' while an objective might be to 'compare the various research methods in use to measure a particular variable'. Ideally objectives will state 'what', 'how', 'where' and 'when' (as appropriate).

ACTION POINTS

4.1 Imagine you are assessing your own proposal. Having completed a draft, answer all the questions in the checklist above for any answers that might be problematic, go back to the proposal and see if you could improve on it, or provide evidence to back up your case.

4.2 List potential thesis or project report titles. Consult other theses and project reports completed recently to gain a feel for the modern style in your discipline. Write down a few options for your own work and ask your supervisor or fellow students what they think of them.

4.3 Create a detailed timetable for your research and writing. Consult **Chapter 6** for advice on managing time and remember to factor in some slippage time. Include suitable milestones; for example, 'finish first draft' (see Table 1.1).

KEY PhD RESEARCH

SKILLS

5

DEVELOPING AS A RESEARCHER

Appraising your skills and gaining proficiency

The UK Research Councils have been active in creating an organisation, Vitae, charged with supporting postgraduate research students in their personal development. Vitae's online resource will help you to outline skills of potential relevance and help you to audit your strengths and weaknesses; in tandem with the training programmes on offer at your own university (or department), you can tailor and fulfil a plan for your own training needs.

KEY TOPICS

→ Relevant personal skills for research

→ Planning your development as a researcher

→ Taking advantage of training opportunities

→ Summarising your development

In the past, PhD researchers had a somewhat patchy experience in gaining skills for personal and career development. Traditionally, PhD training tended to depend on the organisation of department-hosted events such as seminars, and the willingness of their supervisor to help students develop their skill-set. This was recognised as a problem by the UK Research Councils, and, as a result, universities were provided with earmarked resources to tackle this issue. The Research Councils also supported the creation of an organisation to support personal development, Vitae, whose resources can be used to put your institution's training in a personal context.

Vitae aims to 'realise the potential of researchers' by supporting the personal, professional and career development of doctoral researchers and research staff in higher education institutions and research institutes. It is managed by CRAC, the Careers Research and Advisory Centre. Vitae's comprehensive resources are available at **www.vitae.ac.uk/researchers**. Some of the material in this chapter borrows from their approach.

One advantage of creating a single source of generic web-based information is that all postgraduate students can access this kind of support no matter how big or small their institution or the size of a postgraduate's research department.

UK Research Councils

Currently (2013), there are seven Research Councils in the UK:

- the Arts and Humanities Research Council;
- the Biotechnology and Biological Sciences Research Council;
- the Engineering and Physical Sciences Research Council;
- the Economic and Social Research Council;
- the Medical Research Council;
- the Natural Environment Research Council;
- the Science and Technology Facilities Council.

These research councils provide funding directly to UK universities and research organisations.

RELEVANT PERSONAL SKILLS FOR RESEARCH

When embarking on a PhD research project, you will be well aware of the need to carry out certain new activities and to perform them to the required standard. You will probably be keen to develop and add to the skills acquired during your undergraduate days. By engaging with the reflection that this book and the Vitae site invites, you will be preparing for the future and actively taking responsibility for optimising your skill-set in ways that may never be available to you again in your professional life.

Any effort to improve your skills should start from a 'skills audit'. One basic way of thinking about the necessary skills is to divide them into 'hard' and 'soft' skills:

- Hard research skills. These are essential for the progress of your research, and include:

- specific technical skills (for example, the use of software or instruments required in your work);
- methods (for example, analytical lab procedures, survey approaches or design of questionnaires);
- safety training (often required before you can use, for example, radioactive or carcinogenic substances or work unsupervised in a laboratory);
- ethics training (may be required for research involving patients or third-party interviews).

These skills tend to be project- and institution-specific and generally require that you follow a defined procedure or programme relevant to your place of study (that is, your research group, department or university).

● Soft research skills. These also benefit your research, but there is more scope for a variety of approaches. Examples include:
- literature searching;
- writing;
- making presentations;
- teaching;
- teamwork.

In general, many of these softer skills will be transferable to employment.

The essential skill of learning

As a postgraduate, you will be expected to take responsibility for your studies with limited support from those around you. A prescription of how and when to do things that you may have experienced as an undergraduate will be absent. Therefore, how you research, assimilate, analyse, synthesise and retain large amounts of information will be down to you and how you learn best. If the introspection required to understand these 'learning preferences' is novel to you, it is essential that you take some time to audit these characteristics so that you can work to your strengths while reflecting on and developing your less well-developed traits. A recommended online approach to this is available at *www.vark-learn.com*. This includes a simple questionnaire that is used to suggest a personal learning preference (visual, aural, read-write, kinesthetic, or multimodal).

The Vitae 'Researcher Development Statement' (RDS; Careers Research and Advisory Centre, 2010) is a detailed resource which provides postgraduate researchers with a framework for progress. This covers a blend of knowledge, skills, abilities, behaviours and attitudes. It was derived from the Joint Skill Statement of the UK Research Councils (UK Research Councils, 2001). The RDS divides researchers' development needs into four 'domains':

1 Knowledge and intellectual abilities – the knowledge, intellectual abilities and techniques to do research.

2 Personal effectiveness – the personal qualities and approach required to be an effective researcher.

3 Research governance and organisation – the knowledge of the standards, requirements and professionalism to do research.

4 Engagement, influence and impact – the knowledge and skills to work with others and ensure the wider impact of research.

Table 5.1 indicates the sorts of abilities and skills relevant to each of the Vitae domains.

Being aware of the potential skills you might require is the first part of a skills audit. The next is to select and prioritise those abilities particularly relevant to your personality and research area that you might want to develop. Finally, you will need to find both the opportunity and time to undergo the training available to you.

PLANNING YOUR DEVELOPMENT AS A RESEARCHER

The Vitae website's Professional Development Planner (PDP) resource allows you to take each researcher development sub-domain and aspect forward, creating your own targets with the aid of a downloadable spreadsheet planner. For each of the aspects, you are presented with descriptions of three to five phases of development which you can use to self-assess your current position and set future targets (see Figure 5.1 for an example). You are asked to assess or complete the following:

● current phase;

● target phase;

● evidence to support your current phase;

Table 5.1 **Selected knowledge and intellectual abilities within the four domains of the Vitae Researcher Development Statement (RDS).** The three sub-domains for each domain A–D are provided, but only selected (and sometimes paraphrased) aspects of each sub-domain are included. The full statement with its division into domains and sub-domains is available at *http://www.vitae.ac.uk/CMS/files/upload/Researcher%20development%20statement.pdf* (accessed 23 July 2012).

A. Knowledge and intellectual abilities
1 Knowledge base: subject knowledge; theory and application of techniques; information literacy; academic literacy
2 Cognitive abilities: analysis; synthesis; critical thinking; problem-solving
3 Creativity: insight; innovation; construction of arguments
B. Personal effectiveness:
1 Personal qualities: enthusiasm, perseverance; integrity; willingness to reflect
2 Self-management: preparation; prioritisation; time management; work–life balance
3 Professional and career development: career management; responsiveness to opportunities; networking
C. Research governance and organisation
1 Professional conduct: health and safety; ethics; awareness of intellectual property and copyright issues; attribution of ideas
2 Research management: research strategy; project planning; risk management
3 Finance, funding and resources: financial management; infrastructure and resources
D. Engagement, influence and impact
1 Working with others: team-working; collaboration; leadership; equality and diversity awareness
2 Communication and dissemination: methods and media for communication; publication
3 Engagement and impact: teaching; public engagement; enterprise

- how you will achieve your objectives;
- how you will measure it;
- target dates;
- additional comments.

As a novice researcher you may find the descriptions of the higher phases in the Vitae planner to be very demanding – but you would not necessarily be expected to reach these levels of achievement as a research student – these phases represent professional goals for

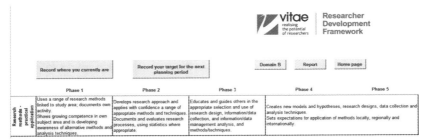

Figure 5.1 Screenshot taken from the downloadable Vitae Professional Development Planner for postgraduate researchers. This shows the five phases associated with the aspect 'Research methods – practical application' of the sub-domain 'Knowledge base' within the domain of 'Knowledge and intellectual abilities' (see also Table 5.1). Note that in this case phases four and five are joint, covering a relatively wide spectrum of status.

experienced research workers, and even then, perhaps at quite an advanced point in their career.

Identifying a set of targets for personal development is one thing, but finding the means and time to achieve them is a different challenge. In some cases, the 'means' will come first, for example, if you spot a suitable training event in your university's postgraduate training scheme. It is then a question of timetabling other activities around this. In other cases, you will need to create both the time and the opportunity yourself. An example for a new postgraduate might be when improving your ability to search for relevant literature, by making an appointment to meet the relevant university subject librarian.

As a guide, Vitae suggests you might spend about a day a month on training, throughout your career in research. It is likely that the progress monitoring system at your university (**Ch 16**) will require you to audit your skills, attend training events and record what you have done. Your university or department may provide their own guidelines for participation (which should take precedence).

As you progress through your studies, you will probably identify new skills to develop or see the need to refine existing ones. Therefore it is important to reappraise your skills from time to time. This may be encouraged either via your department's progress monitoring scheme or as part of the postgraduate training scheme. A good supervisor will also keep you aware of needs and opportunities.

How should I plan my training?

The Vitae website page 'Planning your training' (Careers Research and Advisory Centre, 2012, *http://www.vitae.ac.uk/researchers/1607/ Planning-your-training.html* [accessed 23 July 2012]) suggests that you ask yourself the following questions when prioritising training:

- By what date do I need to have received this training?
- Is it something that I really need to do as quickly as possible to start my research (e.g. learn about databases to be able to store data) or is it something that I need for a particular purpose and that can be scheduled appropriately (e.g. *Viva* training)?
- When is this training available?
- How much time do I want to allocate each week/month to training?
- What are my other time commitments?
- How can I fit my training plan around my research, work and personal obligations?

TAKING ADVANTAGE OF TRAINING OPPORTUNITIES

A typical training scheme will contain a mix of general and specific presentations or workshops. Sometimes, as with learning to use software, the latter will involve hands-on training. The scheme will probably be introduced to you at an induction event, and the programme will probably be available online. A typical training programme will be conducted by a mix of internal and external presenters.

As noted above, institutional training scheme events are not the only way in which you can further your development. Other opportunities include:

- attending conferences, where you can meet other researchers, present interim findings and hear about the findings or views of others;
- making visits to other academics or research groups to discuss matters of mutual interest;
- carrying out specific research objectives in another location (for example, using a specific research instrument or facility; visiting an site of special scientific interest);
- reading books and manuals.

Most of these openings should be discussed with your supervisor before proceeding. Some supervisors are particularly wary of contact with other research groups before research themes or results are confirmed or published.

Typical event titles from a doctoral workshop programme

These examples have been adapted from the University of Dundee's Organisational and Professional Development Programme for 2012 (*http://www.dundee.ac.uk/media/dundeewebsite/opd/documents/OPD%20brochure%20WEB.pdf*) where the target group is highlighted as 'PhD students' or 'All':

■ Communicating science to non-specialists;

■ Communicating through writing – CVs, covering letters and applications;

■ Designing and delivering academic posters – taking a professional approach;

■ Developing as a researcher – launching your PhD (Year 1);

■ Developing as a researcher – making progress in your PhD (Year 2);

■ Developing as a researcher – the end is in sight (final year);

■ Enhancing interview skills – a practical approach;

■ Exploring advanced Excel – functions, tricks and short-cuts;

■ Exploring advanced Word – functions, tricks and short-cuts;

■ Introducing research statistics – SPSS and SIGMASTAT;

■ Introducing research statistics – using SPSS;

■ Learning to use Endnote – effective electronic referencing;

■ Manipulating digital images – understanding Photoshop;

■ Networking effectively – application of social networking tools for professional purposes;

■ Reading at speed – becoming a more efficient reader;

■ Summarising your research for the non-specialist – the layperson's abstract;

■ Understanding intellectual property and commercialisation;

■ Using mind-mapping effectively – principles and tools;

■ Writing and publishing your research.

Benefits of attending training events

As well as the chance to upgrade your skills, training events are an opportunity to get out of your normal working environment and meet other postgraduates. The experience of participating in a group often adds value to your learning. There is a chance to make new social contacts and you may be able to work together to solve each other's personal and research problems. Sometimes you will meet others whose questions and ideas spark new lines of study for you.

It is important to attend training events in a positive frame of mind – so that you and others attending will maximise the benefits. For instance, some information or advice that seems obvious to you may not be at all so to someone from a different culture or background. They might gain from receiving your wisdom in positive discussion. You may note that 'helping others' is part of several sub-domains in the Vitae Research Development Statement.

There may be issues with certain supervisors regarding what they regard as over-attendance at training events. They may feel that you should be spending as much time as possible at your desk or bench. However, you should resist pressure in this direction if you believe you will gain personally from attendance.

What if you have timetabling issues?

You may run into problems if the timetabling of events clashes with other responsibilities. In that case, seek advice about alternative ways to pick up the material – there may be handouts, PowerPoint presentations and other materials you can use.

SUMMARISING YOUR DEVELOPMENT

The work you put in to personal or professional development planning will stand you in good stead when taking part in progress monitoring meetings and later when applying for a job or new research position. It will certainly assist with the vocabulary required to describe your attributes. It will also help you to indicate strengths, weaknesses and areas for development, both when writing applications and orally during discussions or interviews.

There will come a time when you need to summarise your skills and attributes via a *curriculum vitae* (CV) and perhaps in an application letter or statement regarding a specific post you are applying for. The structure and contents of a postgraduate CV are discussed in **Chapter 33**. Meantime, the Vitae Professional Development Planner is recommended as an excellent way of noting your progress and current status if no other personal development planning scheme is promoted at your institution.

ACTION POINTS

5.1 Visit and bookmark the Vitae website (*http://www.vitae.ac.uk*). Download the Professional Development Planner spreadsheet and conduct a personal skills audit.

5.2 Visit and bookmark the webpage for your University's postgraduate training unit. Discuss events you may wish to attend with your supervisor. Be prepared to explain why each will be useful both to you and to your research project.

5.3 Take time to think about the CV details you might wish to have by the end of your postgraduate degree. This will help you to direct your personal development. Desirable aspects may depend on the jobs you might be applying for. If you are unsure about this, it might be a good idea to meet with a Careers Service advisor to discuss possible directions. The earlier you feel able do this, the better.

6

PLANNING AND TIME MANAGEMENT

How to complete your research and write-up on time

Managing your time effectively is an important key to completing a PhD. This chapter provides ideas for organising your activities with tips to help you to maintain focus on the key tasks in the research and writing processes.

KEY TOPICS

→ Diaries, timetables and planners

→ Listing and prioritising

→ Routines and good work habits

→ What to do if you can't get started on a task or can't complete it

→ The value of unstructured time

Successful people tend to have the ability to focus on the right tasks at the right time, the capacity to work quickly to meet their targets, and the knack of seeing each job through to a conclusion. In short, they possess good time-management skills.

As a PhD student, you will need to balance the time you devote to your research, family, paid work and social activities. To a great extent doctoral students are expected to exercise considerable autonomy in conducting their research, hence excellent time management is essential. This is an important professional skill that is implied by possession of a postgraduate degree (**Ch 5**). While you will probably have more freedom over these choices than many others, making the necessary decisions about how to use your time can still be a challenge. Table 6.1 illustrates why good time management is especially important at this level.

Table 6.1 Some of the ways in which PhD students demonstrate poor time management. These are examples of work patterns that don't work well for lengthy projects and possible solutions.

1 **Working long hours for an extended period.** This will probably be the result of being over-ambitious or disorganised. The results can be catastrophic: complete breakdown is not unknown. Even if you are driven by competition or a supervisor with very high expectations you must work out what is healthily feasible within the limits of your project and 'having a life'.
2 **Last-minute completion.** Underestimating the amount of work or failing to focus from the start are two reasons for having to rush at the end. The solution is to be organised, focused and to work at an even, well-judged pace throughout.
3 **Being over-confident.** This can lead to an underestimation of the difficulty or amount of time required to complete a task. The solution is to have a realistic view of your own abilities and what you want to do. This will come from experience, asking others (including your supervisor) what is involved and studying the task in more detail.
4 **Being a perfectionist.** This is a dangerous problem because, on the one hand, carrying out your work to the best of your ability is a hallmark of good postgraduate research. On the other hand, it can lead to a lack of progress as you stall or repeat the same task again and again, looking for the best possible information or result. Sometimes it is better to accept work that is not ideal so you can move on to other tasks.
5 **Not being focused.** Life is full of distractions, but undertaking a PhD effectively means you have to put some of your interests aside to concentrate on a single topic for three years. This does not mean having a lack of outside interests, but it does mean that these need to be kept well in check and, if necessary, scaled down for periods.
6 **Doing too much teaching or outside work.** It is easy to underestimate how much extra work there is in teaching (such as preparation and marking, **Ch 13**) and how tiring it can be. The obvious answer is to keep these activities under control but, if your involvement is partly due to a lack of finances, it is a tricky one to resolve. The same principles apply to outside work.

Time management is a skill that can be developed like any other. Relatively simple routines and tips can help you improve your organisation, prioritisation and time-keeping. Weigh up the following ideas and try to adopt those most suited to your needs and personality. Some may be familiar, but there are always benefits from having a fresh look at your work patterns.

Advantages of being organised

Being well-organised is especially important for large or long-term tasks like a PhD because it seems easier to put things off when deadlines seem distant. If you manage your time well, you will:

- keep on schedule and meet your submission deadline;
- complete work with less pressure, avoid the build-up of stress and fulfil your potential;
- build your confidence about your ability to cope;
- avoid overlapping commitments and having to juggle more than one piece of work at a time.

DIARIES, TIMETABLES AND PLANNERS

Organising your activities more carefully is an obvious way to gain productive time.

Diaries/calendars

A diary or calendar, whether maintained in hard copy or on a mobile, or other on-screen device or software, is the obvious way to keep track of your day-to-day schedule (for example, meetings, seminars and other activities) and to note any deadlines you have.

- For lengthy tasks, work your way back from key dates, creating milestones such as 'finish library work for xxx' or 'prepare first draft of section x'.

- Refer to the diary frequently to keep yourself on track and to plan out each day and week.

- Try to get into the habit of looking at the next day's activities the night before and the next week's work at the end of the week. A diary with the 'week-to-view' type of layout will help you to plan over the longer term.

- Number the weeks, so you can sense how time is progressing over longer periods, such as a term or semester. This may be important if you have teaching activities, so that you can keep in track with the undergraduate year.

In addition, having a written or electronic record of events, meetings or submissions can be helpful if you need to recollect when you did something when you come to write up.

Investigate how you really use your time

Time-management experts often ask clients to write down what they do for every minute of several days and thereby work out how and where the productive time disappears. If you are unsure whether you are optimising time, you might like to keep a detailed record for a short period, using a suitable coding for your activities. When you have identified any time that has been less productive you could try analysing how this has happened. Those of a more numerical bent might wish to construct a spreadsheet to do this and work out percentages spent on different activities. Once you have completed your timesheet, appraise it to see whether you spend excessive amounts of time on any one activity or may not have the balance right.

Timetables

When you have a lengthy task like researching or writing up a PhD, creating a detailed timetable of work can be useful because it helps to ensure you take into account all aspects of the work you have to complete by:

- breaking the task down into smaller parts;
- spacing these out appropriately;
- scheduling important work for when you generally feel most intellectually active (e.g. mid-morning).

One advantage of a timetable is that you can see the progress you are making if you cross out each 'mini-task' as it is completed.

 Always build flexibility into your planning

We often end up rushing things because the unexpected has interrupted a timetable that is too tightly scheduled. To avoid this, introduce empty slots into your plans to allow for contingencies.

Wall planners

These are another way of charting out your activities, with the advantage that you can see all your commitments and deadlines at a glance.

Whiteboards

Some students find it useful to use a whiteboard or other surface to mark up and amend a flexible plan to help them keep track of their commitments, goals and plans.

Thinking ahead

Anticipating events that need to be included in your time planning is important. For example, if you need to book a particular piece of equipment, this clearly needs to be done in advance. Failure to place the booking can upset your planning and waste valuable time – not only your own, but that of others whose work schedules may have been adversely affected because of your last-minute booking.

Similarly, if you need to monitor the subjects of your research, perhaps in a clinic or classroom, then you will need to schedule a visit that coincides with their availability. If you fail to do this, then you may miss the opportunity and damage your research objectives and timetable.

The various milestones of a PhD are listed in Table 1.1. Some of these events, such as seminars and annual reports, will require a lot of preparation. Forward planning is a useful way of avoiding a last-minute rush.

LISTING AND PRIORITISING

At times you may have a number of different tasks that need to be done. Write these tasks down as a list each day, rather than risk forgetting them. You will then have a good picture of what needs to be done and will be able to prioritise the tasks more readily.

Once you've created a list, rank the tasks by numbering them 1, 2, 3 and so on, in order from 'important and urgent' to 'neither important nor urgent' (see Figure 6.1). Your 'important' criteria will depend on many factors: for example, your own goals and submission dates.

Each day, you should try to complete as many of the listed tasks as you can, starting with number one. If you keep each day's list achievable, the process of striking out each task as it is completed provides a feeling of progress being made, which turns into one of satisfaction if the list has virtually disappeared by the evening. Also, you will become less stressed once high-priority tasks are tackled.

Carry over any uncompleted tasks to the next day, add new ones to your list and start again – but try to complete yesterday's unfinished jobs before starting new ones of similar priority, or they will end up being delayed for too long.

This technique works well for practical aspects of researching. Once you get to the writing-up phase, it becomes less easy to

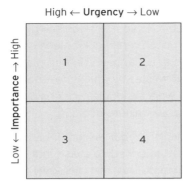

High ← **Urgency** → Low

Low ← **Importance** → High

Figure 6.1 The urgent–important approach to prioritising. Place each activity somewhere on the axes in relation to its importance and urgency. Do all the activities in sector 1 first, then 2 or 3, and last 4.

apply list-making to the writing task itself. However, keeping lists of non-writing things you need to do helps you to deal with each item separately and keep your mind free to focus on the writing in progress.

For example, in normal circumstances, visiting the barber or hairdresser will be neither terribly important nor particularly urgent, but if you have to present a conference poster next week, then the 'shaggy dog' look you have been cultivating may require some attention, meaning that making a salon appointment moves further up your 'to do' list. Hence, priorities are not static and need to be reassessed frequently.

 How can you decide on your priorities?

This involves distinguishing between important and urgent activities.

- Importance implies some assessment of the benefits of completing a task against the loss if the task is not finished.
- Urgency relates to the length of time before the task must be completed.

ROUTINES AND GOOD WORK HABITS

Many people find that carrying out specific tasks at special periods of the day or times of the week helps them to get things done on time. You may already adopt this approach with routine tasks like doing your shopping every Tuesday morning or visiting a relative on Sunday afternoons. You may find it helps to add work-related activities to your list of routines – for example, by making Monday evening a time for literature searching in the library.

Good working habits can help with time management:

- Do important work when you are at your most productive. Most of us can state when we work best (i.e. morning, afternoon or evening). When you have worked this out for yourself, timetable your activities to suit: carry out academic work when you are 'most awake' and routine activities when you are less alert.

- Make the most of small scraps of time. Use otherwise unproductive time, such as when commuting or before going to sleep, to jot down ideas, edit work or make plans. Keep a paper or electronic notebook with you to write down your thoughts.

- Keep your documents organised. If your papers are well filed, then you won't waste time looking for something required for the next step.

- Make sure you always have a plan. Often, the reason projects don't go well is because there is no scheme for the work. Laying out a plan for any academic research or writing helps you to clarify the likely structure behind your efforts. Writing out a fairly detailed plan saves you time in the long run. It is also an aid to consolidating your thinking.

- Extend your working day. If you can deal with early rising, you may find that setting your alarm earlier than normal provides a few extra hours to help you achieve a short-term goal.

- Allocate a specific day each week for 'house-keeping' your research. Taking the time to audit your achievements and progress over the previous week and anticipate your next steps will stimulate your planning for the following week. This can also be an opportunity to catch up on routine tasks such as administration or managing your work space, materials and equipment. Using this strategy means that you start your next research period with a clear desk and a plan of action for the following week.

Create an artificial deadline

If working on a medium-sized task such as a seminar or progress monitoring report, set yourself a finishing date that is well in advance of the formal presentation or submission deadline. That way you will have the luxury of time to review your work, correct errors and improve the quality of presentation.

WHAT TO DO IF YOU CAN'T GET STARTED ON A TASK OR CAN'T COMPLETE IT

People agree that one of the hardest parts of time management is getting started on tasks. Putting things off – procrastination – is all too easy, and can involve the following displacement activities:

- convincing yourself that other low-priority work is more important or preferable;
- switching frequently among tasks, and not making much progress in any of them;
- talking about your work rather than doing it;
- 'helping' others by discussing their work rather than getting on with your own; alternatively, being persuaded to help others with their work to the detriment of your own;
- planning for too long rather than working;
- having difficulty starting a piece of writing ('writer's block');
- spending too long on presentational elements (for example, how a graph looks), rather than the 'meat' of the project;
- finding mundane TV programmes fascinating or being easily persuaded to socialise rather than work.

If you admit to any of these symptoms, you may be subconsciously procrastinating. Becoming more aware of how you might be falling into this trap is the first stage in consciously avoiding it.

Delaying completion of a task, in itself a form of procrastination, is another aspect of time management that many find difficult. It may be that you are avoiding moving on to another, more difficult task. Another possibility is that you are subconsciously anxious about the quality of the final submission and are therefore reluctant to produce the final version.

Procrastination is a special problem for perfectionists. Good time managers recognise when to finish tasks, even if the task is not in a 'perfect' state. As a PhD student, recognising this can mean that the sum of multiple tasks is better, because your attention is divided more appropriately, rather than focusing on a single element.

Tips for getting started on tasks and completing them on time are provided in Table 6.2.

Table 6.2 Tips for getting started on research tasks and meeting deadlines.

1 Improve your study environment.
• Create a tidy workplace. Although tidying up can be a symptom of procrastination, in general it is easier to start studying at an empty desk and in an uncluttered room.
• Reduce noise. It is generally other people's noise that really interrupts your train of thought. A solution might be to go to a quiet place like a library.
• Escape. Why not take all you need to a different location where there will be a minimum of interruptions?
2 Avoid distractions. If you are easily tempted away from study by your friends, you'll have to learn to decline their invitations politely. 'Disappear' off to a quiet location without telling anyone where you will be; or switch off your phone, TV or email.
3 Work in short bursts while your concentration is at a maximum. After this, give yourself a brief break, perhaps a short walk, and then start back again.
4 Find a way to start. When writing, finding a way to start is a very common problem because of the perceived need to begin with a 'high impact' sentence that reads impressively. This is unnecessary, and starting with a simple definition or restatement of the issue or problem is perfectly acceptable.
5 Focus on the positive. You may be so anxious about the end point of your task that this affects your ability to start it. For example, many students are so nervous about the apparent difficulty, or prospect, of writing at PhD level that they freeze in their preparation and put the whole thing off. One way to counter this would be to start writing about an aspect of the topic that excites you. Once you become immersed in this, the writing will become less daunting.
6 In written tasks, don't feel you have to tackle the writing in a linear fashion. Word-processing software allows you work out of sequence, which can help get you going. So, for a PhD thesis, it might help to start on a part that is 'mechanical', such as a reference list or results section.
7 Cut up large tasks. If you feel overwhelmed by the size of the job and this prevents you from starting it, break the task down to manageable, achievable chunks. Then, try to complete something every day. Maintaining momentum in this way will allow you to whittle away the job in stages.
8 Work alongside others. If you arrange to work alongside others, you can spur each other on with sympathy, humour and the promise of a break.
9 Ask for help. You may feel that you lack a particular skill to attempt some component of the task (for example, the ability to use a statistics program) and that this is holding you back. Don't be afraid to ask for help, rather than suffering in isolation: consult a fellow student or your supervisor, or visit one of the many websites that offer assistance.
10 Don't be a too much of a perfectionist. We all want to do well, but doing your very best takes time – a commodity that should be carefully rationed so that all tasks are given their fair share. Also, achieving fault-free work requires progressively more effort, with less return as you get nearer to perfection. The time you need to spend to attain the highest standards for one element will probably be better used on the next part of the task.

THE VALUE OF UNSTRUCTURED TIME

The importance of allowing time in a schedule for contingencies has already been emphasised. Other uses for such 'unstructured' time include:

- carrying out minor tasks, such as tidying, that can improve efficiency and effectiveness;
- observing things or reading text more closely, perhaps for a second time, when new features may emerge;
- reflecting on past events;
- preparing mentally for future events.

Although this chapter stresses the importance of good time management, in PhD research work – whatever your discipline – make sure that you leave some time for serendipity to take over.

Some of the most famous discoveries and inventions occurred during moments when the researcher was thinking about or doing something else (**Ch 17**). So, for example, leave some space in your timetable to browse amongst the library shelves, not looking for anything in particular, but just opening books because their titles look interesting or intriguing. You never know what you may find or what thought process will be sparked by what you have read.

Alternatively, take a walk and look around you – being amongst nature, or even just in the fresh air may help you to arrive at an answer to a difficult problem.

ACTION POINTS

6.1 Analyse your time-management personality. Can you recognise any character traits that might prevent you from organising your time effectively? Might any tips in this chapter help you become better at time management? How could you adapt them to your own situation?

6.2 Experiment with listing and prioritising. If you haven't used this strategy before, test it out for a week or so. Make a list of all your current and future tasks, academic commitments, appointments and social events. Rearrange the list in order of priority. Take special care to take account of events that depend on other jobs being completed. Now try to complete the different components, ticking them off the list as you go. After your trial period, decide how effective the method was in organising your activities and helping you to ensure that tasks were done on time.

6.3 Declutter and reorganise your life. If you reckon that disorganisation is a reason for lack of progress (Table 6.2), make a determined effort to tidy things up. Start with your working environment, and, if necessary, invest in files and boxes to help you organise things. Keep out only that which is relevant to current activities and carefully store the rest. Decide how you can arrange your affairs more sensibly to keep on top of routine tasks. Now you should be in a better mental and physical position to get on with your research.

7

INFORMATION LITERACY FOR PHD STUDY

How to find relevant source material

In researching for your PhD, you will generally be expected to source material for yourself. Your supervisor may suggest some resources to get you started, but after that it will be very much up to you to explore further, according to your specific project aims. Therefore, learning more about your university library from the viewpoint of a researcher is a priority. This chapter offers some suggestions and strategies for using your library resources effectively.

KEY TOPICS

→ First steps for new researchers

→ Basic types of source material

→ How to access your university library's e-resources

→ Obtaining difficult-to-find sources

The library is a key resource in any research project. Modern university libraries are not just repositories of books, journals and archived material. They are information centres that coordinate an electronic gateway to a massive amount of online information. Accessing these resources requires a set of library information skills, sometimes called 'information literacy', that are essential to your research studies. This term has been defined as: 'knowing when and why you need information, where to find it, and how to evaluate, use and communicate it in an ethical manner' (CILIP, 2012).

FIRST STEPS FOR NEW RESEARCHERS

Although you might have studied in higher education for a few years and have used library resources quite extensively for undergraduate

How can I learn more about what my library has to offer?

The library in which you study for your PhD may be a new one to you if you have moved institutions between degrees and may offer different facilities or present facilities in a different way. Apart from contacting the librarian with responsibility for your discipline, you may find that library staff run training sessions on how to use referencing packages or on the use of new or subject-specific databases. Your library's website may also carry useful tips and online access routes to databases and e-journals. Many libraries have hard-copy leaflets providing tips and guidelines for using a range of facilities and resources.

dissertation or project research, your PhD-level studies will probably mean that you need to delve into areas and facilities that you may not have had the occasion to explore or use before. For example, a doctor of medicine undertaking PhD research into euthanasia may find the need to access sources in Law, Philosophy or Theology, all of which would be entirely beyond their prior experience. Indeed, familiarising yourself with a new range of search engines in order to find new material at an appropriate level of detail to support your research may present a major challenge.

Spending time at the start to consider the different aspects of information literacy will bring later rewards. Library experts have identified seven key information skills – see the information tip overleaf. This analysis provides valuable clues about the expectations for your work at this new level, and you should self-assess how well you can carry out each of the seven skills. Essentially, for PhD level research, you will be expected to be able to carry out all of them at a high level of competence. Consult library staff if you feel you need assistance on any specific skill.

Library information systems are constantly changing as your library enters into agreements with new or different suppliers of online information through subscriptions to electronic media, especially e-journals, which are of particular importance in researching. Although you will probably find that your library provides an online information portal dedicated to your subject area, you may find it easier at the outset to contact the librarian with responsibility for collating links to these discipline-specific resources. In some libraries, there may also be librarians with the particular remit of supporting PhD students. Make

The seven key information skills associated with information literacy (SCONUL, 2011)

1 The ability to identify a personal need for information ('identify' information).

2 The ability to assess current knowledge and identify gaps ('scope' information).

3 The ability to construct strategies for locating information and data ('plan' information).

4 The ability to locate and access the information and data needed ('gather' information).

5 The ability to review the research process and compare and evaluate information and data ('evaluate' information).

6 The ability to organise information professionally and ethically ('manage' information).

7 The ability to apply the knowledge gained: presenting the results of their research, synthesising new and old information and data to create new knowledge and disseminating it in a variety of ways ('present' information).

These skills are discussed at various points in this book, most notably in this chapter and **Chapter 8**, but also in **Chapters 9** and **17–21**.

a point of identifying these specialists so that you can explain your research topic and benefit from their guidance and expertise to get your research journey on track. The following sections provide you with some insight into the new or not-so-new resources and techniques that you may find useful in this journey.

BASIC TYPES OF SOURCE MATERIAL

As noted already, you will be expected to research your topic extensively and you should highlight some of the source materials that you may find useful. Some of these materials might be classed as primary sources, while others might be thought of as secondary sources (Table 7.1). This terminology has slightly different interpretations depending on your discipline.

Table 7.1 Characteristics and examples of primary and secondary sources of information.

Primary sources – those in which ideas and data are first communicated.	• The primary literature in your subject may be published in the form of papers (articles) in journals. Such literature is usually refereed by experts in the authors' academic peer group, who check the accuracy and originality of the work and report their opinions back to the journal editors (**Ch 8**). This system helps to maintain reliability, but it is not perfect.
	• Books (and, more rarely, articles in magazines and newspapers) can also be primary sources but this depends on the nature of the information published rather than the medium. These sources are not formally refereed, although they may be read by editors and lawyers to check for errors and unsubstantiated or libellous allegations.
	• Original materials that have been published to provide information to a wide and not necessarily expert audience. For example, White Papers, Financial statements, Public Enquiry Reports and epidemiological reports are all primary sources that differ from other categories in this list in that they provide the 'raw' information without interpretation by others. This kind of material allows you as a researcher to come to independent and perhaps original conclusions. Such documentation is particularly important in the Arts and Social Sciences where incisive interpretation can be an indicator of critical thinking (**Ch 17**) and hence the quality of research.
Secondary sources – those which quote, adapt, interpret, translate, develop or otherwise use information drawn from primary sources.	• It is the act of recycling that makes the source secondary, rather than the medium. Reviews are examples of secondary sources in the academic world, and textbooks and magazine articles are often of this type.
	• As people adopt, modify, translate and develop information and ideas, alterations are likely to occur, whether intentional or unintentional. Most authors of secondary sources do not deliberately set out to change the meaning of the primary source, but they may do so unwittingly. Others, consciously or unconsciously, may exert bias in their reporting by quoting evidence primarily on one side of a debate.
	• Modifications while creating a secondary source could involve adding valuable new ideas and content or correcting errors.

Assumed knowledge

As a graduate, it will be assumed that you will have a working knowledge of how a university library functions, such as:

- how to use an electronic catalogue for your own and other libraries;
- how hard-copy resources are shelved, probably using one of the two commonly used methods – the Dewey decimal system (numerical coding) or the Library of Congress System (alphanumeric system);
- how to find a periodical or journal in hard copy or online;
- the borrowing rules, including the borrowing periods and fines.

If you are unfamiliar with any of these aspects of library use in your institution, you should ask for assistance from a librarian.

CHECKING THE RELIABILITY OF SOURCE MATERIAL

Essentially, the content of source material contains facts and ideas originating from someone's research or scholarship. These can be descriptions, concepts, interpretations or numerical data. At some point, information or ideas must be communicated or published, otherwise no-one would know about them. Generally, the literature in any subject can be categorised as a 'primary' or 'secondary' source. Information and ideas usually appear first in the primary literature and may be modified later in the secondary literature (Table 7.1). Understanding this process is important, not only when analysing and evaluating information, but also when deciding on the evidence or references to cite (**Ch 20**). Logically, the closer you can get to the primary source, the more consistent the information is likely to be with the original.

Typical resources obtainable through your library include:

- Monographs – books on a single, often narrow, subject.
- Reference works – useful for obtaining facts and definitions, and a concise overview of a subject. These include general and subject-specific encyclopaedias, yearbooks and dictionaries, and can be found in the area of the library reserved for reference material. These items usually cannot be borrowed. While some may be available online, others might only exist in hardcopy. It is well worthwhile familiarising yourself with them at an early stage in your studies.

- Research papers – very detailed 'articles' published in journals, covering specific subject areas. Proceedings of conferences where cutting-edge research had been presented would also fall into this category. These may also be available online.
- Reviews – analysis of a research area, often detailed and more up-to-date than books.
- Textbooks – good for gaining an overview of the field.
- Websites – some are published by official bodies and should therefore be reliable in their content; however, other websites without such provenance are not wholly reliable as sources, although they may be useful for comparing viewpoints and sourcing other information.

The value of using more than one source

It is fundamental to the research process that you should consult a number of sources on any given issue. These may corroborate each other, or you may find that they take different views or support different interpretations. Interrogating these different 'schools of thought' is sometimes referred to as 'reading around' a subject. This reading contributes to the analytical processes of critical thinking (see **Ch 18**).

HOW TO ACCESS YOUR UNIVERSITY LIBRARY'S E-RESOURCES

This is normally done via the library's website. Some resources are open-access, but others will require a special password. This may depend on the system used in your library, for example, ATHENS or Shibboleth. Note that different institutions will operate slightly different systems but, if in doubt, ask a member of the library staff.

Many current items are now available online in each of the categories listed above. For example, libraries take out subscriptions to e-book repositories, e-journals, e-newspapers and online dictionaries and encyclopaedias. Your institution will have its own method of giving access to these resources, probably via the library electronic desktop.

The main advantage of this method of accessing information is that it is available 24 hours a day from any computer connected to the

Shibboleth and ATHENS

These are systems that provide a gateway to a number of different databases used by academic researchers (ATHENS is being phased out in some locations). In many cases access is automatic when you are recognised as a logged in member of your university. In some cases you may gain access solely via a library computer. Where these 'automatic' systems do not function, you may have to obtain a password through your institutional library. This will identify you as an authorised user for as long as you are a student.

Internet. Some e-book facilities, such as ebrary, offer features such as searching, note-making and linked online dictionaries.

One point to note is that copying/printing out from such sources is governed by copyright restrictions.

Key online research techniques

Your research skills will now need to become deeper than in your early years of study, because your thesis needs to be based on reliable, refereed evidence that is both up to date and comprehensive in relation to your topic. For example, it will not be sufficient to base your work on a few isolated references, augmented by searches of the Internet or Wikipedia. You will need to identify and access new sources.

To find sources new to you, there are, essentially, three key approaches:

1 **Database searches.** These find sources based on key words related to your research topic. The output is a listing of reference details plus abstract/summary material from a wide range of sources. From this list, you can select references that might be of particular relevance, although it may only be possible to judge how significant they really are when you read the full paper.

2 **Citation-based searches.** With this kind of search, you start with an article and its reference list. From this list, you backtrack through selected references making judgements about their relevance and value and, potentially, in turn looking at items cited in their reference lists. This enables you to gain a perspective on the literature of your subject area, working backwards from the starting point of your most recent source, but it does not enable you to identify more recent research.

3 **Searches using citation indices.** These searches rely on the availability of databases (for example, the *Science Citation Index* or *British Humanities Index*) which give details of publications that have cited a given reference. In other words, they allow you to work forward in time towards more current research. This can be very useful if your original sources are slightly dated.

Should I use a source that I've found by chance on the Internet?

'Browsing' your topic using one of the major search engines will probably produce a wealth of links. This approach can produce good material that has been provided for open access. However, be sure that the sites you enter are authoritative sources and do not contain unsubstantiated and possibly erroneous information. As a ground rule, if the material appears to be useful, then try to triangulate it with references from within recognised academic publications, whether online or in hard copy.

OBTAINING DIFFICULT-TO-FIND SOURCES

Access to the sources identified by any of the above methods is not guaranteed. They may be published in journals to which your library does not subscribe. However, most materials are obtainable via a system of inter-library loans that can be arranged through your own library site by a specialist inter-library loan librarian, although there are cost implications in this process (usually, the cost is borne by the borrower).

Most libraries share resources with those of neighbouring institutions and all are linked to the British Library (www.bl.uk), the national library of the UK. This receives a copy of every publication produced in the UK and Ireland, and its massive collection of over 150 million items increases by 3 million items each year. Some university libraries are designated as European Documentation Centres holding key documents of the European Union (***http://ec.europa.eu/europedirect/ visit_us/edc/index_en.htm***).

Accessing 'raw' data
Electronic databases make it easier to access information from public bodies, and much of that kind of information is also now more readily

available online. For example, statistical population details are available through the National Statistics website (***www.statistics.gov.uk***), while papers and publications produced by the Houses of Parliament can also be accessed electronically (***www.parliament.uk***). Clearly, the types of data in this category that you may wish to access will depend on your research topic. In the Arts and Social Sciences, these types of resource would be categorised as primary sources (**Ch 8**) since they present information without interpretation by others.

Accessing archive material

The use of primary sources is fundamental to research in many disciplines, but especially in the Arts and Humanities. Many universities hold archive material of original documents, collections, artefacts and other source material that can be of particular relevance to PhD study. Your university web page will give you further information about how to access such resources usually through a distinct Archives Service. There it may be possible to speak directly with an archivist to explain your thesis topic and find out what resources might be of possible interest and relevance to your study.

Keeping tabs on web sources

The nature of the Web means that it is a constantly changing environment where material is made accessible very quickly – and can, of course, be altered or even removed with similar speed. Thus, it is important to keep a detailed record of all references you have found online, and provide the 'Accessed' date (see **Ch 20**).

ACTION POINTS

7.1 Spend some time becoming thoroughly acquainted with the electronic library resources available to you. Look, in particular, at any subject-specific resources that are provided on the catalogue system or via the library website.

7.2 Explore the shelves covering your subject area. Identify this area from the library catalogue and the information in the shelving aisles. 'Browsing' the books on foot may reveal interesting resources you might not find by other searching methods. Note that research journals may be stored in a different area of the library.

7.3 Find out about alternative library facilities. In some cases, there may be satellite libraries on different campuses or in different buildings. Some of these may be departmental libraries, containing specialist resources. These can contain duplicate holdings of books in the main library. Importantly, you may find they represent convenient or preferable study areas. Even if they do not cover your subject area, you may find their atmosphere more suited to your mood, learning style or personality.

8

ACCESSING CONTENT FROM THE LITERATURE

How to read and evaluate research publications

A search for information sources related to your PhD topic will bring forward a variety of sources to consider: some relevant, some not so; some reliable, some not so. To evaluate these, you will need to develop the skills of assessing content, reading for meaning, and considering the origin and value of information.

KEY TOPICS

→ The initial survey of potential source material

→ Examining the structure of the writing

→ Text-reading techniques

→ Checking the reliability of source material

→ Identifying bias in text

Whatever the subject of your PhD, the ability to evaluate the information and ideas in source material is essential. This is a key aspect of 'information literacy', involving multi-faceted skills (**Ch 7**).

Your analysis may centre on the accuracy or truth of the information itself, the reliability or potential bias of the source of the information, or the value of information in relation to some argument or case. You may also come across contradictory sources of evidence or conflicting arguments based on the same information. You will need to assess their relative merits.

To do any or all of these tasks, you will need to read the text effectively and appraise the origin and nature of the information you find.

In 'scientific' subjects, you will often need to interpret and check the reliability of data. This is essential for setting up and testing meaningful hypotheses (**Ch 3**), and therefore at the core of the scientific approach. In 'non-scientific' subjects, ideas and concepts tend to be more important, and you may need to carry out an objective analysis of information and arguments so you can construct your own position, backed up with evidence (**Ch 18**).

THE INITIAL SURVEY OF POTENTIAL SOURCE MATERIAL

You will need to be discerning about your reading choice and in this chapter it is assumed that you have found a new text source (**Ch 7**) and wish to evaluate it in order to establish its value to your appraisal of the literature. The focus here will be on the most common sources of information: books, research papers or reviews, and websites, but similar principles apply to other types of source.

You should first carry out a quick survey to familiarise yourself with what the source contains. For books and longer reviews you might find contents or section listing near the front and some websites have site maps, links or tabs that will help. You then can use elements of the structure to answer key questions about the content, as indicated in Table 8.1.

The answers to these questions will help you to decide whether to investigate further; whether you need to look at the whole source, or just selected parts; or whether the source is of limited value at the present time.

> ### Record information about all sources you find
>
> Sometimes, keyword searches and even seemingly relevant titles and abstracts can lead you to papers that are not of immediate value. If this is the case, don't discard these sources, but keep the reference information and brief notes about the content in a filing system – it is very frustrating to forget or mislay details of sources which later transpire to be highly relevant.

Table 8.1 Questions to ask when reading a new source. The individual questions will have greater or lesser relevance depending on the nature of the source (i.e. book, paper/review or website) and your specific area of research

Who wrote it and why?
Details of authorship are usually given alongside the title or on the preliminary pages. The status of the author(s) might be useful (academic qualifications imply some authority and reliability, for example). You might find their affiliation there too (perhaps a university or company). The authors may be well-known authorities in the subject area – or previously unknown to you. Whatever is the case, you should carry out the same rigorous analysis of the content. It can be difficult to find out who wrote a website and indeed parts may have been written and edited by a range of workers. This is especially the case with wikis. The preliminary information may also give reasons for publication (for example, scholarship, publicity, sponsorship) that might influence your analysis.
Who published it?
Well-known publishers have a vested interest in ensuring content is reliable and valid and often put in place rigorous refereeing/reviewing/editing procedures to ensure this is the case. Websites may be sponsored or part of a bigger web presence and have the same controls.
When was it written?
This is usually obvious from the title pages. The date of publication will help you to put the source in its context and decide, for example whether its assumptions, methods or conclusions remain valid. Old material can remain valid for a surprising amount of time in some disciplines, but be outdated very quickly in others. Web-based material can be difficult to date as it may be modified frequently after its first appearance (**Ch 20**).
Can I rely on the information within?
You will get clues from the author's affiliation (see above) and publisher, but you will need to focus on the content too. Your judgement should be influenced by: standard of presentation; the methods used; analysis with statistics; and the support given to the position within by the literature that is cited (**Ch 20**).
What does it say?
The title (and abstract for a paper or review) should be informative, but they may mislead because key aspects may have been omitted for space, or because the authors wish to make a headline-grabbing statement. For books, the contents listing or index may be helpful to find relevant material. There is quite frequently a mismatch between what the author(s) think(s) or say(s) they've done and what you may feel after reading the main body of the paper or book.
How does it fit with my current interests?
This clearly depends on your research question (**Ch 3**) and the part of the overall thesis structure that you are working on. If you have used a pictorial or tabular structure to lay out your key thoughts on relevant issues, then you can add the citation alongside or in a parallel structure. Those who like to use reference cards (**Ch 9**) may like to lay these out over a desk or table to find groupings or trends.

Learning how to access the content of academic texts quickly will be of significance in saving time as well as giving you a grasp of the main thrust of a text you plan to read in full.

Well-structured academic texts usually follow a standard pattern with an introduction, main body and conclusion in each element. Sometimes the introduction may comprise several paragraphs; sometimes it may be only one paragraph. Similarly, the conclusion may be several paragraphs or only one. Figure 8.1 illustrates a model layout for a piece of text with five paragraphs, comprising an introduction and conclusion with three intervening paragraphs of varying length.

Within the structure of well-written academic text, each paragraph will be introduced by a topic sentence stating the content of the paragraph. Each paragraph performs a function. For example, some may describe, others may provide examples, while others may examine points in favour of a particular viewpoint, others points against that viewpoint. The function of these paragraphs, and the sentences within them, is usually signalled by use of 'signpost words' that guide the reader through the logical structure of the text. For example, the word 'however' indicates that some contrast is about to be made with a

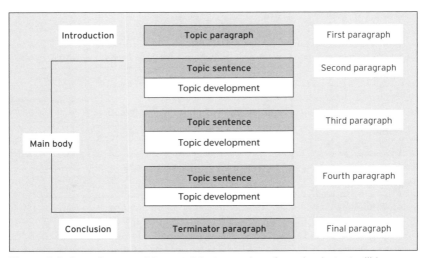

Figure 8.1 Sample textual layout. Most samples of academic text will be similarly organised.

point immediately before; 'therefore' or 'thus' signals that a result or effect is about to be explained. Examples of signpost words are shown in Table 8.2. You can use this knowledge of the structure of writing to establish the substance of a piece of text.

Reader as author

The points in this chapter about the organisation of printed material and the structure of text are important for you as a reader or 'decoder' of text. This awareness should also come into play when you act as an academic author yourself and have to write about your own ideas in your thesis or research papers.

TEXT-READING TECHNIQUES

With good technique, your searches will provide plenty of information to assess. There will be much to read, and you will need to develop the skills of doing this quickly, while simultaneously abstracting meaning

Table 8.2 **Examples of signpost words and phrases used to indicate and manage the flow of writing.** These are sometimes called 'discourse markers' or 'cohesive devices' because they contribute to the construction of the discussion within a text (**Ch 27**).

Type of link intended	Examples of signpost words
Addition	additionally; furthermore; in addition; moreover
Cause/reason	as a result of; because (mid-sentence)
Comparison	compared with; in the same way; in comparison with; likewise
Condition	if; on condition that; providing that; unless
Contrast	although, by contrast; conversely; despite; however; nevertheless; yet
Effect/result	as a result; hence; therefore; thus
Exemplification	for example; for instance; particularly; such as; thus
Reformulation	in other words; rather; to paraphrase
Summary	finally; hence; in all; in conclusion; in short; in summary
Time sequence	after; at first; at last; before; eventually; subsequently
Transition	as far as … is concerned; as for; to turn to

and assessing relevance. As a graduate student, you will probably have developed speed-reading skills to some degree but may not have been truly attuned to the underlying principles of the 'shape' of academic writing before now. Relevant strategies to help you 'access' the content of text include:

- Picking out the topic sentences. Read the topic and terminator paragraphs, or even just their topic sentences, to gain a quick overview of that element. Follow this by reading the topic sentences for the intervening paragraphs to provide an overview of the entire section or chapter you are evaluating. This will aid your understanding before you study-read the whole text. At this point, you will already have made judgements about whether this text is appropriate and how you rate it as germane to your research for whatever reason.

- Skimming. This is where you pick out a specific piece of information by quickly letting the eye run down a list or over a page looking for a key word or phrase, as when seeking a particular name or address in a phone book. This might help you to judge whether the text you are reading is in the register (tone) and genre (format) appropriate to research level study (**Ch 26**). For example, if key 'jargon' or technical words are missing, then it is possible that the text is not tackling the issue at the level you require.

- Scanning. Here, you let your eye run quickly over a section, for example, before you commit yourself to study-read it. Sometimes headings and sub-headings may be used, which will give some indication of the sequence being followed in delivering information. This will help you to gain an overview of the content before you start.

- Identifying the signpost words. As noted in Table 8.2, these help guide you as the reader through the logical process that the author has mapped out for you.

- Recognising clusters of grammatically allied words as well as subject word 'strings'. Subliminally, good readers group words in clusters according to their natural alliances. This helps the reader to make fewer fixations (see tip overleaf). A similar characteristic applies to reading texts used at PhD level since these often contain specialised word 'strings' that form a single meaningful concept (**Ch 27**); looking for such word strings will help you to assimilate content and hence evaluate its merit more quickly.

The essence of speed-reading

Fast readers tend to operate by using their peripheral vision (what you see, while staring ahead, at the furthest extreme to the right and the left). This means that they absorb clusters of words in one 'flash' or 'fixation' on the text. A reader who does this is reading more efficiently than the reader who reads word-by-word. Research has indicated that people who read slowly word-by-word are less likely to absorb information quickly enough for the brain to process.

- Taking cues from punctuation. As you read, you will gain some understanding by interpreting the text using the cues of full-stops and commas, for example, to help you gain understanding of what you are reading.

To be effective, reading quickly must be matched by a good level of comprehension. Clearly, you need to incorporate tests of your understanding to check that you have understood the main points of the text. One method of reading that incorporates this is called the SQ3R Method – Survey, Question, Read, Recall and Review (Table 8.3).

Assessing sources of facts

Some sources and facts can be considered very reliable. In the sciences, one interpretation of reliability is that the observation or experiment can be repeated by a competent peer – well-established 'textbook' knowledge usually falls into this category. In other areas, reliability may be bound up with the track record and authority of the person making the assertion, or in the nature of the evidence which is cited to support a case.

One important method of establishing reliability is whether the original source has been 'peer reviewed' (Table 8.1). This is where the material is reviewed by one or more academics ('referees') working in the same field, prior to being accepted for publication. This helps to ensure that:

- the material is original;
- all relevant past work is quoted;
- conflicting theories and opinions are mentioned;

Table 8.3 Reading for remembering: the SQ3R Method. The point of this method is that the reader has to engage in processing the material in the text and does not simply read on 'autopilot' where very little is being retained.

Survey stage
• Read the first paragraph (Topic Paragraph) and last paragraph (Terminator Paragraph) of the relevant section of text
• Read the intervening paragraph topic sentences
• Focus on the headings and sub-headings, if present
• Study the graphs and diagrams for key features
Question stage
• What do you know already about this topic?
• What is the author likely to tell you?
• What specifically do you need to find out?
Read stage
• Read the entire section quickly to get the gist of the piece of writing; finger-tracing techniques may be helpful at this point
• Go back to the question stage and revisit your initial answers
• Look especially for keywords, key statements, signpost words
• Do not stop to look up unknown words – go for completion
Recall stage
• Turn the text over (or look away from the screen) and try to recall as much as possible
• Make relevant notes
• Turn over the source again
• Check over for accuracy of recall. Suggested recall periods – every 20 minutes
Review stage
After a break, try to recall the main points

- any data and calculations are checked;
- interpretations of information and data are valid.

Such reviews cannot guarantee reliability, and it can be argued that they may act to entrench 'established' viewpoints: radical new ideas often encounter extreme resistance when they are first put forward. It is the journal editor's task to ensure that a balance between freedom of expression and satisfactory reasoning is maintained.

Other sources can be a lot less reliable. They may not cite evidence, or this may not be available for examination by others. In the worst cases, evidence may be fabricated or impossible to assess or test.

What you read could be misquoted, misrepresented, erroneous or based on a faulty premise. The data presented may carry no indication of error levels. These risks are particularly important for of Web-based information, as this is less likely to be refereed or edited.

An obvious way to check reliability is to make cross-referencing checks. 'Triangulating' in this way involves looking at more than one source and comparing what is said in each. The sources should be as independent as possible (for example, do not compare an original source with one that is directly based on it). If you find the sources agree, you may become more certain of your position. If two sources differ, you may need to decide which is better.

The quality of academic work is often indicated by the extent and quality of citations provided by the author. This applies particularly to articles in academic journals, where positions are usually supported by citations of others' work. These citations may demonstrate that a certain amount of research has been carried out beforehand, and that the ideas or results are based on genuine scholarship. If you doubt the quality of the work, these references might be worth looking at. How up-to-date are they? Do they cite independent work, or is the author exclusively quoting him- or herself or the work of one particular researcher?

This leads to another form of cross-referencing, which is to look at who else has cited the author's work, and how. In many subjects, you can use the *Web of Knowledge*, ***www.webofknowledge.com***, to find out how often an article or author has been cited and by whom. You may then be able to consult these sources to see how others have viewed the original findings. Reviews of a subject area published after your source may also provide useful comments.

How can you check whether a source is peer reviewed?

For academic journals, this may be in or close to the 'information for authors' section which appears every three months or so in current (unbound) volumes, or on specific web pages and may provide valuable insights and background information about the submission, refereeing and editing process. Some journals also indicate who edited or refereed specific articles. In books, the acknowledgements section may indicate whether a peer has assisted by reading a draft.

IDENTIFYING BIAS IN TEXT

In many subjects it is important to differentiate fact from opinion. To do this when reading material that is unfamiliar, you may need to answer the following questions:

- To what extent has the author supported a given viewpoint?
- Has relevant supporting information been quoted, via literature citations or the author's own researches?
- Are numerical data used to substantiate the points used?
- Are these data reliable and can you verify the information, for example, by looking at a source that was cited?
- Might the author have a hidden reason for putting forward biased evidence to support a personal opinion?

At some point, you should concentrate on analysing the method being used to put the points over, rather than the facts themselves. This will help you detect fallacious arguments and logical flaws (**Ch 18**).

Analyse the language used

Words and their use can be very revealing. Have subjective or objective sentence structures been employed? The former might indicate a personal opinion rather than an objective conclusion. Are there any tell-tale signs of misinformation? Bias might be indicated by absolute terms, such as 'everyone knows...'; 'I can guarantee that...' or, a seemingly unbalanced consideration of the evidence. How carefully has the author considered the topic? A less studious approach might be indicated by exaggeration, ambiguity, or the use of journalese and slang. Always remember, however, that content should be judged above presentation.

You should look closely at any data and graphs that are presented and the way they have been analysed. If the information you are looking at is numerical in form, have the errors of any data been taken into consideration, and, where appropriate, quantified? If so, does this help you arrive at a conclusion about how genuine the differences are between important values? Have the appropriate statistical methods been used to analyse the data? Are the underlying hypotheses the right ones? Have the results of any tests been interpreted correctly in arriving at the conclusion? Look closely at any graphs. These may have been constructed in such a way as to emphasise a particular viewpoint, for example, by careful selection of axis starting points (**Ch 21**).

Don't be blinded by statistics. Leaving aside the issue that statistical methods don't actually deal with proof, only probability (**Ch 21**), it is generally possible to analyse and present data in such a way that they support one chosen argument or hypothesis rather than another (as in the adage 'you can prove anything with statistics'). To deal with these matters, you will need at least a basic understanding of the 'statistical approach' and of the techniques in common use (**Chs 21** and **23**).

ACTION POINTS

8.1 As a new PhD student, gain a feel for the primary literature in your subject area. This may be shelved in the library building or you may be expected to access it online (or both). Read one or two articles to gain a flavour of the format, style of writing, language and sources used. Initially, expect to find some of the subject matter relatively impenetrable; as you progress, you will master much of the jargon used.

8.2 Use the questions in Table 8.1 to assess a source about which you are uncertain. If you are unable to establish its reliability, you should research further around the topic.

8.3 Practise analysing excerpts of text for their underlying structure. Can you identify the types of paragraphs and sentences being used? Can you identify how where signpost words are being used to direct or redirect your thoughts as a reader? Understanding how these methods are used in practice is a valuable route to developing your own proficiency in writing.

9

ORGANISING RESEARCH MATERIALS

How to collect and file information and details of references

You will come across a large amount of potential source material in your researches. If you wish to copy this, you will need to take account of copyright law as it applies to copying for 'educational purposes'. Whether you create a copy or not, you will need effective note-making techniques to abstract the key points as these relate to your research topic.

KEY TOPICS

→ Copying or printing out source material

→ Making research notes from sources

→ Themed research notes

→ Indexing and organising your resources and research notes

Over three or more years of PhD research, you will consult all manner of source materials. You will copy or print out some sources and take notes from others. All this paperwork and related information needs to be organised so that you can retrieve it easily when necessary. In addition, comprehensive reference details will be required for those sources you quote in your thesis and any research publications. Formats for citation and reference lists are discussed in **Chapter 20** – this chapter deals with ways in which you can keep the detailed information required for creating reference lists.

COPYING OR PRINTING OUT SOURCE MATERIAL

Having a paper copy of your source material can be extremely convenient. You can view this at your convenience, annotate it and store it for later reference. It can take the form of an original printed version, a photocopy, a scan or a printout. Increasingly, digital media are used for these purposes, but although computerised filing and annotation systems offer convenience, they are unlikely to supplant paper copies entirely.

When you copy or download any resource, you must take account of copyright law. This 'gives the creators of a wide range of material, such as literature, art, music and recording, film and broadcasts, economic rights' (UK Intellectual Property Office, **www.ipo.gov.uk**). Copyright infringement is regarded as equivalent to stealing, and legal rights are sometimes jealously guarded by companies with the resources to prosecute.

In the UK, authors have literary copyright over their material for their life, and their estate has copyright for a further 70 years. Publishers have typographical copyright for 25 years. This is why the copyright symbol © is usually accompanied by a date and the owner's name. For example, you'll find this information on the publication details page at the start of a book (as in this one).

Use of the copyright symbol

The © symbol indicates that someone is drawing your attention to the fact that something is copyright. However, even if © does not appear, the material may still be copyright.

You will be at risk of breaking the law if you copy (for example, photocopy, digitally scan or print out) material to which someone else owns the copyright, unless you have their express permission, or unless the amount you copy falls within the limits accepted for 'fair dealing'.

'Educational copying', for non-commercial private study or research, is sometimes allowed by publishers (they will state this on the material, and may allow multiple copies to be made). Otherwise, for single copies for private study or research, you should only copy what would fall under the 'fair dealing' provision, for which there is no precise definition in law.

Established practice suggests that you should photocopy no more than 5 per cent of the work involved, or:

● one chapter of a book;

- one article per volume of an academic journal;
- 20 per cent (to a maximum of 20 pages) of a short book;
- one poem or short story (to a maximum of 10 pages) from an anthology;
- one separate illustration or map up to A4 size (note: illustrations that are parts of articles and chapters may be included in the allowances noted above);
- short excerpts of musical works – not whole works or movements (note: copying of any kind of public performance is not allowed without permission).

Private study or research

This means exactly what it says: the limits discussed here apply to that use and not to commercial or other uses, such as photocopying an amusing article for your friends.

These limits apply to single copies – you can't take multiple copies of any of the above items, or pass on a single copy for multiple copying to someone else, who may be in ignorance of the source or of specific or general copyright issues.

In legal terms, it doesn't matter whether you paid for the source or not: copyright is infringed when the whole or a substantial part is copied without permission – and 'substantial' here can mean a qualitatively significant section even if this is a small part of the whole.

Approved copyright exceptions

Some copying for academic purposes may be licensed by the Copyright Licensing Agency (CLA) on behalf of authors. Other electronically distributed material may be licensed through the HERON (Higher Education Resources On-Demand) scheme. In these cases you may be able to copy or print out more than the amounts listed in the text, including multiple copies.

Your university may also 'buy in' to licensing schemes, such as those offered by the NLA (Newspaper Licensing Agency) and the Performing Rights Society. As these can refer to very specific sources, consult your library's staff if in doubt.

The same rules apply to printing or copying material on the Web unless the author gives explicit written clearance. This applies to copying images as well as text from the Internet, although a number of sites do offer copyright-free images. A statement on the author's position on copying may appear on the home page or a page linked directly from it.

Complexity of copyright law

Note that the material in this chapter is a summary, and much may depend on individual circumstances. Note also that copyright legislation is the subject of international cooperation and is supported by a network of international agreements.

MAKING RESEARCH NOTES FROM SOURCES

Whether you have a copy or not, keeping a record of the content and your interpretation of source material is essential. You will have developed note-making skills during your undergraduate studies and will probably have a preferred method for doing this that suits your learning preference (for further information see the VARK online resource, **Ch 5**). If you feel that now is the time to experiment with different forms of note making, a range of techniques is discussed in McMillan and Weyers (2012).

Why are you taking notes?

The reason why you are taking the notes may be to:

- frame an overview of the subject;
- record a sequence or process;
- enable you to analyse a problem;
- extract the logic of an argument;
- compare different viewpoints;
- borrow quotes (with suitable citation – **Ch 20**);
- add your own commentary on the text, perhaps by linking key points with what has been discussed in a lecture or tutorial.

The style, format and detail of your notes will depend on the purpose.

One of the pitfalls of making notes is that these can become too detailed. To avoid this, the trick is to:

1 identify your purpose;

2 scan the section to be read;

3 establish the writer's purpose, for example:

- a narrative of events or process
- a statement of facts
- an explanation of reasoning
- an analysis of an issue, problem or situation
- a logical argument
- a critique of an argument;

4 work out their 'take' on the subject, and how this relates to your purpose;

5 make minimal notes that are sufficient for you to summarise the above, using an appropriate note-making style and layout.

Essentials of note-making

1 On all notes record the source, namely:
- Author(s) surname(s) + initials
- Title in full with chapter/journal title and pages
- Date of publication
- Publisher + place of publication

You will need this information to enable you to cite the source if you decide to use it in your own writing (**Ch 20**).

2 Add the date(s) you made the notes as this may prove helpful in back-tracking for information.

3 Personalise your notes by using, for example, underlining, highlighting, colour coding and so on. This will help to make your notes meaningful in six days, weeks or months.

When making notes, always write down your sources. As discussed in detail in **Chapter 20**, you may risk plagiarising if you cannot recall or find the source of a piece of text. Avoid this by getting into the habit of making a careful note of the source on the same piece of paper that you used to summarise or copy it out.

Always use quote marks ('...') when taking such notes verbatim from texts and other materials, to indicate that what you have written down is a direct copy of the words used, as you may forget this at a later time. You do not need to quote directly in the final version of your work, but if you paraphrase you should still cite the source.

THEMED RESEARCH NOTES

The volume of material that postgraduates have to handle means that most try to introduce some short-cuts. This suggestion helps avoid the frustration of 'losing' a particular note or idea. The method involves creating a file for a particular aspect of your research and within that single document creating a template in the form of a small table as illustrated in Figure 9.1(a).

As this mini-database develops, you will have a composite record of related material that you will be able to use when you reach that particular aspect in your writing. Figure 9.1(b) shows how this might look as the record of notes grows. You might choose to handwrite such notes, but the time spent typing them up will enable the details to be searched, copied and pasted. Either printed out as hard copy or viewed on the screen, they can be shuffled around to help group and visualise connections between sources. The key advantage is that you have all the related material in easily readable format in one place.

INDEXING AND ORGANISING YOUR RESOURCES AND RESEARCH NOTES

Research projects have the potential to generate a considerable quantity of source material either in hard copy or in printouts/photocopies, in addition to e-sourced material read online. This presents three related problems:

1 How to file and organise the hard copies you have obtained (usually by photocopying, but sometimes directly from an author).

2 How to cross-reference your notes on the material, so you refer to the right references in the right places.

3 How to create a database that allows you to create a reference list of all the references you cite.

(a)

Theme	
Publication details	
Direct quotation or paraphrase	
Importance/relevance/ Anticipated location in thesis	
Personal appraisal	

(b)
Source 1

Theme	Disadvantages of eco systems in house building
Publication details	Green, A. 2012. The EcoHouse. London: Earth Press.
Direct quotation or paraphrase [with page reference]	"Eco measures will only work if the home owner understands the underlying principles of the materials and services incorporated in the building." Page 59.
Importance/relevance/ Anticipated location in thesis	Need for eco education for home owners. Could be included in disadvantages. Either in intro. or critique chapter.
Personal appraisal	Useful as recognition that as eco homes become more the norm, their efficacy has to be matched with owner's knowledge.

Source 2

Theme	Disadvantages of eco systems in house building
Publication details	Brown, B. 2010. Building green. Ely: Fens Press.
Direct quotation or paraphrase [with page reference]	"The builder has to engage with the eco concept for successful project completion." Page 25.
Importance/relevance/ Anticipated location in thesis	Need for eco education of trades involved in construction. Could be included in disadvantages. Either in intro or critique chapter.
Personal appraisal	Supports idea of need for commitment from all stakeholders in the project.

Source 3

Theme	Disadvantages of eco systems in house building
Publication details	Black, H. 2009. Financing green-ness. Dublin: Green Press.
Direct quotation or paraphrase [with page reference]	"Financial houses need to be included in 'green education' so that mortgage applications for eco homes can be sympathetically appraised." Page 95.
Importance/relevance/ Anticipated location in thesis	Need for eco education for business. Could be included in disadvantages. Either in intro or critique chapter.
Personal appraisal	Useful as recognition that as eco homes become more the norm, their efficacy has to be matched with owner's knowledge.

Figure 9.1 Examples of layout of entry for composite note-making strategy: (a) template; (b) examples of the template in use.

Hard-copy approaches

One simple 'low-tech' method for storing hard copy and related reference information involves creating a record card for each item. Each hard copy document is given an 'accession' number in sequence (1, 2, 3...) and is stored sequentially in boxes or files so that frequent reorganisation is not required as your collection expands. Each document is matched by an index card of the same number. On the card you write essential bibliographical information and any comments you want particularly to note, for example, a composite note as discussed above. You then store the cards in alphabetical order by author. Thus, if you recall that an article written by E. Burke (2003) is relevant, you can find the card, identify the accession number and immediately retrieve the relevant document from your filing system.

This method will help you become more familiar with your material and its content. The accession numbers or the record cards themselves can be used as a way of grouping references in different topic areas, and the cards can easily be re-ordered alphabetically when writing up your reference list. This system is labour-intensive and has the disadvantage that the final list will probably have to be typed up as a single exercise; nevertheless, it might suit some learning styles better than the computer-based models described below.

Personalised computer-based approaches

Following the 'accession number' approach in the hard-copy model, an alternative, computer-based system involves creating a file folder in which you insert sub-folders arranged by themes or aspects within your work. In each sub-folder (theme) you create a word processor file that contains a simple table such as that of Fig. 9.1(a) in which you list bibliographical references of each source in order of 'accession number' and record alongside notes of your thoughts about the content and findings in relation to your own study. Some people find that a spreadsheet rather than a Word table is more suited to this purpose. Within the same folder, you might wish to keep any detailed quotes that you have taken directly from source material; any downloaded materials on that theme; and any pieces of ongoing written work. When creating a reference list, the reference information can then be cut and pasted into a word processor file and sorted alphabetically or numerically, eliminating any duplication. This method has the advantage of allowing on-screen manipulation of bibliographical data and interpretations.

Both the hard-copy and computer-based methods have the disadvantage of requiring extensive cross-checking and proof-reading of the final list to ensure that all the conventions of the referencing method are applied consistently.

Using commercial bibliographic software

This is another possibility, as these systems offer great potential for organising citations within your text and for preparing your reference list. In order to use the systems, appropriate bibliographic data must first be entered into fields within a database (you can also search online databases and import reference data from these). The database can then be searched and customised in the style of your choice to create a consistent reference list for your thesis or for any papers you may write. Research notes, as described above, can also be added.

One advantage is that the database system will help you to avoid punctuation inaccuracies in the final version. In addition, most packages offer the functions of inserting citations according to different referencing methods and output can be altered to suit different requirements for different publication contexts. However, on the negative side, you have to consider whether the effort taken to learn how to use whichever package is available to you (for example, EndNote, Reference Manager or ProCite) is worthwhile in a research project that may have relatively few references. If you decide to use this type of software, it is worth attending a training course if one is offered by university staff or seeking guidance online. Be sure that servicing your database doesn't become an end in itself.

Chapter 20 covers key aspects of documenting sources and appropriate ways of recording and citing quotations and ideas taken from them.

The golden rules of effective note-making

Whatever method of making notes you choose, ensure that the information is:

- easily recorded;
- easily sourced;
- easily read;
- easily understood long after you've made the notes.

9.1 Next time you are in the library, read the documentation about photocopying often displayed beside the photocopiers. This will provide detailed information about current legislation and any local exceptions. The library website may also be a useful source of information, for example, about copyright-licensed material.

9.2 Review how you currently store information. If this is in note form, consider storing like with like, for example, in folders by theme or topic. If you have print-out material, consider whether you need to create box file storage that groups materials again by topic and theme. Although this may not seem important at early stages of the research process, at later stages these decisions could have time and labour-saving implications.

9.3 Review your note-making technique. Consider how this will come into play when you start pooling your sources and writing thesis material about them. Will your current methods be fit-for-purpose? Perhaps the themed notes method might be a more appropriate way of synthesising and collating related information. When your ideas become blocked or you are not sure of the next step, then reading over these composite notes may help to open up new strands of thinking or writing.

INTERACTIONS WITH OTHERS DURING A RESEARCH PROGRAMME

10

SUCCESSFUL POSTGRADUATE–SUPERVISOR RELATIONSHIPS

How to make the most of this important collaboration

The relationship between a postgraduate student and their supervisor is vital to the success of the research activity from both points of view. The student wants to obtain the degree and the supervisor has an interest in ensuring that this happens. Thus, it is essential that both parties work together to ensure that their mutual and individual aims are achieved.

KEY TOPICS
→ The self-directed nature of postgraduate research
→ The duties and responsibilities of a supervisor
→ The pressures on your supervisor's time
→ Supervisor and student personalities
→ The supervisor's role in writing up your work

Arriving at a good working relationship with your supervisor is a vital component of successful postgraduate research. In many cases, this association develops easily through the various phases of the degree and lasts well beyond into later employment. In others, there may be a mismatch between the expectations of either party and problems may ensue. This chapter aims to clarify the ground-rules for supervised research and to provide suggestions for remedying any difficulties that arise.

THE SELF-DIRECTED NATURE OF POSTGRADUATE RESEARCH

Postgraduate study is not intended to be an exercise in the student awaiting direction on the one hand and the supervisor dispensing instructions on the other. The student has to learn to exercise a degree of autonomy in a number of ways. This involves recognising a number of important responsibilities, as discussed in **Chapter 2**.

Firstly, you will need to take responsibility for your own research by planning your time and pacing your work so that you achieve objectives on time (**Ch 6**). However, autonomous work in itself is not enough. It must be supported by independent thought. You are expected to be able to produce fresh ideas which you can develop and defend in discussion (**Chs 17** and **18**). Although you will probably start by 'working to instruction', increasingly you should become the expert and it should be you, rather than your supervisor, who drives the research.

Your period of postgraduate study will involve the development of a number of personal transferable skills, for example, advanced presentation techniques. It is your responsibility to explore the means of developing such skills. For instance, this might involve using appropriate software tools to help you present your work competently at conference level. Most universities provide a series of workshops to assist with this and other skills development (**Ch 5**).

Writing skills are vital to your progress and ultimate success (**Chs 25** and **26**). Many post-docs and lecturers will readily admit that their postgraduate experience led to major improvements in their abilities in this area and that their supervisor's guidance was a major influence on their progress. You should take a proactive role by reacting positively to feedback (**Ch 16**), adapting your writing to the style adopted in your subject area, and learning new writing skills from relevant courses (**Ch 5**), writing manuals and reference works (**Ch 26**).

Key expectations of supervisors

These are the main qualities a supervisor will expect you to display:

- honesty;
- autonomy (once trained);
- hard work;
- ability to write effectively;
- openness about problems.

THE DUTIES AND RESPONSIBILITIES OF A SUPERVISOR

For you, as a postgraduate student, your supervisor will probably be the most important person in your working life. He or she will be in a position to help you in many ways.

Before you even started your research, your supervisor's role in your work may have included some of the following:

- Obtaining the funding that will support your studies. This might have included negotiating a studentship for your position from a departmental quota or applying for a grant that will pay your stipend or salary and other expenses.

- Creating or assembling the components of your working environment. In the sciences, for example, your supervisor may have obtained vital equipment through research grants. In other areas, they may have accumulated vital resources or evidence that will underpin your work, such as old books, manuscripts and papers. They may have had to negotiate desk and/or lab space for you and the raw materials you will need to conduct your study.

- Providing or bringing together the ideas that will form the basis of your work. In some cases, these may be defined in great detail as part of a research grant proposal (for example, proposing hypotheses and laying out clear milestones). In others, they may simply be a general area of study and associated intellectual framework, encapsulated perhaps in a project title and single descriptive paragraph, that you will be expected to develop in a detailed proposal or plan (**Ch 3**).

When you begin as a researcher, your supervisor's role will probably include some of the following:

- helping you settle down at the University when you first arrive – for example, by providing guidance on finding accommodation, matriculation, and finding your way around your department and important facilities such as the library;

- supporting you in developing appropriate skills to pursue your work – these may include, for example, guidance on how to use software, or a particular set of analytical techniques, or tips on assembling a reference collection (**Ch 20**);

- assisting you to develop the research project from the initial ideas, perhaps helping you to refine hypotheses or ideas on the basis of your early results or findings (**Ch 17**);
- putting you in touch with those locally or at a distance who can help with your studies or contribute to your work.

Once your work gets going, your supervisor's role may include some of the following:

- ensuring that you work safely at all times;
- being available for discussions and meetings;
- providing guidance on obtaining the resources you need to carry out your studies;
- providing pastoral care, if required, or to put you in touch with those who can help you;
- enthusing you about the work in hand and helping you get through the inevitable low points when everything seems to be going wrong (**Ch 11**);
- making sure your work does not end up in a dead end and that you do have something to write up when you finish;
- keeping you informed about the various deadlines within your study periods (such as those for writing reports);
- helping you interpret the rules and regulations and Codes of Practice that govern your studies;
- helping you to analyse your findings;
- giving you feedback on your research and the related written work you produce;
- helping you publish your findings or to disseminate them via posters, seminars or conference presentations;
- providing guidance about the *viva voce* exam and other assessments.

Always go to meetings with your supervisor well-prepared

Have all your materials well organised and neatly written up. Create a list of discussion points beforehand, and if you have questions, be prepared to show you have made some attempt to answer these independently.

Key responsibilities of supervisors

The key responsibilities of a supervisor are to:

- ensure you work safely;
- provide adequate resources and facilities for your work, including training in necessary skills;
- give you positive feedback on results and ideas and maintain your enthusiasm;
- provide help when things go awry;
- monitor your progress and help you to write up on time;
- support your onward progress when your studies are finished.

When you have finished your PhD studies, your supervisor may:

- give you guidance on possible careers and to help you find a job after your work is finished (**Ch 33**);
- write references for you when you apply for jobs (but you should always inform your supervisor about jobs you are applying for and provide them with an up-to-date CV).

THE PRESSURES ON YOUR SUPERVISOR'S TIME

All of the above duties and responsibilities of a supervisor take time, and it is important to realise that your supervisor undertakes these duties while contemporaneously and sometimes simultaneously carrying out a wide range of other tasks. Typically, these could include:

- carrying out his or her own research;
- working with other postgrads, post-docs and technical staff;
- teaching undergraduates;
- marking exam papers or conducting oral exams;
- carrying out departmental administration;
- attending University committees and working groups;
- writing up other research work;
- refereeing others' work;
- applying for research funding;
- going to seminars and conferences;
- (if they are lucky) having some sort of private life.

This means you should make sure your notion of the amount of time your supervisor can spend with you is realistic. After all, postgraduate study is primarily about learning to work and think on your own.

That does not mean that your supervisor can ignore you. It might mean, for example, that you will have to be patient in waiting for feedback on drafts of your work. Normally, you will have a good idea of the context in which your supervisor is working and can adjust your expectations accordingly. Just before a lecture might not be a good time to ask for a considered opinion on your work; in the run-up to an important conference, all of your supervisor's attention might be on putting together his/her contribution; and in vacation periods, he/she may go away from the lab or office for several weeks.

Time your approaches to your supervisor

Be sensitive to your supervisor's working patterns and to any one-off tasks they are doing. If possible, suggest diary dates in advance.

SUPERVISOR AND STUDENT PERSONALITIES

Although there may be times when you will doubt it, supervisors are human beings and hence are fallible. They may be near-geniuses and have heroic research achievements to their name but at the same time they may have difficulty empathising with students or seem rather abrupt. In the majority of cases, this simply requires adjustment on the part of the postgraduate student. Table 10.1 lists some supervisor types, the sorts of qualities they may display and some strategies for accommodating these.

While you will inevitably focus on your supervisor's traits, he or she will also have a view on your personality. The focus may be on qualities he or she is pleased to see, such as being:

- hard working;
- punctual;
- focused;
- technically adept;
- intellectually bright.

What should you do if you do not feel your supervisor is giving you enough of their time?

1 Compare notes with others in your department to see whether you are relatively disadvantaged in this way.

2 Try to be more proactive in setting up meetings, perhaps by helping to set up diary dates or a regular meeting slot.

3 Raise the matter informally at your progress monitoring meetings.

4 As a last resort, you might wish to consult the chairperson of the department's research committee, the head of department or your faculty dean. Many of these people will be quite happy to have discussions on an informal basis and you can trust them to respect confidentiality if agreed beforehand.

A supervisor will probably not want to deal with personal matters extraneous to the research itself. Examples might include: lack of motivation; being homesick; financial problems or issues with relationships. Nevertheless, because these issues may have a direct effect on your progress, you should explain your feelings frankly – but don't expect a lot more than sympathy in return. Your supervisor is not a social worker and his or her attention will nearly always be directed to the outcomes of your work. If you need further help, consult the relevant student services unit directly.

There will inevitably be ups and downs in the student–supervisor relationship (**Ch 11**). What is important is to recognise that you share a common goal and may need to compromise a little to achieve it.

What should I do if I have more than one supervisor and they give me conflicting advice?

This is a difficult situation, and one that can only really be resolved by discussion with all parties present. You should confront an issue of this kind as soon as possible as it could lead to huge problems nearer to submission. If things are not resolved easily, it might be a good idea to have confidential chat with the head of department or postgraduate dean (or equivalent).

Table 10.1 Some supervisor types with likely approach to your research, typical supervision styles and suggested strategies for working successfully with them. Note that, as with any stereotyping exercise, the real situation will be more complex: a specific supervisor may demonstrate more than one trait and/or may change between modes at different points in the academic year.

Supervisor type, approach to your research and supervision style	Suggested strategies for successful relationships
The big hitter – an established researcher with a considerable reputation and track record. Able to pick the very best PG students. Will have exceptionally high expectations for work-rate and results. Your research project is likely to fit into a well-established programme of work, possibly as part of an extended group. Unlikely to be able to devote much time for day-to-day supervision and may delegate this to other team members.	• Ensure that your commitment and hard work are evident • Ensure that you stick to your plan and avoid deviation from it as this will not be appreciated • Present the key points from your work well in meetings by taking along a prepared list of queries. Meetings may be brief and feel more like an interview than a discussion, so ensure that you make best use of them • Be prepared to snatch discussions at every opportunity • Seek detailed feedback on your written drafts from others as your supervisor may not have time or feel it is their role to give detailed feedback on grammar, style and word use
The overworked academic – has many calls on his/her time: teaching, administration and, if lucky, research. Probably keen on your project but frustrated by inability to offer you as much supervision as he/she would like. Variable engagement with you, and especially poor during crunch times of academic year, e.g. when teaching or examining.	• Make good use of 'times of plenty' and develop strategies for times when contact is infrequent • Expect meetings to be re-scheduled or cancelled at busy times due to conflicting tasks. Try to timetable meetings within your supervisor's diary • Expect long waits for drafts to be returned, possibly with variable quality of feedback
The theorist – your project could be part of his/her grand plan and your results could be expected to uphold a pet theory. Will *not* like any results or conclusions that conflict with his/her predictions. May tend to over-supervise as above.	• Make sure you are on very safe ground if you disagree on key issues with opposing research groups at conferences and during oral exam • Be prepared for conflict with opposing research groups at conferences and during oral exam

The at-a-distance manager – a supervisor primarily by name only, appointed mainly so you can fulfil university or external requirements. May not be interested in your project or be able to contribute much. Meetings will be infrequent and you will largely be expected to work by yourself.	• Understand your situation from the start and lower your expectations • Try to make use of whatever alternative support networks are present in the department or university • Press for meetings and discussions and be prepared to ask questions or to be referred to someone who can help • Be prepared to make contact with outside experts, e.g. by email
The one who'd rather be doing your research – your project is a pet topic but time and status no longer allow him/her to carry out the work. May over-supervise at times – interfering in your work, expecting impossibly high standards for someone of your experience, dictating approaches and expressing irritation if you do things in your own way. May take over when work due for publication.	• Try your best to work to his/her standards • If you disagree with the expected approach, be prepared to present a well-argued case for your preferred method • Don't come to rely entirely on his/her analysis and interpretation – you must be able to defend your own thoughts under oral examination
The father/mother figure – often an experienced and noted researcher in the twilight of his/her career. Relishes opportunity to pass on wisdom in a supportive, friendly manner. Approaches may be slightly outdated but will generally be sound.	• Make sure any information provided is up-to-date – supervisor may be a little stuck in the past • Keep up to date with current literature in your area • Relish the opportunity to learn from all his/her wisdom and knowledge – 'old' does not necessarily mean 'out-of-date'
The technocrat – has built current career on knowledge of a specific approach, technique or instrument. May expect you to be as methods-savvy as him/her. Methods may churn out results but may be limited in applicability.	• Be aware of other approaches and try to fit these into your work to 'round' your experience • Take advantage of results-churning by writing plentiful papers – the window of opportunity may be narrow • Try to gain a wider knowledge of the topic beyond the immediate methodology

Continued overleaf

Supervisor type, approach to your research and supervision style	Suggested strategies for successful relationships
The would-be superstar – highly ambitious, and your work may be part of his/her grand plan for advancement. Likely to be impatient and will expect results yesterday.	• Work hard – you may be able to coat-tail on his/her upwards trajectory, possibly moving between institutions along the way • Resist tendency for quality to suffer in the demand for instant results – keep your own standards as far as possible, as you will be judged by them
The introvert – a talented researcher but one who lacks people-skills. May have succeeded so far as a loner and may be a reluctant supervisor (see below). Not good in meetings or in passing on wisdom and personal advice.	• Work at making him/her comfortable in discussion • Be prepared to gain information in short sharp meetings
The slightly reluctant supervisor – may have been pressed into having you as a student, may resent the commitment of time involved and may not be entirely interested in your research topic.	• Try to be as pleasant as possible and to minimise his or her workload by preparing well • Try your best to enthuse him or her in your subject material • Try to find other sources of advice and encouragement
The novice – new to this task. Likely to be keen, friendly and interested. Research field may be fresh but uncertain. May not have developed the required person-skills for supervision and may be unfamiliar with procedures, rules and regulations. May be paired with a more senior co-supervisor.	• Take advantage of the enthusiasm a novice supervisor can provide • Capitalise also on other sources of advice and encouragement: most universities will arrange for co-supervisors for staff unfamiliar with this role • Be prepared to double-check on procedures and timing • Recognise that, although the age differential between you and this type of supervisor may be narrow, you need to keep a certain amount of distance and avoid over-familiarity

THE SUPERVISOR'S ROLE IN WRITING UP YOUR WORK

Communicating your work in writing is a vital part of any postgraduate study programme (**Ch 25**) and you can expect your supervisor to take a keen interest in this. In all probability, you will gain mutually from this writing by enhancing your respective CVs and reputations. Perhaps because of the importance of placing your work on record, the interactions that take place during this process often involve some thorny discussions and it is important that you understand the reasons for these.

How much will your supervisor help you in writing up?

Misunderstandings on this issue can act as a major source of dissatisfaction. International students particularly, who may be paying large fees for the postgraduate experience, might expect that this is in part a payment for help with writing up. It isn't, normally. Moreover, most supervisors will be unable to have the time to help with putting your ideas into scholarly English. For this, you may need to consult a specialist writing centre in your university.

While you will be asked to sign a statement to the effect that your thesis is all 'your own work', there is necessarily an element of collaboration between student and supervisor. You will be expected to write your thesis, taking into account feedback provided by your supervisor. The *viva voce* exam is designed to ensure that the thesis is your own work, and that you fully understand what has been written. Despite the need for autonomy, you should have a legitimate expectation of guidance and constructive criticism concerning your efforts.

However, your supervisor may insist on including material you do not agree with or insist on removing material you think is important. Before getting too annoyed with this, do bear in mind your supervisor's experience and wisdom. He or she may well have good reasons for adopting a particular stance – perhaps sensitivity to the 'political' aspects of your research, or knowledge of the key figures working within your research area (that is, potential examiners or referees) and how they might react to what you propose to write.

Your supervisor may feel that aspects of your work are not ready for publication. He or she may insist that you repeat your procedures several times; or that you analyse it in greater depth. Again, you should respect their wisdom in such matters. If your results are important or go against other work it might be extremely important for have a high level of confidence before going public. Do not feel insulted if another person in the research group is asked to repeat your work; again, this is part of the double-checking that may be vital before publication. Your supervisor will be well aware of the rigour with which referees will look at your work and the sorts of comments they are likely to make and may wish to forestall most of these.

Deciding on authorship of published work

Authorship details can be a source of disappointment or resentment. It is best to discuss and decide such matters before anything gets written up for submission to a journal.

- In the Sciences, it is the norm for any papers arising from 'your' work to be jointly authored. It is widely accepted that the supervisor 'co-owns' the intellectual property that you develop in partnership.

- In the Arts, it is usual for postgraduate students' publications not to carry the supervisor's name as an author, although, of course, their contribution should be acknowledged in the appropriate thesis section.

There will probably be 'local rules' for whose name will go first on any joint paper. In some cases, this is decided alphabetically. In others, the supervisor's name usually goes first, whilst elsewhere it will appear last, indicating seniority. In some research groups, the pattern will be to alternate names in a sequence of papers.

Expect some differences to emerge in your writing styles. Your supervisor will probably have had a different type of schooling/training from you and therefore may write in a different way – perhaps one that you feel is overly formal and pedantic. Almost certainly, however, your supervisor will have the same or a better qualification that the one you aspire to and a greater experience of writing in academic style. Listen and learn. Writing your thesis may be the single most important period in your life as far as learning about English is concerned. There is much to be gained from sensible discussions about the issues that arise. It is not uncommon, for example, for there to be lengthy supervisor–student discussions on the use of commas or sentence or paragraph construction. Even if you disagree with the style being proposed, you should go along with what your supervisor advises, and accept that learning to write in different ways is an important skill to emerge from your studies.

ACTION POINTS

10.1 Analyse how your personality will interact with that of your supervisor. Decide what type your supervisor appears to be (Table 10.1). Reflect on how you might forestall or respond to the challenges you feel might emerge in your continuing relationship and plan the tactics necessary for this. What kind of postgraduate student are you? Imagine a classification of postgraduate student types that supervisors might develop: what traits do you display that they may like or dislike?

10.2 Think about the skills you need to develop to become more independent from your supervisor. Look at the opportunities available to you for improving the skills of an autonomous researcher, and sign up for any relevant training sessions or workshops in your institution.

10.3 Investigate the regulatory framework surrounding student–supervisor relationships. This will be published within a 'code of practice for supervised research' or similar within your institution. The aim in doing so is not to become a 'barrack-room lawyer', but to clarify for yourself the realistic expectations for both parties.

DEALING WITH THE HIGHS AND LOWS OF BEING A POSTGRADUATE

How to respond positively to events and feelings

Your mood is likely to oscillate while researching for a PhD. This is common and is a function of the difficulty and amount of work expected, which inevitably impact on health, relationships and feelings. Everybody feels stress differently. It is important to recognise likely causes and to consider potential solutions.

KEY TOPICS

→ What to expect

→ Responding positively to stress

This chapter aims to help by alerting you to possible reasons for highs and lows in your PhD studies. You will then be in a position to recognise what might be happening and your feelings about this, and in some cases to forestall or accommodate the underlying issues. This applies as much to the highs as the lows – and it is sometimes dealing with the contrasts of life that leads to tension, stress and depression.

 Personal feelings are individual

We all respond in different ways to the challenges of life, and so it is with those of PhD research. For example, one person might find a certain aspect stressful, such as delivering a seminar, while another would thrive on this task. The corollary is that solutions are also personal, and you will have to work to find a way to deal with your state of mind at any given time.

One aspect that every PhD student must be fully prepared for is sustained and intensive work. At times this will seem like sheer hard labour and it will frequently involve a degree of tedium. However, no prize worth earning is easily gained, and this applies also to the results of research: if the central question were easy to answer, someone would already have done so. The secret, if there is one, is to be ready for this effort and to spread out the work as evenly as possible rather than creating overload in the final stages. Good time management and planning (**Ch 6**) will be essential.

Nearly all postgraduate students experience up and downs during the three or more years in which they are researching for their PhD. In other words, if you feel particularly low at any point, you will not be alone – it is almost part of the rite of passage for this qualification. The highs of PhD study, however, are well worth waiting for, as they will involve some of the most rewarding academic experiences you will ever have.

Highs

The highs of PhD study are intense and recognising this is probably why you signed up for the degree. The ultimate achievement of your period of postgraduate study will be walking up to receive your degree at the graduation ceremony. This is the vision to keep in mind when the going gets tough. However, there will be many other highs along the way that should sustain you during this lengthy period of study. Some examples might include:

- Gaining good feedback from meetings. If your supervisor or progress monitoring committee members are supportive, this can give you a welcome boost. You may increase the value of the experience if you go into such meetings well prepared (**Chs 10** and **16**), and perhaps with a series of queries, rather than attending with a passive outlook,

- Obtaining an excellent piece of data or making a breakthrough in understanding. With good fortune and effort, such events will occur relatively frequently. You will probably feel an urge to share these moments. However, don't be surprised if your enthusiasm leaves others somewhat bewildered; this will probably be because they don't understand the technical significance of your finding.

- Finding an important new reference or information source. Sourcing new papers that are relevant can be extremely helpful to the progress of your work (although they can sometimes present a challenge if the results or ideas disagree with your own). This will usually give a boost to your efforts.

- Taking part in creative discussions. A 'meeting of minds' can occur with your fellow students, a supervisor, a colleague or a fellow researcher. This can lead to breakthroughs in understanding and the generation of new ideas. Take full advantage of the 'buzz' that follows such meetings by writing down your immediate thoughts and reactions as soon as possible.

- Delivering your first seminar or paper. This will probably feel stressful in the run-up to presentation, but after the event, you will nearly always have a feeling of elation. Aim to capitalise on the greater insight and understanding you may have after explaining your topic to others. Learn from any questions that are posed.

- Completing your write-up. Submitting your thesis to the relevant office will be a great moment. It will be the culmination of months of single-minded effort, and the initial elation may be followed by slight deflation. Remember to start preparing for your *viva* soon after this point. When reading through your thesis, do not be depressed by any errors you find. Everyone makes some mistakes. Note these and present them at the *viva*.

- Having a successful outcome from your *viva*. The oral exam is without doubt a stressful experience for many, but it needn't be if you are well prepared and understand what to expect (**Ch 31**). You won't always know the formal result with certainty, but will usually have a very good idea (the chair or external examiner may phrase it as 'we will be making a recommendation...' to the relevant university committee). Enjoy the celebration!

- Having a research publication accepted. This will mark your contribution to the body of knowledge and understanding in your area, and should be a very proud moment. It will probably represent the culmination of years of work and should be fully savoured.

Keep a reflective diary

If you don't want to share your feelings with others, share them with yourself. Reflect on the positives and negatives and use this written formulation of your situation to find greater understanding and to note potential solutions where these are required.

Lows

Low points can occur for a number of reasons. These include:

- Lack of progress. This is probably the most frequent reason for negative feelings during PhD research, and can probably be conquered only by reapplying yourself to the work. It can occur for a variety of reasons, depending on the project. Examples could be: when an experiment doesn't work; when you find a reference that negates a cherished idea; or when your supervisor doesn't like what you have done. You simply need to dust yourself down and try to respond positively.

- Lack of confidence. This may be especially acute in the first months of research. You will meet others who seem cleverer and more proficient, and who seem to come up with results with ease. You may even question whether doing a PhD was the right choice for you. Gain assurance from your past achievements and the fact that others have judged you capable of working at this level. A good supervisor will be very supportive if you explain your feelings.

- Not meeting your own or others' high expectations. You may have set yourself a high target for the quality of your work and you may feel worried that you are not able to meet this. Your supervisor or sponsors might also expect high things of you. Accept that there is no shame in trying and failing, only in not trying. Remember, your thesis doesn't need to present an Earth-shattering conclusion; and that 'negative results' can be valuable as part of a bigger picture.

- Poor working relationships. These can occur with your supervisor, fellow students or other people on whom you depend for progress, such as technicians and university officials. Be aware that there are always two sides to any story and try to see things from the other side. The general advice here is (a) to explain your feelings where appropriate, and/or (b) to be twice as nice back in return for any slight you may feel. Both strategies often result in a positive dividend.

- Feeling isolated. You may feel, for example, that you have had a lack of supportive contact with your supervisor, or that family members do not understand your situation. Talk to them. Talk to others. This will help relieve both the symptom and potentially the cause.

- Deterioration in personal relationships. This may occur because of the amount of time you are spending on research or because you are tired when you return from your studies. One solution is to ring-fence time for your significant other(s), possibly by timetabling this in your week. Make an effort to show you care and, in discussion, focus on the potential rewards to you both from your qualification. You'll return refreshed to your work and those around you will feel that their needs are also being recognised.

- Hating the writing. Many postgraduates thrive on the research phase of a PhD but abhor the writing-up. They may have always disliked this aspect of university work or may have a condition like dyslexia that makes it particularly tough. The tips in later chapters of this book may help with this problem.

The highs and lows of postgraduate study may be played out on a longer timescale, but are inevitably more extreme than those of your undergraduate days. After all, you have more invested in your PhD project – at the end it will seem like an extension of your personality. It is by recognising that there is always a cycle of ups and downs, and by responding in a positive fashion, you will cope with all the lows and move on to success.

Break out of your routine if you are feeling low

Perhaps you need to try something new to create a more positive feeling. Examples might include:

- trying a new method or approach;
- reading a different source;
- going away, perhaps to a conference or seminar;
- speaking to someone with a different perspective;
- starting work on a new part of your write-up.

Returning to an old problem thereafter may help you to tackle it with renewed enthusiasm.

RESPONDING POSITIVELY TO STRESS

Feelings of 'stress' represent a way humans have evolved to cope with difficult situations, by placing the brain and body under a condition of 'high alert'. Understanding these feelings will help you channel them so you perform better. Research shows that students perform better under a certain amount of stress, while too much, or too little, results in a weaker outcome. Learning to cope with stress is also a skill that will be useful in later life.

Stress means different things to different people and involves a wide range of emotions and feelings, so an all-encompassing definition is hard to produce. Stress usually involves some form of external pressure, resulting in mental or emotional strain, typified by worrying, fretting and agonising. Most people feel stressed at some point in their lives; equally, it is true that one person's worrying threat may be another person's stimulating challenge.

What if I feel really, really bad?

For some, the stresses of postgraduate student life are such that they consider dropping out or even feel suicidal. Talking about your situation is the best way to counteract these feelings. You can do this anonymously and/or confidentially through:

■ The Samaritans (***www.samaritans.org.uk***);

■ Nightline (***www.nightline.niss.ac.uk***);

■ or through your university's medical or counselling services (find this via ***www.studentcounselling.org/***).

These sources provide contact telephone numbers and 24–7 online guidance.

Recognising when you are under stress, or likely to be so, is important because it allows you to adopt avoidance strategies. Common physical symptoms associated with stress include: breathing difficulty, comfort eating, diarrhoea, dry mouth, feeling of panic, headaches, nausea, shaking hands and sweating. You may also show behavioural changes, such as displacement activity, irritability, loss of appetite and sleeplessness. All of this is normal and something that even outwardly confident people need to work their way through.

There are many positive strategies to deal with stress. You may find one or more of the following tips appropriate to your situation and/or personality. They are in no particular order.

● Try not to worry about things over which you have no control. If necessary, recognise your personal limitations. Accept life as you find it and try to find positive ways around each problem.

- Share your problem. Simply talking about your problems ('verbalising') can help you confront problems, put them in perspective or work out a solution, while bottling things up may make them worse. You might wish to open out your feelings to a friend; talk to a receptive member of academic staff; or seek a session with one of your university's counsellors.

- Find out more about what's bothering you. There may be books available about your problem, and there will almost certainly be a website somewhere. You may be able to work through a solution yourself.

- Participate. Seek out ways of getting involved and busy. Join a club or society. Ask someone to go along with you, or ask if you can accompany someone who is already participating.

- Learn to prioritise. If you are stressed because you have too much to do, make a list of tasks and put them in order based in urgency and importance (**Ch 6**).

- Put things in perspective. Look around you and see how others are coping. There is always someone worse off than you are, and some people battle through against amazing odds. If they can manage, why not you?

- Try to forget about your problem. Some problems (not all, certainly) simply disappear with time as event move on or circumstances change. What was a problem on Friday morning may have disappeared by Monday morning. Watch a film for some escapism. Get some sleep and see how you feel in the morning. Inspiration sometimes comes at the most unexpected times (**Ch 17**).

- Try not to be a perfectionist. Accept a lesser standard if this means your life is more balanced.

Make an appointment to see a doctor or nurse if your problem involves your health

These professionals have seen nearly every problem before and are expert at helping to find solutions – or can refer you to someone who can. You may need to register with a local practice (ask around to see which doctors have a good reputation) or you could use your University's Health Service.

- Confront your problem. OK, so the fact that you have reached a particularly tough part of your research is causing you grief. Well, start studying or writing! Or if someone is being a pain in the neck, tell them so, explaining why their actions are causing you problems. Do this calmly but firmly; becoming angry will only increase your tension and add to your negative feelings. Similarly, running away from a problem merely means you avoid the issue rather than facing it and add to your sense of negativity and tension.

- Do something physical. This is great for removing the symptoms of stress. Go for a jog or swim or join a fitness class. This will provide an outlet for all the jangled nerves and hormones that your body has unconsciously prepared in anticipation of a stressful event.

- Don't be afraid to have a good cry. This is a very natural way to relieve stress in some situations – and this applies to everyone.

- Learn how to meditate. Try out yoga or other methods of relaxation. Some people find this is a great tool for de-stressing.

- Change your working pattern. If you are getting into problems because of excessive hours at the bench or desk, the remedy is obvious. On the other hand, if you can confess to slacking, then increase your work rate. Decide to work longer hours or work the same hours more effectively. Cut out activities that are preventing you from achieving your goals.

- Try to manage your time better. If an apparent lack of time is causing stress, see if you can organise yourself better (**Ch 6**).

- Recognise that you can't please everyone. Accept that you may have to act selfishly or in a focused way. You may find that others are far more accommodating than you thought they would be, if you simply explain and apologise.

- Treat yourself. Instead of feeling that you are always doing things you don't like, or find hard, or take ages, give yourself a break and do something you know you will enjoy. You will probably find that when you return to your stressful task you are in a much better frame of mind to conquer it.

- Make a conscious effort to see problems in a more positive light. Regard them as challenges that you *can* manage and accommodate.

11.1 If you can, make sure you influence matters. You may be able to remove the cause of stress. For example, simply speaking to your supervisor about a worrying issue may clear the air and result in an agreed path out of a problem. This may require determination and assertiveness on your part. Putting the blame on others is tempting, but you may have the solution in your own hands. For instance, you may think others are being unfriendly, when in fact you are expecting them to make all the running, rather than being outgoing yourself.

11.2 Use your university's counselling service if in need of help. The mere fact that a counselling service exists should tell you something: others have been here before. This service will be staffed by professionals, expert in their job. They will make you feel at ease; assist you to work out your own solution; and put you in contact with others who can help. You can rest assured that the service will be fully confidential and independent from the academic side of university life.

11.3 Participate fully in the postgraduate culture. Having the chance to talk informally about your research can put things in perspective, can be invigorating and can help establish friendships and networks that will endure long past your study years. Even if you are the only student in your department doing a postgraduate qualification, there will be institutional opportunities for you to meet other PhD students through seminars, training courses and through your on-campus Postgraduate Society – in some cases there may even be a Postgraduate Society especially for students in your discipline (if not, why not start one?). Alternatively, there are online postgraduate sites active within the UK and elsewhere. Such opportunities should not be seen as time-wasting but a chance to meet with others who are facing similar challenges to you.

12

WORKING IN A RESEARCH TEAM

How to balance research cooperation and autonomy

Some PhD students will work on their own, while others will work as part of a research team. All students will be members of a wider group forming the academic community that is the essence of a university or research institute. Understanding team roles and the contributions made by others can make your passage through the system easier.

KEY TOPICS

→ Advantages and disadvantages of researching in a team

→ Understanding team roles and associated skills

→ Working within the wider academic community

→ Taking part in extracurricular activities

For some, PhD research is essentially a solo activity carried out in a library and possibly with minimal contact with a supervisor. This can lead to particular issues associated with isolation, some of which were discussed in **Chapter 11**. Others will be joining a research team. This can bring attendant advantages, but also some disadvantages. Being aware of these and considering appropriate responses can help you make the most of this situation and forestall potential issues. Even if you consider yourself a solo researcher, you will still be part of a dispersed academic community in your department and university, and may benefit from analysing the responsibilities and interactions inherent in team situations.

ADVANTAGES AND DISADVANTAGES OF RESEARCHING IN A TEAM

If you join a research team it is likely to be led by a highly able, motivated and respected individual, perhaps of professorial status.

He or she will have already established their academic credentials through hard work and talent. The funding that supports you will probably have been awarded only after a rigorous review process of his or her grant proposal. The team they will have assembled might include a range of members including other PhD students, possibly at different stages in their studies. Many will have been part of the team for a number of years. You will start at the bottom of a pecking order.

Typical members of a large research group

- The research group leader;
- Other 'permanent' research staff;
- Associate staff, perhaps with a predominantly teaching role;
- Administrator and secretary;
- Technicians;
- Postdoctoral staff;
- Other PhD students.

In smaller groups multiple roles may be carried out by the same person, or the role may not exist.

Nevertheless, as a PhD student in this situation, you will be rewarded with a number of advantages arising from this cooperative environment:

- There will probably be adequate finding and resourcing for your work.
- There will be access to equipment to carry out analyses.
- There will be other PhD students and colleagues to talk to.
- The working environment will be lively and possibly even competitive, yet supportive.
- You will fit into a well-established programme of study.
- The methods and equipment you use are likely to be well-tested and reliable.
- You may be credited on team research publications, and possibly as a co-author.
- You will gain from the reputation of the lab or research team when applying for new jobs.

These, inevitably, come with some disadvantages:

- It can be difficult to be autonomous in a team (see below).
- The research you are asked to do may be tedious and uninspiring.
- You may have little freedom to explore your own interests.
- You may feel like a small cog in a large machine for producing results.
- You may feel you won't get the full credit for your work or ideas.
- There may be personality clashes and cliques within the team that might draw you in on one side or another.
- Your supervisor may be busy, so you will hardly see him or her.
- The general expectation for work-rate will be exceptionally high.
- The focus may be entirely on research, with little scope for teaching activities.
- Others may feel they should be co-authors on your papers.

The key to a successful PhD experience will be the balance between gaining assistance from the research team environment and the need for autonomy in your own project. The latter is not only important for establishing the expected academic outcomes of the PhD degree (**Ch 2**) it will also impact on your personal development (**Ch 5**), which in many ways is the important personal outcome.

Role of the research group leader

To a great extent, the impact on you of the potential problems of carrying out a PhD within a research group will depend on the team leader, who will probably also be your supervisor. An effective leader/supervisor will understand what these issues are and take steps to counteract them, especially when you first join the group.

UNDERSTANDING TEAM ROLES AND ASSOCIATED SKILLS

Research suggests that there are many distinct team personalities and that each of us has a 'natural' team role. Thinking about your group activities will help you develop as a team member. What you find out about yourself may even influence your eventual choice of career and job.

Meredith Belbin, a researcher in this area, has classified nine or even more roles that people tend to play in teams (Belbin, 2012). His analysis recognises that there are both 'good' character traits and 'allowable weaknesses' for each role. The second notion is valuable, because it reduces the feeling that any one role is intrinsically superior. By its very nature, a research team has a natural leader – usually also your supervisor. However, others in the group may assume certain leadership roles in the absence of the supervisor. For example, acting as the interface between the group members and the supervisor, associate staff or postdoc members may assume informal leadership roles from time-to-time.

Table 12.1 offers a simplified version of Belbin's analysis as it might apply to research teams. As a PhD student, there is little doubt about your initial position in this classification – you are, and will primarily be regarded as, a 'worker'.

A part of the tension in being a research team member is that you, or a fellow member, may be asked to play a different role from the one that is 'natural' to you. This can lead to problems as people try to adapt to the requirements of the role, or when someone tries to assume a different role from the one they have been assigned. Also, when people work in a small research team, they may be asked to play multiple roles or to switch between roles at different times as the project progresses.

You can see from Table 12.1 that many skills are required for effective teamwork. Table 12.2 focuses on some essential skills for you as a member of a research team and provides brief tips for carrying these out successfully.

 Capitalising on your existing skills

You may already have built up considerable teamwork skills. Perhaps you have played team games, been a member of a fund-raising group, organised a social event or been employed as part of a team. This experience will help greatly as you learn more about your character as a research group team worker and transfer the necessary skills to this situation.

Table 12.1 Research team roles. The content of this table is derived from the work of Belbin, with adjustments to fit the research team situation. Belbin's analysis subdivides most of the roles shown and includes key attributes and allowable weaknesses not shown here. Consult Belbin (2012) if you wish to learn more or find out about the research that supports his analysis.

Research team role	Key attributes and beneficial functions in a research team	'Allowable weaknesses'
Group leader	Makes the team work towards its shared goal. Good at spotting others' talents and delegation. A dynamic go-getter who is eager for results. Good at generating action, trouble-shooting and imposing a pattern. Provides drive and realism to team activities. Takes a balanced view and displays sound judgement.	May be less creative than others and have no special expertise. Can be impatient with others.
Creative person	A source of originality for the group's activities. An intelligent, ideas person, who generates solutions to problems and often uses unusual approaches. An extrovert, communicative sort, who enthusiastically investigates new information and ideas. Good at exploiting resources and developing external relations.	May work in isolation and ideas may be impractical. May not communicate well. Can be over-optimistic and may have a short attention span.
Organiser	Turns ideas into actions. Good at making sure things get done. Uses energy, discipline and common-sense to solve problems. Good focus on fulfilling objectives. Painstaking, orderly and well organised. Conscientious and anxious that all tasks are completed their own high standard.	May lack flexibility and resist new ideas. Can be obsessive about details and may wish to control quality and outcome.
Critic	Analyses what the team is doing in a detached and unemotional way. Good at evaluating the group's ideas and making sure they are appropriate.	May lack drive and have a low work-rate. Critical comments may act to de-motivate others.
Worker	Willing to support others and provide cohesion to the team. Diligent. Provides essential expertise and skills to the group. Adds expertise but can be single-minded and may not see the wider picture.	Narrow outlook, focused on own work. Can be obsessed by technical detail and not see the big picture. Doesn't like to lead or make decisions.

Table 12.2 Tips for being a successful research team member.

Behaviour
Give-and-take is essential to team function at many levels. To succeed as a group you will have to get along together. This may require diplomacy and tact. Team membership requires everyone to be able to give and receive criticism constructively and not to view it as personal disapproval. • Be willing to compromise • Be considerate – respect the different abilities and contributions of others • Be positive, and praise others' inputs whenever you can • Respect the leadership of the group and the roles of others in the group • Don't form or take part in cliques within the group • Remember that if someone has flaws in some areas, they may be compensated for in other areas (and perhaps at a later time) • From time to time, reflect on your contribution to the team
Communication
The success of any team depends on its ability to communicate. The larger a research group, the more important this becomes. Group members need to understand what is expected of them by the team and its leader. Time frames have to be defined, as do team roles, and other arrangements such as for the interchange of information. Face-to-face meetings are usually important; email is also a useful way of keeping in touch. At an early stage, try to understand how these communication channels work in your research team. • Make sure you talk to other team members and try to encourage them to talk to you • Be prompt with replies to messages • Talk through all problems as soon as possible • Understand that other team members may be shy or nervous • Contribute if your team has to present its work or answer questions on it • Learn to listen to others and recognise that views that differ from your own may have value • Don't monopolise discussions or impose your views
Focus and commitment
Teamwork can be demanding in time and effort; everyone needs to show dedication and a high work-rate if the highest standards are to be achieved collectively. With the help of its leader, your research group must keep its collective eye on its goals and targets to ensure that it meets these, otherwise team output and future funding might suffer. • Try to 'do your bit' and don't be a lazy team member • Understand your part in the overall research group goal • Ensure your work is up to the standards set for group (and even better, if this does not compromise your targets) • If you feel your contribution is overloading you or is disproportionate to the contribution of others, then try to discuss this openly and without attributing blame • Keep the final objective, your PhD thesis, in mind at all times

Time management in research teams

Research teams will have targets and milestones to reach to justify their funding. Creating and managing these is an important responsibility of the team leader and the 'organiser' figure. In small groups, both roles may be assumed by the head of the team, whereas in large groups a research administrator may assist. There will always be a deadline for your personal contribution within the team and this implies that individual time management and planning will be required to meet your goals (**Ch 6**).

WORKING WITHIN THE WIDER ACADEMIC COMMUNITY

Whether you work in a research team or not, you will be part of the wider academic community in your university or research institute. Members who you are likely to interact with as a postgraduate student include:

- Research academics working outside your area. These may be members of your progress monitoring committee, or perhaps attendees at your research seminars. They may be able to provide useful advice or facilities for your work.

- Teaching staff. These may be the same as the above or a specialised group, depending on departmental organisation. They may be involved in your own teaching activities – either by setting up the undergraduate curriculum or managing your contribution to it. Such staff may have been active researchers in the past and can be valuable sources of academic wisdom.

- Departmental administrative staff. These may assist you in the formal aspects of PhD study, including reminding you about progress report deadlines and organising any contributions to teaching you may make. Some may have important roles to play in the resources and facilities you use, such as IT. The departmental secretary is always central to the organisation's activities and will usually know what you should do or who you should contact if you have a problem.

- Librarians. Most university libraries allocate responsibility for specific subjects to certain staff and these subject librarians can be an essential source of assistance in your researches. They may conduct induction or information sessions for postgraduate students that are well worth attending.

- Technicians. These staff are important in the sciences and may support your work in a very direct way, perhaps by maintaining complex analytical instruments, or perhaps indirectly by looking after a chemical store or making up stock solutions.

- Postgraduate office staff. The postgraduate office is usually a central facility administering all the university's PhD programmes. Its staff will be involved in the formal aspects of your studies, including thesis submission and the examination. Normally the office will publish a set of rules for postgraduate study and examination that you should read.

- Other officials. These include staff involved in such areas as intellectual property, legal matters, accommodation, student support, postgraduate training, students' union facilities whom you might come into contact with, depending on your area of work.

One special group in the university community could play a vital role in your time working on a PhD and that is your peers, both in your department and across the institution. These other postgraduate students can support you, motivate you, be your ally, and generally keep you going when times get tough. The success of this relationship depends as much on you as on them, so you should try to be proactive in joining in, organising meetings and helping others. Many will become lifelong friends.

Many others are involved in the university community, from the Vice Chancellor (Principal in Scotland) to the janitors and cleaners. All will play a role in your studies. All deserve respect and politeness.

Be considerate to administrators and other staff

Bureaucracy can be irritating and inefficient but it is a necessary evil. Expect to have lots of forms to fill in, sometimes covering the same information, but often fulfilling an important institutional or even legal purpose. Furthermore, you will have a single-minded interest in your own project and thesis and many staff cover a range of different roles and responsibilities. Their current agenda and associated priorities may be different from yours and you may need to be patient when waiting for a response.

TAKING PART IN EXTRACURRICULAR ACTIVITIES

The high work rate expected of PhD students may limit how much you can take part in outside activities, but these can provide a valuable release from postgraduate life.

You may choose to pursue activities such as a sport or skill with others who share their interest; you may wish to carry out charitable work, or you might opt to become involved in student representation through the Students' Union or Association or your Postgraduate Society. Participating in these kinds of non-study activities is important because it can help you to develop new and different relationships and also bring a sense of balance to your life. It can also provide you with insights and experiences of teamwork that may make useful additions to your CV.

Some extracurricular activities can complement your research – for example, participating in a debating society if you are studying politics, attending language classes if you need to translate key references, or joining a hill-walking club if your research has an ecological aspect.

The danger in taking part too enthusiastically in extracurricular activities is that you will lose track of your academic responsibilities. This should not be a problem if you limit your involvement carefully and use appropriate time-management approaches (**Ch 6**).

How can I play a part in university decision-making?

Representing your fellow postgraduate students can be considered to be a special type of extracurricular activity. You can contribute in two ways:

1 Become involved in school/department boards or committees at higher levels. To take part in these, you might need to become elected as a local representative.

2 Stand as a postgraduate candidate for the executive committee of your students' union or association.

Some might regard this type of committee activity as boring, and it often is, but it gives you a chance to see the bigger picture, to observe the conduct of meetings and to make a difference for your fellow postgraduate students.

12.1 If you are joining a research group, think about how it is constructed and who performs the roles described above. Conversely, if you are a 'solo researcher', think about who can take the place of these people, where relevant, in your situation.

12.2 Attend teamwork workshops. If you are interested in learning more about this topic, you will probably find sessions offered in the postgraduate training programme.

12.3 Look into the postgraduate support services in your university. Ensure you know what each officer's responsibilities are and how to contact them, when and if needed.

TEACHING AS A POSTGRADUATE

How to make the most of opportunities to tutor, demonstrate and lecture

Teaching duties are generally considered to be an important aspect of postgraduate training. They offer the opportunity to refine skills, add to your CV and, in some cases, top up your bank balance. There are distinct benefits to such work, but also some drawbacks. You should approach opportunities to teach with a considered view of how this will impact on your current and future prospects.

KEY TOPICS

→ Pros and cons of carrying out teaching

→ Acting as a tutor

→ Acting as a demonstrator

→ Delivering lectures

→ Assessing student assignments

As a postgraduate, you will probably be invited to carry out various types of teaching duties. These may include the following:

- tutoring – small group teaching centred around discussions on a prescribed topic or answers to problems related to an aspect of their course;

- demonstrating – lab- or field-based teaching, again to small groups, helping them to achieve the goals of a practical or field visit;

- lecturing – one-to-many teaching, usually in a seminar room or lecture theatre and generally supported by presentation tools, such as PowerPoint (**Ch 14**);

- assessing – appraising, providing feedback and marking student work, usually to specific marking criteria.

Assessment of your teaching

You should be aware that your teaching efforts will be appraised, either by direct observation by a colleague, or by formal or informal feedback from the students. This information may be used for references when you apply for a job.

PROS AND CONS OF CARRYING OUT TEACHING

The main advantages of carrying out teaching as a postgraduate are:

- the prospect of learning new skills related to teaching;
- the opportunity to see whether a career involving teaching would suit your personality;
- in some cases, the better understanding of your subject area which comes from having to explain it to others;
- the financial remuneration, where you are paid for the work.

On the other hand, teaching involves a commitment of time and energy. It will probably take more preparation time than you imagine and there may be additional assessment duties that also require your attention for long periods. You will also find intensive teaching surprisingly tiring. It might therefore affect your research by temporarily lessening your enthusiasm and drive. Your supervisor may not like the fact that you are distracted from your project – and some supervisors strictly limit the time their students can take to teach.

Successful teaching involves a range of complex skills which it is easy to underestimate. When new to this role, there is a temptation to rely on your past experience as a student, taking the best model of teaching you experienced as an undergraduate, and trying to emulate this. Of course, you may not have observed all possible methods in action, so there is merit in studying the theoretical background to teaching, to try to improve your proficiency. However, effective teaching requires a range of practical classroom skills and the best way of learning these is through experience and practice. Thus, to create a effective personal approach it is best to aim for a combination of attending workshops on teaching 'theory' and trial and error in front of real students.

What commitment might my teaching involve?

When you are asked to undertake tutoring or demonstrating, ensure that you check exactly what this will involve. Asking the following questions could be useful.

- What is the total time requirement?
- What training will be given?
- Will any materials or directions be provided?
- How many classes/labs/tutorials will this involve?
- How often will tutors/demonstrators be expected to see students beyond that commitment?
- What are the mechanisms for returning work, that is, do tutors/demonstrators have to return work to students in one-to-one tutorial sessions?
- What are the departmental rules on students' non-attendance for tutorial/lab/feedback sessions? Are there any sanctions? If so, who has responsibility for invoking these?
- How many teaching-related meetings will have to be attended?
- Are there any reports I will have to complete regarding my tutoring/demonstrating, including reports on individual students?
- What are the mechanisms for submitting/recording marks?
- What is the rate of pay?

ACTING AS A TUTOR

Your main task ahead of running a tutorial is mastering the subject material so that you can both ask and answer relevant questions. You may need to allocate time for reading around the topic, and you may need to seek the advice of those creating the syllabus to track down relevant sources or to ensure that your explanations are 'on message' to fit with other parts of the course. Assuming you have gained this understanding, the remaining challenges are related to ensuring that the tutorial engages and informs all the students present.

Because tutorial group sizes are small, you can adopt a relatively relaxed presentational manner. It is vital to the success of tutorials that the students feel comfortable with the other people in the group – and that includes the tutor. At an early meeting of the group, introduce an

Find a suitable tutorial location .

If you can influence this, try to ensure that the room in which you are teaching is suitable for the number of students (enough chairs) and the type of teaching expected. For example, if you wish to use presentation aids, ensure that suitable facilities are present.

activity in which students get to know each other. For example, get them to find out five things about a partner and then introduce them to the group. This type of 'warm-up' activity takes time, but it will pay dividends: it is easier for participants to engage in a discussion if they know the names and backgrounds of the others present. If you involve yourself in this activity, it could encourage your tutees to see you as approachable and human. However, there is a fine line between being friendly without becoming over-familiar. Remember that you will have to assess their work.

Agree a code of conduct for tutorials

When dealing with novice tutees, it is a good idea to establish some ground rules, for example:

- only one person speaks at a time;
- everyone contributes;
- all ideas and opinions are respected and are permitted an airing;
- often there are no 'right' or 'wrong' answers;
- all ideas are worth discussing, provided that they can be supported by evidence;
- note-taking is expected.

Explain the aims of the tutorial. Either clarify how you wish to allocate the time available to the topic or get the students to allocate the time they think appropriate to the aims as outlined. The advantage of involving the tutees in this is that it gives the students 'ownership' of the tutorial and makes it less easy for them to be passive. It also enables you to retain an element of control: you can invoke the agreed timetable as a means of moving on.

The normal method of initiating discussion is to ask the whole group a few questions related to the topic, perhaps starting with something unlikely to be challenging. If such 'round table' discussion is not working, either because no one speaks or a few students dominate the discussion, try dividing the students into groups and asking each group or pair to discuss an aspect of the tutorial topic. Working in this way helps to create a situation where the students feel confident about giving a personal opinion. When one student is asked to report back to the whole group, then everyone in that group shares some of the responsibility for the ideas expressed. In this way, the quieter students feel less intimidated, embarrassed or helpless.

Beware of digressions in tutorials

Some students may think that the tutorial session is an opportunity to discuss points of their own choosing or a chance to ask questions about lecture topics. If this happens, stress that tutorials and the tutors who run them have a prescribed agenda and that you cannot digress from this. Point out that most lecturers have 'office hours' when they can seek clarification on other points.

A common problem is that some students will have failed to do the preparatory reading. You may then find that those who have done this are left to 'carry' the tutorial, while others 'ride' on the work of others. One strategy to overcome this problem is to get each student to write a couple of sentences about one of the resources they have read. They must name the resource. Give the group a few minutes to do this right at the beginning of the tutorial. Ensure that they put their names on the sheets of paper and collect them in immediately. This will embarrass those who have not done the reading as they are unlikely to be able to write much. A quick glance will show you:

- those students who have done the reading;
- those who have not done any reading, or not very much;
- the key ideas that students have drawn from their preparation.

You may wish to draw attention to the level of preparation at that point; or you may wish to pass no further comment at this stage. Proceed with the discussion or other activity as you had planned, or use the students' key ideas as discussion prompts. Ensure that you finish the tutorial with five minutes to spare and then redistribute the papers and ask the students to write down three additional points arising from the discussion. Collect these in and review them later. These observations may give you, as tutor, some insight to the learning that has taken place in the tutorial. At this stage you may wish to point out that the reading is a prerequisite for effective tutorial participation and that you will be repeating the exercise again. This strategy often has a remarkable effect on those students who have failed to do the reading and will help the students who have prepared to feel that their hard work has been recognised.

At the end of the tutorial, leave time to sum up the issues that have been raised and the key points as you see them. Advise students of further reading which may be useful.

Dealing with shy or incompatible group members

If you feel that certain people do not 'mix' well, then do not be afraid to rearrange the seating, or the order in which the students sit – even to the extent of reading out a prepared list of pairings. This strategy can help you to split up cliques and encourage the participation of students who might not know anyone else. Explain that the pairings will differ for each meeting. This means that, if there is a pairing that did not work well, you can undo it for the next session.

ACTING AS A DEMONSTRATOR

Again, preparation is essential to good performance. There is often a demonstrators' session ahead of a lab session where you can familiarise yourself with the material, pick up tips from academic staff and ask any questions. This might reveal gaps in your knowledge that can be filled by a little reading ahead of the session. You should also read though the schedule ahead of time so you can:

- gain an idea of the overall timing, and be ready to hurry students up if necessary;
- identify potential sticking points where your help may be needed;
- note critical procedures where you will need to ensure that the students follow the instructions to the letter.

Ahead of any lab or field visit, you should make a special note of any safety information provided – you might be held to account if anything goes wrong.

Ensure basic safety procedures are observed, for example, that:

- students can use the equipment properly and safely;
- students are all wearing the necessary protective clothing and lab spectacles;
- where chemicals are in use, you know which students are wearing contact lenses;
- all students in the lab are aware of the fire drill procedures;
- all students clear up after their laboratory session.

Once the session starts, get the students to their allocated bench space as quickly as possible. Don't distract them if a staff member is introducing the session. Ensure that they understand the task they have to fulfil, the sequence in which to work, and that they all have the correct equipment and materials or know where to obtain them.

Look out for potential stragglers

Especially at the start of a laboratory session, keep a look-out for students who are struggling – these often the quiet ones who never ask questions. A helpful intervention at this stage can often improve their experience and yours.

When the session is running, move around your lab area systematically. From your comments and attitude, try to send the message that you are approachable. Although the unskilled actions of some students may frustrate you, avoid talking down to them. Treat them as equals and strike a balance between creating a relaxed informal atmosphere and pursuing a serious work activity. Encourage questions and be patient. Try not to show exasperation with 'simple' queries. For you, it may be the fifth time you have answered the same question in one session, but for the individual student, it is the first time.

When listening to the answers to your questions, check that the students understand what they are doing and why. Avoid giving the answers yourself when students cannot. Instead encourage them to work things out from first principles. Get them thinking for themselves, but be prepared to give them some pointers to get them there.

Finally, experiments and observations can fail to work for a variety of reasons. If you feel that the student has not really tried, then you may be able to take a firm position and instruct them to repeat their work.

However, there are times when you may need to exercise discretion. For example, when the student has worked really hard to find the answer, but has not been able to get a good set of results, then give them permission to use the results from another group so that they can complete the calculations and submit their report.

DELIVERING LECTURES

Delivering a lecture or series of lectures is probably a more daunting task than leading a tutorial or acting as a demonstrator. You'll probably be nervous speaking to tens, if not hundreds, of students and will need not only well-prepared material, but a fair amount of self-assurance. Often these two are linked, so there is a need to work through the subject matter and decide your approach beforehand.

Chapter 14 provides advice about delivering a seminar or paper and much of this guidance applies to teaching undergraduates. However, there are some key differences that you must allow for:

- The course syllabus and its learning outcomes. You are likely to be filling a 'slot' in a well-defined programme of lectures and other teaching formats such as practicals and tutorials. This syllabus may not have been of your making, but, despite this, you must pay attention to the learning outcomes for your specific lectures and the teaching context before and after them. Otherwise, you would be in danger of repeating material or teaching inappropriate material. If the learning outcomes inform the students' assessment, as they should, then if you do not teach to these, the students may suffer if, for example, exam questions are set by others.

- The level of interest of the audience. When delivering a seminar, a fair proportion of those listening to you will be interested in your topic or will at least be polite enough to feign attention. A body of undergraduates will almost certainly include a proportion of students who are simply there to gain a pass or who regard it as 'cool' not to seem interested. You will need to enliven proceedings to gain and retain their attention and possibly employ a number of 'crowd control' techniques to avoid losing control of proceedings.

- The size of the venue. Often lectures are delivered in quite large lecture theatres and you will need a loud and clear voice to be understood throughout. Generally, supporting your spoken explanations using PowerPoint or similar presentation software will help as key terms and phrases can be printed out to avoid misunderstandings. A large lecture theatre presents challenges in keeping up eye contact with those present – an essential aspect of body language if you wish to engage students.

- The duty to be intelligible to the majority. In a postgraduate seminar, you can generally make assumptions about the knowledge and understanding of your audience. Indeed, after the usual introductions, you will be expected to cover your topic at the highest possible level, often going into great technical detail. This will almost certainly not be the case in undergraduate lectures. Here, you must spend more time ensuring that you cover the basics, before leading on to more complex material if this is relevant. It is essential to gauge from student reactions (for example, facial expressions) when you need to repeat something, or find a different way to explain it.

- The need for the audience to take notes. Your material needs to be paced carefully so that this can occur. Do not fall into the trap of putting all the material on a PowerPoint slide and then handing this out in 'notes' form. This will not only bore your audience as you read from the slides, but will not actually help them to understand. A key step in the latter process is the rephrasing in one's own words that note-making represents. Watch to see whether most students have stopped writing before moving on to your next point. Where necessary, repeat key pieces of text or even dictate them. Vary your delivery style so that students can realise when something is worth taking down *verbatim*. Don't be bullied by students or staff into releasing your full notes for electronic access. These are your intellectual property and, even if this practice is departmental policy, a single sheet of headings should provide enough guidance for students who attend the lecture whilst indicating to students who skip lectures that they will not be spoon-fed.

Sometimes, you will be asked to deliver the lecture using a prepared set of notes or slides created by someone else. It is rarely easy or successful using someone else's material. You won't feel entirely at home with the content and will probably not know what would have been said 'between the lines' by the originator.

Although it is more work, it is a far more gratifying experience to construct your own material and approach to the topic. You will probably have quite a lot of freedom to decide how to do this. Everyone develops their own style, and being able to experiment with this is a major reward of carrying out lecturing duties as a postgraduate. It is conceivable that you will judge it appropriate to provide a continuous monologue, but it is more likely that you will recall how this type of lecture generally failed to keep your attention and will therefore want to try something different. Table 13.1 provides some tips for alternative approaches to the standard 50-minute lecture slot.

Develop a personal pedagogy

A specific approach to teaching is known as a pedagogy. For example, some prefer to lecture with the support of presentational software, using this as 'scaffolding' to keep a structure to their explanations; others prefer a more free-form speaking style, only occasionally referring to notes. Some like to 'tell a story' of a particular development, personalising it with anecdotes about the people involved and how they arrived at their discoveries and ideas; others prefer to create an objective conceptual framework within which they can hang information and ideas in a logical fashion. You can experiment with your experiences of teaching to develop a personal methodology – one that suits you, your subject material and your students.

ASSESSING STUDENT ASSIGNMENTS

Assessment is a skilled and responsible task which you may be asked to carry out. Marking assignments can be a task that is time-consuming, although as you build up experience you will find that you become more efficient. The main objects of the exercise are to:

- assess the student's knowledge and understanding of the topic area;
- judge the extent to which they have met the requirements of the task;
- provide the student with constructive feedback on their work.

Often, your work will be moderated by others, but you should bear in mind that the marks you give and what you write in feedback might affect someone's future.

The work of assessing student assignments actually involves three distinct processes:

1 Appraising – which relates to evaluation of the content of the submission.

Table 13.1 A selection of approaches for delivery of teaching during a standard 50-minute lecture slot. These examples of variants of the 'standard continuous delivery' are intended to involve students in the lecture; make them think about and discuss the lecture material; and keep their focus for specified periods of intensive concentration.

Approach	Description	Commentary
Standard continuous delivery	The lecturer speaks more or less continuously over the full period. May use written notes or PowerPoint or similar slides to structure the content.	Students often find this dull and uninspiring, requiring a feat of concentration and tiring amounts of note-making.
Punctuated delivery	As above, but session is divided into (say) three, with a different type of activity in the shorter middle part. This could be: discussing matters with a partner; answering a quiz; viewing a video.	Breaks up lecture allowing for the theoretical average concentration period of 20 or so minutes. The integrated activity can engage students with the subject material.
Use of a personal response system (PRS)	The PRS system is used to allow students to respond to questions throughout the lecture. The lecturer can use this to test student understanding or engage students with the material.	Requires investment and can be tricky to set up, but many systems fit well with, e.g., PowerPoint slideshows. Capable of enlivening lectures and raising student interest.
Scaling opinion	The lecturer identifies some key debating points to be covered. Students have to score their support for each viewpoint on scale 1(low) to 5 (high); lecture is delivered; then students reassess their viewpoint post-lecture and then if time permits pairs discuss and explain any changes in their viewpoint or justify their original assessment.	This can be a useful way of helping students to develop analytical, reasoning and arguing skills. It can also help weaker students to gain some insights into the thinking processes of others (perhaps more able students).
Group discussions with feedback	The lecturer introduces a topic or topics, following which the class is divided up into groups to discuss defined points under a time limit. The groups may report back to the lecturer whose task is to tease out and summarise the key themes.	Involves all students but they may drift off theme during discussion. Does not suit all topics or all presenters.
'2s and 4s' technique	In a variation on group discussions, students are asked to discuss a point in pairs and then two pairs come together to exchange views and come up with a collective answer/viewpoint.	Engages all students; makes students develop skills of explanation and argument. Should be time-limited but if used in the first part of lecture, then students become more engaged with substance and points in later lecture material.

2 Grading – which means allocating a mark (grade) to the work based on university guidelines and any marking scheme provided in addition.

3 Annotating the script – which involves correcting and providing feedback comment on the script using a marking code so that the students are directed to comments on their work.

You will need to be aware of the distinctions across these activities. For example, just because a student has submitted a paper that is poorly presented in terms of layout, typing or handwriting, punctuation or spelling, this should not mean that the paper is immediately downgraded in terms of content, and vice versa.

The language of assessment and marking: some definitions

- **Assessment** – often used as a catch-all term to mean the act of marking (grading), but also used specifically (as here) to indicate the combined act of appraising, grading and annotating (see text for definitions).

- **Assignment** – generic term for a piece of work submitted for marking and feedback, such as an essay, a lab report or a set of answers to problems.

- **Feedback** – a term that has several meanings and contexts, but all relating to comments (both positive and negative) on the standard of work produced by a student or group of students. It could involve relatively casual face-to-face comments or formal written comments on submitted work. The most useful feedback is constructive and contains and tips on how a student might improve.

- **Formative assessment** – task where the work is submitted for a mark and comment, but not for inclusion in the final course mark. The rationale is that completing a piece of work for formative assessment gives the student some indication of the standard required and a chance to improve later.

- **Summative assessment** – usually conducted at the end of a period of study and aims to assess the student's assimilation of new learning. The assigned mark will be included in the final mark for the course.

[Note that sometimes assignments that are primarily formative include a summative element – the distinction is not wholly rigid.]

For many assignments, there are sets of guidelines for marking scripts whether these are essays or reports. Where these exist, you should follow the guidelines as closely as possible. If no detailed guidelines are available beyond the standard grading of marks, then you should seek guidance from the course director or other academic teachers on the course. If your department or school uses a marking schedule or sheet for providing feedback on undergraduate written work, then this will probably provide you with some specific aspects to consider in your marking.

Think back to your own student days: did the feedback you receive help your learning? Many students invest a huge amount of meaning into what markers write on the scripts and so you should think carefully about your choice of words. Important aspects should include:

- comments related to the learning objectives of the exercise;
- systematic use of marking schemes and/or marking criteria;
- written observations that are constructive, focusing on positive aspects as well as negative aspects of each student's work;
- an indication of the balance placed on different aspects of the assignment (e.g. presentation, structure, standard of English) in the particular exercise being marked;
- consistency, that is treating each student in the same way.

You should also be a realist about marking. After you have burnt midnight oil on the marking exercise, and proudly returned the marked scripts to the departmental office, do not be surprised to find that a significant percentage of students do not actually collect their work. This can be dispiriting to any marker. However, many departments now adopt a policy requiring students to be seen by their tutors or demonstrators for the return of work. Make sure that you establish whether this will be expected of you before you agree to undertake the work and decide whether you are willing to do this. Doing the tutoring/demonstrating/marking/returning of work may be much more of a time commitment than you are able to make. This will depend on the stage of your postgraduate study and whether the financial gain is commensurate with the time invested. You also need to consider whether the loss of time is outweighed by the value in terms of experience for your CV.

Table 13.2 provides tips for carrying out these assessment activities.

Table 13.2 Tips for appraising, grading and annotating student assignments. These three activities are as defined in the text.

Appraising the work

- **Find out about the departmental guidelines on marking of assignments.** There may be two versions: one for the students and one for the tutors.
- **Ask for any marking scheme that exists.** If none, decide on your own general criteria: what you consider to be the aspects of the answer including key points to be covered in the content of each question and the proportion of marks to be awarded to each. Be aware (and make students aware) that there are often no 'right' answers, and that the marker is required to make an assessment of the extent to which the assignment constructs a case for the viewpoint it expresses, noting any factual inaccuracies and errors.
- **Start by assessing a topic that you favour personally.** This gives you a chance to read work that should be familiar and should help you judge the ability band of the group of students whose work you are assessing.
- **Look out for plagiarism.** Plagiarism is generally penalised and you should follow the relevant departmental or university guidance on this, using software like TurnitIn if advised. Students are often unaware of what constitutes plagiarism and how to avoid it; course handbooks should offer guidance on plagiarism avoidance. You should be alert to the potential for plagiarism which the Internet invites.
- **Where relevant, check the submitted bibliography/reference list.** Assess whether references are appropriate to the task, up-to-date, sufficiently broad to cover the topic and are authenticated (e.g. not simply non-refereed websites).
- **Be aware of special cases.** For example, dyslexic students may be eligible to add stickers identifying their work as that of a dyslexic person. In these cases you should discount spelling, punctuation and syntax errors according to the university rules (which you should locate and read).
- **Always aim to be consistent.** Students may compare their marks and feedback and will complain if discrepancies exist.
- **Don't try to solve deep-rooted student problems.** Where a student appears to have significant problems in producing academic writing of the required standard or adopting an analytical and objective approach to the work, then refer them to relevant support services.

Grading the work

- **To get the 'feel' of a paper, read it right through and allocate a 'first reaction' mark.**
- **Read the paper over again, adding annotations (see below).** Allocate marks as appropriate, that is, according to the criteria you have been given or that you have developed for yourself. Remember that you will be assessing university-level essays which, even at first year level, should demonstrate analytical thinking and an ability to evaluate the key issues through well-written and logically structured text. Essays should certainly go beyond narrative description and reiteration of facts from books.
- **Arrive at a final grade for the paper**, if appropriate summing part marks (always double-check your maths). Recalibrate your grade against the department or university grade descriptors and, if necessary, the marking scheme if provided.

Annotating and providing feedback

- **Check whether the work you are marking is a piece of formative or summative assessment.** This may affect the way that you wish to write your comment on the paper.

- **Choose what sorts of errors to correct.** In particular, decide whether you are going to correct mis-spellings and incorrect/missing punctuation and make sure that anything *you* write on a script is free of error in these respects.

- **Ensure that anything you write on a script is legible.** People who are visually impaired may need to have printed corrections.

- **Use a pen that distinguishes your writing from that of the student author.** There is a school of thought that suggests that red is not a good colour to use, as students are discouraged by copious amounts of red on their work. Remember, too, that red and green are difficult colours for people who are colour-blind (usually male), while both these colours have unfortunate significance for some members of non-British cultures. For example, in some cultures red indicates death. Note also that if it is the departmental custom to photocopy marked scripts for their archive file, then some colours are not reproduced well when copied.

- **Use relevant marking shorthand.** If there are no particular 'marking codes' provided by the department, then you could use some of the marks used in *Hart's rules* (Ritter, 2005; see **Ch 29**). Whether you choose to follow Hart's rules or whether you decide to develop your own, it is essential that you explain your 'codes' to the students before the work is returned to them. Do not assume that all staff use the same codes or that students will understand them without explanation.

- **Create a generalised feedback sheet.** One strategy that saves time and makes the marker's comments more accessible to students is to use a system of numbering. On the script, mark each point with a numeral and, on a separate piece of paper (possibly copied for all students), list each error by number. In this way the student can cross-reference the point you have made on the separate sheet with your list.

- **Remember that, under data protection legislation, students can ask to see any written records.** Ensure that anything you write on a script or in records is not defamatory in any way.

- **Explain.** Writing comments such as 'poor' or 'weak' is not particularly helpful to the student. Explain your reasons for making such comments.

- **Provide constructive feedback – legibly written or word-processed.** Offer positive feedback as well as negative. Counterbalance any negative comments with positive suggestions for turning each aspect round. Whatever you write should be helpful – even if you have to hunt for a positive attribute in the paper, take time to try to find one. Remember that you may be the nearest a student gets to interaction with anyone on the academic side of the university. What you write could be critical to the student's learning, their progress, their decision to continue with the subject or their decision to give up the whole university experience. In some circumstances, you may feel that it is more appropriate to discuss the issue face-to-face.

13.1 Take advantage of training opportunities. Don't assume you can instantly walk into the classroom and teach – even if you can already do the basics of presentation, you may be missing out on deeper pedagogical understanding that could make your work (and feedback) so much better.

13.2 Create 'open office hours' when students are allowed to contact you. This time-management tip will help to ensure that your own work is not constantly interrupted.

13.3 Make the most of teaching opportunities. Find out from your teaching experiences whether a job involving this activity would suit you in a potential career. For example: are you comfortable speaking in front of large classes? Do you find it satisfying to impart knowledge and increase understanding in others? Is it rewarding for you to create new ways of explaining difficult concepts? Use your experiences as a chance to add to your CV; you can also mention these in job applications and interviews.

14

GIVING A RESEARCH SEMINAR OR PAPER

How to deliver an effective spoken presentation

At various points in your PhD studies you will be required to deliver spoken presentations. These might be contributions to small meetings, seminars for the whole department or even presentations to large conferences. This chapter focuses on good groundwork and the basics of presentation, to help you prepare well and communicate your points effectively.

KEY TOPICS

→ Planning and preparing your script

→ Effective speaking

→ Using presentation software such as PowerPoint

→ Answering questions

→ Pointers towards a successful presentation

You may be expected to give a spoken presentation in several different situations – from a brief and relatively informal presentation to a journal club to a full-blown paper at a national or international conference. Your talk may be relatively casual or it may be supported by high-tech visual aids. In all cases, good preparation is the key to success. This chapter will focus on more formal types of presentation, although similar principles apply elsewhere.

PLANNING AND PREPARING YOUR SCRIPT

Whatever, the occasion, it is important to be well prepared. Having a well-thought-out plan, good supporting material and a clear picture of your main conclusions will boost your confidence and improve your audience's experience. However, over-rehearsal can lead to a dull and monotonous delivery and you should also try to avoid this.

Identifying the purpose of your presentation

On the surface, this may seem simple, but there are several facets to consider. Identifying your key aims at an early stage is essential to help you with the outline framework. Next, defining the reason for giving the presentation and your likely audience will help you to pitch the content in terms of depth, detail and density – these will differ depending on circumstances and getting them wrong will lead to a poor experience for both you and your listeners.

Structure

Every substantive presentation should have a beginning, a middle and an end. The old maxim '*say what you are going to say, say it, and then say what you have said*' conforms directly to this structure and you need search no further for an outline plan.

1 Introduction. Your task here is to introduce yourself, state the aim of your presentation, say how you intend to approach the topic and provide relevant background information. Start your talk with the basics – don't forget to begin with the seemingly obvious, such as definitions of key terms. Not all of your audience may have the same background in the subject as you. If they aren't on the same wavelength, or don't understand key terms, you may lose them at the very beginning.

Keep your introduction positive

Never start a talk by being apologetic or putting yourself down. For example, you may be tempted to say you are unprepared or lack expertise. This will lower your audience's expectations, probably unnecessarily, and get you off to a weak start.

2 Main content. This will depend on the nature of the talk. For a talk about research in the Sciences or Engineering, you might start with methods, and then move on to results, perhaps displayed as a series of graphs which you will lead your audience through. For a spoken paper in the Arts, you might discuss various perspectives on your topic, giving examples or quotes as you go.

3 Conclusions. Here, your aim is to draw the strands of talk together, explaining how all your points are related and giving ideas of where

things might develop in the future – for example, suggestions for further research or different angles to approach the subject. Finally, you should recap your whole talk in a series of 'take home' statements and then thank your audience for their attention.

Aspects to consider when preparing a talk – a checklist

❏ **Audience**. Will they be experts, peers, lay people or a mixture?

❏ **Arrangements**. What is the date, start time and period allocated for your talk?

❏ **Venue**. How might the location and nature of its layout affect your delivery?

❏ **Facilities**. What equipment and audio-visual aids are available?

❏ **Context**. Who will be preceding and/or following you? What introduction to you and your topic might be given?

❏ **Presentation style**. Do you want to use 'chalk and talk', overhead transparencies or PowerPoint?

❏ **Delivery**. Will you use a detailed script, prompts or simply improvise?

❏ **Requirements**. What might you need to bring? Which equipment might you need to practise with?

❏ **Liaison**. Who should you contact to confirm details or make special requests?

Creating a script or series of prompts

Most presentations begin as pieces of writing that evolve through several stages:

1 Creating a brainstorm or concept map of what you need to cover.

2 Laying out themes or headings with brief explanatory note.

3 Producing a script – more or less the full text of your talk with 'stage directions' and an indication of timing.

4 Reducing the script to a set of key words and bullet points – your prompts.

As you become more experienced, you will find you can move directly from stage 2 to stage 4, perhaps thinking through appropriate phrasing in your head rather than writing down the exact words.

Working from prompts, sometimes called 'cues', is recommended, whether they are produced as headings on cards or as bullet points in a PowerPoint slideshow (or similar). These basic headings provide the structure of your talk, so that you don't ramble or lose your place. They also help to promote an air of informality that will draw in your audience. All you need to remember is roughly what you intend to say around each point. However, be wary of running over time if you adopt this free-ranging approach. Ask a colleague in the audience to time your presentation and signal to you if you are over-running.

Reading your talk from a written script is probably a bad idea, even though you may feel more confident if you know in advance every word you are going to say. This kind of delivery always seems dry; not only because it results in an unnatural way of speaking, but also because you will be so busy looking at your script that you will almost certainly fail to make eye contact with your audience.

For similar reasons, you should probably not memorise your talk, as this will take a lot of effort and may result in the same flat or stilted delivery as if you had scripted it word-for-word. There is a happy medium where a talk has been practised enough for the speaker to be confident, yet still convey an air of spontaneity.

Practice makes perfect

It is always a good idea to practise your talk beforehand. This will help you to:

- become more confident in the material;
- identify any complex parts that you cannot easily put into words, and practise these independently;
- find out whether your presentation will fit the allotted time.

If you present the 'draft' talk to a friend or peer, they can provide useful comments on your audibility and clarity, presentation style (including gestures), and use of visual aids.

EFFECTIVE SPEAKING

This is more than speaking loudly enough to be heard and pronouncing your words clearly so that the audience can make them out. These skills are fundamental – although you will already realise that many speakers fail even at this hurdle. Ask a friend to check and comment on your diction to make sure you meet these basic criteria.

Good speaking not only ensures that information is transmitted, but also engages the audience. You can do this in two main ways – through your actions and body language, and through the approach you take.

Developing your own speaking style

Every speaker has their own idiosyncrasies, but some elements of style can be learnt. Consider the different ways other speakers present their material. Some will be good and some not so good. Adopt techniques you admire and try to work these into your personal style.

First, don't just stand still and speak robotically. Aim for an element of variety to keep interest levels high:

- Move around a little – but make sure you face the audience so you will be heard and do not pace up and down excessively.
- Use moderate hand gestures to emphasise your points – but don't wave your hands around like a windmill.
- Ensure you make eye contact with the audience – but don't stare at one person or area all the time.
- Liven your talk by shifting between modes of presentation, for example, by drawing a diagram on the board or presenting a visual aid – but don't overdo this or the audience may be distracted from your theme.

Second, try to involve your audience. Use rhetorical questions to prompt them to think, even though you will be supplying the answers. Ask them direct questions, for example, *'Are you all familiar with this article?'* then follow up with prepared response of your own, such as, *'For the benefit of those who haven't, I'll just recap on the main points'*. If it would be relevant, ask them to do an activity as part of the presentation. This takes confidence to handle, but it can work well and is especially valuable to break up a longer talk and engage the audience.

USING PRESENTATION SOFTWARE SUCH AS POWERPOINT

The standard method of supporting a talk with images and information is now via software such as Microsoft PowerPoint. These systems provide flexibility and allow you to incorporate digital images with ease, but do require functional hardware. If you are planning to use this type of software, always check whether appropriate digital projection facilities will be available in the room or can be borrowed or booked.

You can select from a variety of designs for each PowerPoint slide, most of which help you to structure your talk around a series of bullet points and to mix text with images or graphs (see Figure 14.1). This may help you to organise your prompts, but you should make sure you don't simply read them word for word from the slide. Few things are more boring than a speaker reading out what you can already see on a screen.

If you doubt your ability to speak freely around the bullet points, you can use the notes facility within PowerPoint to write down information you might not remember. You can then print out each slide and associated notes together on a single A4 page to act as a support during the presentation. Use the 'Print > Print what: Notes Pages' command, but select 'Pure Black and White' under 'Colour/greyscale', or your printout (including slide backgrounds) may appear in colour, possibly wasting printer ink.

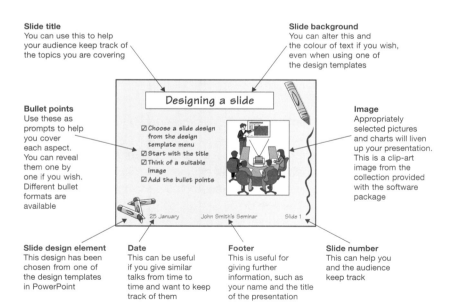

Figure 14.1 Elements of a typical PowerPoint slide. Similar features are available using other software.

A step-by-step tutorial for setting up a PowerPoint presentation is beyond the scope of this book, but once the basics have been learnt, for instance from a handbook or online self-help tutorial, the tips shown in Table 14.1 may be useful. Always check that your version of PowerPoint is compatible with the relevant computer system.

Allow plenty of time for preparing digital presentation slides

The technology is helpful but, especially with complex material, each slide can take a lot of effort to set up. However, because of the flexibility of this system, you can save some time by merging the planning and writing phases of your talk into one session. For instance, once they are constructed it is relatively easy to change the order of slides or to alter formatting.

ANSWERING QUESTIONS

This is a part of a talk which many people worry about, as they have no control over what may be asked, and feel they might look stupid if they don't know an answer. Tips for dealing with this element include:

- Prepare for likely questions. Think through what people might ask and have an answer ready.

- Ask for clarification if you don't understand a question fully. You could also ask the questioner or chair to repeat the question if a part of it was indistinct or didn't seem to make sense to you.

- Repeat the question for the benefit of those who might not have heard it. The questioner will be facing you, not the audience, and their voice may be indistinct. This will also buy you some time for composing an answer.

- Think before you answer. Rather than blurting out the first thing that comes to mind, take time to weigh up the different aspects. You may feel the necessary pause is long, but this will not be how the audience perceives it.

- If you don't know an answer, say so. Everyone will see through a speaker who is waffling. Try saying 'I don't know the answer at the moment, but I'll find out and get back to you ...' if you want to say something rather than leaving a pause.

Table 14.1 Tips for constructing slides with presentation software such as PowerPoint.

Aspect	Comment
Background and text colouring	Choose a background or slide design template with care. A lighter background with dark text will attract attention, but will be hard to concentrate on over the long term, whereas a darker background with light writing will be more restful on the eye.
Slide design	The standard PowerPoint designs are tried and tested, and are especially useful if you have little time to prepare for a talk, but many of your audience will have seen them before. You can easily be more original, for instance, by incorporating an image into the background, but be aware that this will take time to set up.
Slide numbering	Inserting the numbers on slides can help your audience to make reference to a particular point at the question and answer stage of a presentation.
Text size and font	The standard PowerPoint text size defaults to values that mean that it is difficult to get much information on each slide. You can override this feature, but there is a good reason for it: cramming too much into each slide is bad practice. A point size of 28 is probably the lowest text size you should use. Sans-serif fonts, such as Arial, are said to be easiest to read on-screen.
Use of images	If you can, try to include an image in at least half of your slides. Even if these are only partially relevant, they help to maintain audience interest. A text-only presentation consisting of nothing more than bullet points will seem very dry. Use images from copyright-free web resources if you don't have images of your own. Avoid 'clip art'.
Revealing your points one by one	Use the 'animation' feature to build up your slide line by line as you wish. This will help you to pace your talk and ensure that the audience is listening to you, rather than reading ahead on the slide. You may find it advantageous to copy a slide with headings and repeat this after each 'section' to show where you are in the talk.
Use of special features	You can uses special features for introducing each new slide and, within each slide, you can make text enter from different directions in different ways and even accompanied with noises. You can also link to websites (if your computer is appropriately connected) and run digital video clips. Resist the temptation to go overboard with these 'bells and whistles', however, because although such features can make a talk livelier, they tend to distract from your main message and may run counter to the preferred approach in your field or department.
Handouts	Think about providing your audience with a handout of the slides. In PowerPoint, you can use the File > Print > Print what > Handouts > 6 slides per page option to do this. When printing, it is best to select 'pure black and white' from the Colour/greyscale options, or all of the slides may print in colour, including the background. Numbering your slides (see Figure 14.1) will help your audience keep track with the handout.

How can I deal with nerves?

A certain amount of apprehension is normal before speaking. Experienced speakers know that being slightly nervous is important, because this creates energy and sparkle when delivering the material. Their view is that if the adrenaline isn't flowing, their presentation will probably lack vitality. Turn any anxiety you may have to your advantage by using it to energise your preparation and thinking of it as something that will work for you rather than against you when you are talking.

POINTERS TOWARDS A SUCCESSFUL PRESENTATION

The time immediately before a talk always seems rushed, and this may add to your natural anxiety. The key is to prepare carefully and methodically. Table 14.2 provides a checklist of points to consider. To improve your confidence in your ability to speak effectively, the following pointers may help:

1 Dress appropriately for the occasion. You should look smart, but should feel comfortable in what you wear. Turning up in casual clothes may be interpreted as showing a lack of respect to your audience and may lead to the expectation of a sloppy presentation.

2 To reduce tension, take deep breaths. This can be done both before you address the audience and during pauses in your presentation.

3 Make sure you can be heard. At the start of your talk, ask the audience if they can hear at the back. When practising, try to use the room where the presentation will take place and ask a friend if they can hear you. If you know someone in the audience, you could ask them to signal to you if you are talking too quietly (or too loudly).

4 Make sure your audio-visual aids can be seen. If you are using some kind of projection system, make sure that you – or your shadow – don't block out the projected image. It's a good idea to ask your audience if they can see clearly before you start.

5 Don't speak too quickly. This is a common response to nerves. Make a determined effort to slow yourself down and speak clearly.

Table 14.2 Quick checklist for giving a presentation.

1 Purpose and aims	2 Plan, leading to content	3 Practise with a dry-run	4 Predict the unexpected
Identify why you are doing the presentation, e.g. • for assessment • for passing on an idea • for passing on new information Think about the context e.g. • the area of study • the audience What are you trying to achieve? e.g. • explanation • description • persuasion • construction of an argument	• Brainstorm • Decide on a structure for delivery of your material • Decide what to include/exclude • Take the level of the audience into account • Take into account the time at your disposal • Decide on materials required • Collate results/facts/figures/ lines of argument/evidence • Make conclusions • Make recommendations (as appropriate) • Summarise key points	Decide on a strategy for constructing your notes e.g. • Cue cards • PowerPoint • Slides • Models • Realia (physical items) Prepare methodically, e.g. • Highlight and sequence your notes • Perform the whole presentation as a 'dry run' using audio or video tape, a mirror, or a friend • Focus on complicated explanations: practise these more • Time your dry run so you know exactly how much to cut or add	• What will you need in the way of equipment? • What will you do if something breaks down? • What will you do if you are overcome by nerves? • What can you do if you 'dry up'? • What questions may be asked? • How could you deal with these questions? • Can you prepare answers? • Be prepared to be flexible. • If you have had to formulate an argument, anticipate the counter-argument(s)

5 Produce visual aids	6 Performance and delivery	Pointers for success	Predicaments to avoid
Preparation of visual aids • Check for readability • Sequence visual aids • Ensure diagrams are clear, neatly presented, and visible from the back of the room • Aim for simplicity • Build up diagrams rather than trying to put in too much detail to begin with. Presenting visual aids • Don't block the view for the audience • Make the presentation memorable • Explain terms • Allow time for note-taking	Organisation • Be aware of how to use platform or classroom equipment • Check out the accommodation beforehand Vocal • Speak clearly • Control speed of delivery • Have a watch/timer available • Organise your notes so that you do not lose your place Body language • Establish eye contact • Smile • Avoid irritating mannerisms • Let your enthusiasm generate interest in your audience	• Time your talk beforehand • Speak clearly and slowly • Define subject matter • Engage with the audience • Explain your aim • Explain outline of your talk • Follow a logical sequence • Summarise • Anticipate questions • Prepare answers • Prepare your material thoroughly; spend 95% on preparation; 5% on delivery • Perceive nerves are normal • Gain experience • Use readable visual aids	• Going over allotted time • Gabbling or whispering • Memorising • Reading your text aloud – remember that written language never sounds as memorable as spoken language • Overloading slides • Overplanning – allow for disasters, queries, interruptions and relevant questions • Being fazed by the audience taking notes • Panicking – take a deep breath and console yourself that it will soon be over, but it would be better to try to enjoy it – then your audience will do so also

6 Engage the audience. Speak directly to them, not to the floor, your notes, the screen, or a distant wall. Look at their faces and take cues from their reactions. If they don't seem to understand what you've said, repeat it in a different way. If they look bored, speed up, or ask a rhetorical question to engage their thoughts. Imagine the members of the audience are your friends – speak to them with enthusiasm, warmth and genuine feeling. They will respond in kind.

7 Pace your talk. As you speak, check how you are doing and speed up or slow down as necessary. In some cases, the real talk will take longer than you anticipated when practising. This will either be because the initial business of getting set up has used up some of your allotted time, or because you have relaxed during the presentation and said more than you thought you would. In other cases, you may find that slight nervousness means you have spoken faster than intended.

8 Have a 'plan B' if your talk over-runs or the projection system fails. Plan things so that you can miss something out from the main section of the talk if you are under time pressure (for example, by skipping over a few PowerPoint slides). This is preferable to being unable to complete your conclusions – people may be more interested in those than in the detail of your presentation – and they can always ask about the skipped material at the end. Print out the PowerPoint slides, perhaps in handout, or note form, so you can still use these if the projection system fails.

9 Anticipate questions. Think through how you would answer them and, where appropriate, anticipate and forestall them in the presentation itself.

10 Try to enjoy the occasion. If you seem to be taking pleasure from speaking, your audience will also enjoy the session. Conversely, if you don't seem to be interested, why should they be?

ACTION POINTS

14.1 Improve your knowledge of presentational software. Even if you have no talk to give in the near future, time spent learning how to use PowerPoint could improve your presentation. You may wish to attend a relevant postgraduate training workshop.

14.2 Learn from other speakers. Every time you attend a seminar or listen to a speaker, think what makes the good ones good and the bad ones bad. Think about which elements of good delivery you could adapt and use yourself.

14.3 If you feel shy, take small opportunities to practise speaking so you can build up confidence. These might include making a comment at a meeting or asking questions at other talks – anything that gets you used to hearing your own voice speaking in a formal situation. You might explore the possibility of joining a local Speakers Club in your area. In the United Kingdom the Association of Speakers Clubs (*www.the-asc.org.uk*) promotes 'Public speaking development among friends'. There are clubs throughout the UK whose members meet monthly – sometimes separate groups for male and female members. Students who join these groups can develop their skills, enjoy the challenge of speaking to a supportive group and benefit from the practice and feedback.

15

PREPARING AND PRESENTING A POSTER

How to summarise and communicate your findings

Research posters are often used at conferences as a medium for summarising findings and ideas. They maximise the number of people who can see your work and the timetabled poster sessions provide a valuable forum for informal discussion. This chapter explores the design features that make up an effective poster and gives guidance on 'defending' a poster.

KEY TOPICS

→ Deciding on a title, abstract and content

→ Designing your poster

→ Constructing and setting up your poster

→ Defending your poster

The idea behind a poster display is to present a summary of research or scholarship in an easily assimilated format. Poster sessions are common at academic conferences, particularly (but not exclusively) in the sciences; students in Arts and Humanities subjects are increasingly being asked to contribute this kind of material. The purpose is to allow presenters to:

- report findings or ideas within a single session;
- provide opportunities for people with similar interests to meet and discuss detailed information inappropriate for wider discussion;
- report on work in progress as well as ready-to-be-published material;
- focus on methods as well as results;
- showcase the essence of their work;
- develop their presentational and other 'soft' skills desirable in doctoral candidates.

In some departments a poster session may be used to allow PhD students in their first or second years to report their progress. The advice presented here will assume that your poster is for a research conference, but similar principles apply to other situations. Poster presentations at conferences often take place over lunch-time or morning/afternoon breaks. Sometimes there is a rota of posters, so that over a two- or three-day conference a number of presenters will be given a time slot to display and defend their particular poster.

DECIDING ON A TITLE, ABSTRACT AND CONTENT

If you are submitting a poster to a conference committee, you will probably have to fill in a form beforehand so that your proposed contribution can be vetted and, if accepted, assigned to a poster area or session. The information you provide may also appear in the conference programme, allowing participants to decide which posters to visit. The form will include the expected administrative details such as name and department, but the two most important sections will be for the title and the abstract. A possible problem will be that you may have to submit the form so far in advance that you cannot be entirely sure of what you will be able to present.

Typical components of a poster

- **Title:** phrased in a way that will inform and attract visitors.
- **Author information:** names, affiliation and a contact number or email address.
- **Abstract or summary:** stating the approach taken and the main conclusions.
- **Introduction:** providing brief background information essential for understanding the poster.
- **Materials and methods:** describing experimental or field research, background theory or historical overview.
- **Results:** key findings or examples.
- **Conclusions:** giving the 'take-home messages' of your study or research.
- **Acknowledgements:** stating who has funded and/or helped you.
- **References and sources:** only those that are essential.

Title

This is important because conference delegates will be scanning a large number of titles and you will want to present them with the key words that will let them select appropriately from the options so they can use the poster session most efficiently. At the same time, you will want to make a striking statement about your work. Assuming word limits do not prevent this, a two-part title can be used to draw the reader in – the first part being a 'hook' and the second giving more detail. The chapter titles in this book are examples of this approach.

Beware of 'mis-selling' your poster content

You may raise expectations though an attention-grabbing poster title and abstract that implies you have achieved more than is the reality. This will probably backfire when visitors to your poster are disappointed in what you present. Better to take a more measured approach and impress them through the quality of your work.

Abstract (Summary)

This will be limited in length and you need to communicate exactly what visitors can expect. You might consider single sentences for aims, methods, key findings and conclusions, for example. The style should not be verbose and words should be chosen carefully to provide the impression of interesting, well-conducted work. You will be communicating to a knowledgeable readership so jargon and technical words are acceptable.

Content

Although a striking take-home message is important, you should also bear in mind the need for visual impact in your poster when making your choices for content – this may attract casual readers.

You should not feel that your poster has to include all the work you have done. By omitting some information you are giving people the opportunity to engage with you and your poster by asking for further information. Background elements, such as technical elements of materials and methods, can be explained to those who are interested during the poster session. Even seemingly narrow subjects will have scope for different presentational approaches.

You will normally be allocated a limited space to set up your poster (typically 1.5 m wide and 1 m high) and although this may initially seem a large area to cover, you will probably have to select carefully what to include. This is because your poster needs to be legible from a distance of one metre or so, and the large font size required for this inevitably means fewer words than you might otherwise prefer. When thinking about content, therefore, it is best to assume that space will be limited.

DESIGNING YOUR POSTER

The key design principle for any poster is to generate visual impact. Your poster needs to stand out among the others in the session and provide a striking visual feature to draw a spectator towards the academic content. This can be achieved in several ways:

- a striking overall design concept related to the topic;
- effective use of colour or a prominent colour contrast between the background and the poster elements;
- a large eye-catching image at the centre of the poster;
- some form of visual aid attached to the poster, such as a large model related to the topic.

Examples of imaginative poster design

- A poster about forest ecology where the text is presented as 'leaves' on a model tree.
- A study of urban geography where the poster has the appearance of a close-up street map with aspects written within each building.
- A physiology poster where an organ like the liver is drawn at the centre with elements (correctly) attached to it via arteries and veins.

Posters can be composed of a single sheet or of a mosaic of smaller sheets or shapes. These sheets or 'panels' will be attached to the main poster board, usually by drawing pins or Velcro pads – and their size or shape may place a constraint on your overall design – check the overall dimensions as soon as you can, to work out your options for arranging these sheets.

The next important aspect to decide is how your reader will work their way through the material you present. Each section of text will be read left to right in the usual way, but the route through the elements may not follow this rule. Various options are shown in Figure 15.1. Whichever you choose, it is important to let your reader know which path to take, either by prominent numbering or by incorporating arrows or guidelines into the design.

The ideal text size for your poster title will be about 25–40 mm high (100–170 point size) for the title, 15–25 mm for subtitles (60–100 point) and 5–10 mm (25–40 point) for the main material. If you only have an A4 printer at your disposal, bear in mind that you can enlarge to A3 on most photocopiers, although this may limit you to black and white text. Linear dimensions will increase by 1.41 times if you do this.

Once point size and panel dimensions are known, you can work out a rough word limit for each component. Besides being succinct, your writing style should make it easy to assimilate the material, for example, by using bullet points and sub-headings.

At an early stage, you should draw a diagram of your poster, mapping out the main components to scale. You may also wish to create a mock poster to the exact dimensions to gain a better idea of what the final version will look like.

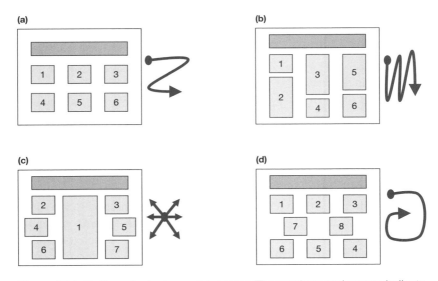

Figure 15.1 Options for laying out a poster. The numbers and arrows indicate the route taken by the reader, while the hatched bar at the top would contain the title and author details.

Tips for creating better posters

- **Check out the font and point sizes you plan to use.** Print out a specimen sheet and stand one to one and a half metres away. You should be able to read the material easily from this distance. Copy some random text (e.g. from a website) onto a sheet at the same font size and carry out a word count to gain an idea of what your word limit will be for each component.

- **Your poster should be able to 'travel well'.** You should think about how you take it from the point of construction to the display venue. The components should be portable and packaged in a weather-proof way.

- **Remember that 'white space' is important in design.** An overly fussy presentation with many elements covering the entire area will be difficult to assimilate. In this case, 'less can be more' if it helps you to get your central message across.

- **Consider colour combinations carefully.** Certain colours are difficult to see against others and some pairings may be difficult to distinguish for those who are colour blind (for example, red and green). Bold, primary colours will attract the eye.

- **Use language to draw the reader in.** For example, if the titles and subheadings are given as a series of rhetorical questions, a casual viewer will naturally want to read the text to find out the answer.

- **Don't provide too much detail.** Keep the wording sparse, and be prepared to talk further about matters raised in the text during the poster defence.

- **Use a handout, if you have too much detail to cover.** If you've done loads of research but have to cut some interesting parts out of the final design because of space constraints, consider giving readers a short handout to cover these aspects. This should contain your contact details.

- **State your take-home message clearly.** Leave your reader in no doubt about your conclusions. You could, for example, list them as a series of bullet points at the end.

First aid for posters

Create a poster 'repair' kit to take with you. This could include scissors, sticky tape, Velcro pads, Blu-tack or drawing or map pins. Posters can become damaged in transit and organisers do not always supply these items, or underestimate the quantity required.

CONSTRUCTING AND SETTING UP YOUR POSTER

Each part of the poster will need to be printed or copied according to your design brief. Using panels as described above makes it easier to construct the poster as a series of independent components and to bring these to the poster session for final assembly. These can be attached to your board directly or pasted onto card first.

The panels for a poster can be printed professionally from a digital file or using a laser or similar quality office or home printer. Good quality paper should be used, and it is a good idea to laminate or plasticise this so it will be unaffected by dirt or liquids such as rain or coffee.

Where a poster is to be printed from a digital file, you will probably find presentation software such as PowerPoint easier to use than a word processor like Word. These programs allow the different text elements and figures to be created, uploaded and moved around more easily. The size of the area can be adjusted to be realistic for the final printout size with 'View' adjusted so you can see relevant parts on screen.

 What are the standard paper sizes?

These halve in area as you go through the series:

- **A0:** 841 × 1189 mm (1 m² total area)
- **A1:** 594 × 841 mm   **A2:** 420 × 594 mm
- **A3:** 297 × 420 mm   **A4:** 201 × 297 mm

DEFENDING YOUR POSTER

At the poster session, delegates mill around the posters, quizzing the authors about their work. These sessions can be very stimulating for all involved, and collaborations and even job offers may result. Taking a few copies of your CV or business cards with you may be useful in this context.

The atmosphere, at least superficially, is usually very relaxed. Despite the informality, expect probing questions to find out about your research, and not just about the details you have chosen to display. However, do not expect a large proportion of the delegates to be interested in your specialised area. They will most likely be focusing on the one or two posters most relevant to their own research area.

Allow visitors time to read the text of your poster before engaging them in conversation. Thereafter, you may wish to ask them a question yourself to break the ice. If delegates are wearing name tags you may be able to work out which institution they come from, which may help with an opening conversational gambit.

Typical questions about your poster that you should be ready to answer

- Why did you take this approach to the topic?
- How did you do the research?
- Can you give me more detail on the methods used here?
- Can you explain this figure (or table)?
- What does this mean for...?
- Why did you arrive at that interpretation?
- How does this finding relate to...?
- How does this relate to xxx's findings?
- Do you think this is applicable to...?
- Where next for this topic or research area?
- What are you going to do next?

ACTION POINTS

15.1 Find out the dimensions of your poster space and draw this out to scale. If you copy this sheet you can use it to sketch out a range of possible designs.

15.2 Have a critical look at research posters in your department. These are often put up on display after they have been used at a conference. Learn from good and bad aspects of what you see.

15.3 If you are worried about defending your poster, hold a mock event. Prime a friend or peer with a series of likely questions (see the checklist above), then try to answer them as you would to delegates. As well as getting you used to speaking aloud about your work, this should help remove any nervous feelings. It will also allow you to find out what you *don't* know, in time for some quick revision.

16

BEING APPRAISED

How to respond to progress monitoring and other feedback on your work

At various points in your postgraduate research your work and approach to it will be reviewed in a constructive manner. It is important that you respond positively to any observations and take appropriate action when required.

KEY TOPICS

→ Arrangements for progress monitoring

→ Other types of feedback

→ Learning from feedback

Many people and groups have a vested interest in your success as a PhD researcher and in the quality of your experience as a postgraduate student. The list starts with yourself, obviously, but includes your supervisor, your sponsors or funding body, the department, the university and those who assure the quality of UK higher education. As a result, most universities have organised training and review schemes to ensure that you have every opportunity to gain from a research degree.

This approach is not unique to universities since appraisal systems are commonly used in industry and other organisations as a means of ensuring that employers and employees are working towards the same ends to maintain good working and welfare practices. Table 16.1 indicates the types of attribute that are considered in generic workplace appraisals. During the postgraduate progress monitoring appraisal, these aspects of your performance may well be considered alongside your technical and academic progress. Progress monitoring and skills development schemes (**Ch 5**) therefore give you a flavour of the professional appraisal and development planning you may experience later in your career.

Table 16.1 A comparison between progress monitoring and workplace appraisals. This listing is a generic listing derived and adapted from a number of sources.

Attributes in appraisal	Progress monitoring context	Workplace contexts
Commercial judgement	Not applicable	✓
Product knowledge	Not applicable	✓
Technical knowledge	✓	✓
Time management	✓	✓
Planning	✓	✓
Budgeting and forecasting	Not applicable	✓
Reporting	✓	✓
Administration	✓	✓
Communication skills	✓	✓
Delegation skills	✓	✓
IT/equipment skills	✓	✓
Meeting deadlines	✓	✓
Meeting commitments	✓	✓
Creativity	✓	✓
Problem-solving	✓	✓
Decision-making	✓	✓
Team-working	✓	✓
Developing others	✓	✓
Energy and determination	✓	✓
Work-rate	✓	✓
Steadiness under pressure	✓	✓
Leadership	✓	✓
Integrity	✓	✓
Adaptability and flexibility	✓	✓
Personal appearance and image	✓	✓

ARRANGEMENTS FOR PROGRESS MONITORING

All universities should have systems for monitoring the progress of individual PhD students. These schemes may go by a variety of titles, but the generic term 'progress monitoring committee' will be used here. The general format is that you will make written submissions to that group, and probably meet them, roughly twice each academic year. Arrangements and their timing will differ, but may include some or all of the following:

- an introductory meeting to get to know the members of your review committee, including perhaps any co-supervisor or second supervisor assigned to you;
- submission of forms giving your personal information and other details of your study;
- submission of your research proposal (**Ch 4**) and feedback on this;
- submission of various reports, for example, a literature review and/or annual reports;
- reviews of your personal development and training schedule;
- meetings where progress towards your previously agreed targets will be discussed, and new goals established;
- a meeting after a year of study where a decision will be made on whether you move on to PhD studies for a further two years or are asked to work towards a Master's by research degree;
- a meeting where your thesis plan will be discussed;
- meetings where your progress in writing up will be discussed;
- notification of intention to submit.

You should receive oral and written feedback after each meeting or submission, and often this will be quite detailed. Some progress monitoring outcomes result in the production of an 'action plan' negotiated with student and supervisor.

Supervisor's reports

You should be aware that at the same time as you are submitting reports for progress monitoring, your supervisor may be completing parallel forms for the committee to review.

Who will be on my progress monitoring committee?

In some, but not all institutions, your supervisor will *not* be a member. The committee will comprise at least two people, normally both experienced academics: someone with knowledge of your subject area and someone from outside your school, faculty or department. Secretarial or administrative personnel may also be present.

These progress monitoring meetings are intended as a two-way process. On the one hand, they will create milestones and benchmarks for you to work to and (as emphasised in **Ch 6**) help to even out the rate of your work, so that it is not a hectic sprint at the end. However, they will also allow you to discuss any difficulties you may be having, or ways in which you might be helped to move forward.

OTHER TYPES OF FEEDBACK

The formal progress monitoring scheme is not the only place where you can obtain valuable feedback. Other avenues include:

- Meetings with your supervisor. Depending on your subject and the personalities involved, these may take place at relatively lengthy intervals or on a daily basis. Your supervisor is the person in the best position to advise on technical points or details of your study area. They are likely to provide feedback on draft materials, including submissions for progress monitoring.

- Discussions with other academics and research students. Explaining your work to other people is always valuable because it forces you to put your thoughts into words. The give-and-take of informal discussion is useful for floating new ideas in a non-judgemental environment.

- Seminars and poster presentations. Here, you will obtain feedback from those knowledgeable in your field, but with additional perspectives on the subject. The questions and observations of those attending may help you to see how, for example, your explanations or data presentation might be improved, especially where a misunderstanding has arisen. These may be provided both during the relevant event, and also later, in the aftermath, where it can be given during an informal one-to-one discussion.

- Referees' reports. When you submit posters or papers for inclusion in a conference or publication in a journal, these will usually be peer-reviewed. Particularly in the case of papers, this will often involve a set of quite detailed comments: someone very knowledgeable in your area will have looked over your work very closely and so you can expect very meticulous and technical feedback.

LEARNING FROM FEEDBACK

The natural inclination when you receive negative feedback is to treat it as possibly unjustified criticism of your efforts. There will possibly be times when this is true, but mostly those providing you with feedback will have your best interests at heart. Academics in particular tend to depersonalise discussions as part of their training, whereas you may feel that you have made a personal investment in the work upon which they are commenting. Hence, their criticism may hurt initially. Perhaps only on reflection will you appreciate that their comments were fair.

A positive mind-set is essential and you should think about how you could address the issues raised. Even if you feel vehemently that the comments are incorrect, this could indicate that you have not communicated your original points clearly. Your immediate thoughts should be along the following lines:

- Do I fully understand the comment?
- How can I seek clarification (when a comment is obscure)?
- What should I do to make an improvement?
- What can I learn from this?
- How can I move on (what is my action plan)?
- Do I need help or advice and where can I get it?

 Learning from others' perspectives

You will frequently find that other people approach an issue in a different way from you. They may interpret information differently or view it in a different way as result of their experience, knowledge base or subject background. Their position will help you take a more rounded view of your subject, and may even offer new avenues for study.

It may be a good idea not to respond to feedback too quickly. Think things through again after time for reflection. With due consideration, trying to look at both sides of the discussion, do you still feel the same? Perhaps an informal discussion with a third party might help resolve some of the issues. Certainly, airing your feelings to an independent party is one way to put the disappointment of negative comments behind you, before you make a formal, and perhaps more diplomatic, response.

Yourself as your own best critic

A crucial element of the academic autonomy expected at PhD level is the ability to self-criticise. This covers personal behaviour and research skills, but in this context chiefly relates to the written word. In particular, you will need to develop the ability to review and edit your own writing (**Ch 29**). As you develop this skill and your work becomes more in tune with discipline norms, you will find that you will receive fewer comments on your work.

ACTION POINTS

16.1 Find out about the full scope of your university/ departmental progress review scheme. Don't just react to the immediate task ahead of you – take a longer-term view, so you can anticipate what to expect and can plan your preparation (including attending training events, **Ch 5**) well in advance. Ensure that you respect the process by devoting adequate time to prepare yourself for the meeting and for compiling your report and any other written work required.

16.2 Decide what to do about feedback comments on your writing. The high standards expected of PhD writing may mean that you have to take steps to make improvements. For instance, does your supervisor always comment about your spelling or grammar; or make suggestions about citation and referencing? If so, look at relevant guidance books and reference works, to see if you can adjust appropriately. Attend workshops or visit guidance staff, where these might assist you.

16.3 Improve your knowledge of editing and proof-reading marks. When you submit written work and receive it back you may find it annotated with proof-reading marks indicating where changes could be made (**Ch 16**). Most of these may be familiar to you from your undergraduate studies, but if not, it will repay learning about them (see Ritter, 2005, for example, or ask your supervisor whether he or she has a copy of proof-marking rules from past submissions of papers or books). These coded marks are also useful to know so that you can speed up the editing of your own drafts.

RESEARCH METHODS

17

CRITICAL THINKING

How to apply method to arrive at valid, original ideas

The ability to think critically and with originality is fundamental to PhD research and thesis writing. This chapter introduces concepts, methods and pitfalls to watch out for when trying to improve your analytical capabilities.

KEY TOPICS

→ The importance of thinking skills in PhD research

→ Thinking at the appropriate level

→ How to approach a critical thinking task

→ Being original in research

→ Putting forward a balanced and unbiased analysis

→ Fallacies and other common pitfalls in thinking

Critical thinking can be defined as the ability to analyse a problem and present a solution to it. Your undergraduate studies will have given you a chance to develop this skill. You will hone it even further both during the research phase of your PhD project and when you write it up. The aim of this chapter is to help you to do this through a deeper understanding of relevant thought processes.

THE IMPORTANCE OF THINKING SKILLS IN PhD RESEARCH

We routinely think without really contemplating what we are doing. It is perhaps only when decisions are particularly difficult, or, in relation to research, when positions and conclusions need to be explained, that we focus intensely on the logic and evidence behind them. Laying out your analysis or argument in words is thus a key stage in critical thinking. Expressing thoughts in written (or spoken) language requires you to:

- refine and clarify your thoughts;
- lay out the logic of your thinking so that it can be followed and understood by others;
- understand and make use of the connotations and meanings of phrases and words;
- find the right expressions to explain your meaning to others;
- use language to persuade.

It follows that the skills of writing and speaking are important for critical thinking and hence for PhD research (**Ch 25**).

---

i

Contexts for thinking critically

Examples of PhD activities requiring higher-level thinking skills:

- making judgements on the reliability of sources;
- evaluating the content of sources;
- designing experiments, observations and surveys;
- selecting and using numerical or statistical methods to analyse data;
- deciding how to present results;
- constructing arguments;
- arriving at a position and supporting it with evidence;
- drawing conclusions.

THINKING AT THE APPROPRIATE LEVEL

Benjamin Bloom, a noted educational psychologist, working with several colleagues, identified six different processes involved in thinking within education:

- knowledge acquisition;
- comprehension;
- application;
- analysis;
- synthesis;
- evaluation.

Bloom *et al.* (1956) showed that students naturally progressed through this scale of thought processing during their studies (Table 17.1). Looking at this table, you may recognise that your school work mainly focused on knowledge, comprehension and application, with only some analysis, while in your later undergraduate years, there would be greater expectation made of you with emphasis on analysis, synthesis and evaluation. At PhD level, the requirement is to refine these more advanced skills yet further. While there will always be elements of fact-finding, comprehension and application in any thesis, what you will primarily be judged upon is your ability to analyse evidence, synthesise new ideas and evaluate situations, problems and evidential material.

Thinking about thinking in this way involves an advanced level of insight, known as 'metacognition'. Understanding thought processes at this 'higher' level will allow you to place your activities at a 'lower'

Table 17.1 **Classification of thinking processes by Bloom *et al.* (1956) with corresponding potential actions.**

Bloom's taxonomy of thinking processes (in ascending order of difficulty)	Typical activities characterising each level
Knowledge. If you know a fact, you have it at your disposal and can *recall* or *recognise* it. This does not mean you necessarily understand it at a higher level	• Defining • Describing • Identifying
Comprehension. To comprehend a fact means that you *understand* what it means	• Contrasting • Discussing • Interpreting
Application. To apply a fact means that you can put it to use	• Demonstrating • Calculating • Illustrating
Analysis. To analyse information means that you are able to break it down into parts and show how these components fit together	• Analysing • Explaining • Comparing
Synthesis. To synthesise, you need to be able to extract relevant facts from a body of knowledge and use these to address an issue in a novel way or create something new	• Composing • Creating • Integrating
Evaluation. If you evaluate information, you arrive at a judgement based on its importance relative to the topic being addressed	• Recommending • Supporting • Drawing a conclusion

level into context. Thus, rather than aimlessly trying to achieve a goal, you are able to recognise the type of activity necessary to meet your target and then adopt methods that have previously been successful for that sort of task. In short, an awareness of academic thinking at this new level should aid you in performing better in all aspects of your research. Such understanding will help you to meet the expectations of those who monitor and appraise your academic performance as a postgraduate.

 Definition: metacognition

This has been defined as 'knowing about knowing'. In the context here, it includes understanding how you think and how you might apply different thinking processes to different tasks.

HOW TO APPROACH A CRITICAL THINKING TASK

Suppose you recognise that critical thinking is required to solve a specific problem within your PhD research or to arrive at a position within your thesis. The pointers below should help you to arrive at a logical answer. Although presented sequentially, you should regard this listing as a menu rather than a recipe – think about the different stages and how they might be useful for the specific issue under consideration and your own style of work. Adopt or reject them as you see fit, or, according to your needs, change their order.

● Define exactly what the task or problem is. An important preliminary task is to make sure you have identified this properly. Write down a description of the problem or issue, taking care to be very precise with your wording.

● Organise your approach to the problem. You might start with a 'brainstorm' to identify potential solutions or viewpoints. Typically, this might consist of three phases:

1 *Open thinking*. Consider the issue or question from all possible angles or positions and write down everything you come up with. Don't worry at this stage about the relevance or importance of your ideas. A 'spider diagram' or 'mind-map' can be used to lay out your thoughts.

2 *Organisation.* Next you should try to arrange your ideas into

categories or subheadings, or group them as supporting or opposing a viewpoint.

3 *Analysis.* Now you need to decide about the relevance of the grouped points to the original problem. Reject trivial or irrelevant ideas and rank or prioritise those that seem relevant. This involves several further activities discussed below.

● Assemble background information and check your comprehension of the facts. You will need to gather or rearrange relevant information and ideas to support your viewpoint or position, provide examples or suggest a range of interpretations or approaches. You also need to ensure that you fully understand the evidence you have gathered by using dictionaries and technical works to find out the precise meaning of key words or discussing the ideas with your peers or supervisor.

● Check relevance. Now consider the information you have gathered, your thoughts and how these might apply to your problem. Now, marshal the evidence you have collected – for example: for or against a proposition; supporting or opposing an argument or theory. You may find it useful to prepare a table or grid to organise the information and help you balance your thoughts. Be ruthless in rejecting irrelevant or inconsequential material.

Always ask yourself questions

One of the keys to critical thinking is to ask 'why?' when coming across any new fact, concept or theory. Developing this habit of questioning means that you are constantly seeking the underlying reasons for things being the way they are. In research, you must rarely take anything for granted and seldom rely on someone else's views.

● Think through your argument, and how you can support it. Having considered relevant information and positions, you should arrive at a personal viewpoint, and then construct your discussion or conclusion around this. When writing about your conclusion, you must take care to a avoid value judgments or other kinds of expression of opinion that are not supported by evidence or sources. This is one reason why frequent citation and referencing is demanded in academic work (**Ch 20**).

● Write up your thoughts. Once you have decided on what you want to say, writing this up should be much easier.

BEING ORIGINAL IN RESEARCH

Finding a new way of looking at a topic or a novel solution to a problem is vital for the advancement of knowledge and understanding. Such original thinking tends to result in small-scale changes in academic understanding. Occasionally, however, major 'paradigm shifts' occur after important new ideas, concepts or discoveries come to the fore. These events sometimes involve a period of intense opposition from proponents of 'established' understanding (**Ch 3**). Even with small-scale changes in thinking, differences of opinion are part-and-parcel of academic debate and often aid the development of an idea by requiring the proponents of different ideas to defend the logic of their position.

Overcoming barriers to creative, original thought

This kind of thinking proceeds best when you:

- have a good all-round understanding of the topic – making it possible to synthesise something new from these building blocks;
- make connections – for example, using approaches from one discipline in another;
- aren't afraid of failing – and approach your subject with confidence;
- are willing to take risks – and be unconventional in your approach;
- have a personal technique for generating ideas – and for overcoming being 'blocked';
- do not act as a perfectionist – and are willing to build on imperfect starting points;
- do not procrastinate – and find a way of starting.

Do not allow thoughts about practicalities to stifle your initial thoughts. What is required for originality is an initial focus on the *generation* of ideas, without these being constrained by theory or feasibility. You should delay the process of selecting those ideas which are viable as a secondary process.

Many new ideas involve 'lateral thinking', a concept first introduced by Edward de Bono. This means jumping out of past thought patterns and concepts ('thinking out of the box'). It involves challenging the assumptions or limitations that apparently define a situation, and choosing a new perspective on the problem. Unsurprisingly, then, it is important to support free and unfettered thinking. This involves resisting or moving away from the influences of others' prior arguments or work, one's own preconceptions or apparent boundaries. Finding a personal route to liberate your thoughts is essential for turning on your creativity.

However, thinking with freedom should not be confused with being ignorant about your topic. New ideas rarely arise independently from a framework of understanding. This mental 'scaffolding' is important to understand the problem, the underlying principles and the language in which a solution might be described. You need to find a balance so your fresh thoughts are not overly constrained by these influences.

Your brain needs stimuli to come up with ideas. You can select these stimuli and try to focus your thoughts or set up conditions that support unpredictable new thinking. However, the results may not be immediate: sometimes original thoughts come in unusual places and at unexpected times. Table 17.2 describes some methods of producing ideas.

Reading and note-making as adjuncts to originality

Sometimes when you have no ideas, it is because you lack the seed to grow them. You might need to read around the subject to find out more about it. If stalled, finding a new source with a fresh approach might kick-start your own thinking. It is important not simply to read: you need to make notes, so you keep things active and retain your thoughts. Your notes should be of three main types:

1 notes about the subject material (**Ch 8**);
2 details of the sources, so you can cite these and avoid plagiarism (**Ch 20**);
3 your own ideas, as these appear through association as you read.

It is a good idea to keep a written summary of the problem alongside these notes and refer to it from time to time, so that your mind remains connected with the problem.

Table 17.2 Six methods of stimulating fresh thinking.

1 Brainstorming

This is probably the most commonly used technique for generating ideas. It means coming up with a range of thoughts about a topic before trying to making sense of them. The advertising executive Alex Osborn, who coined the term, proposed that the four keys to effective brainstorming are:

- think of as many ideas as possible – the more you generate, the greater the chance of finding an answer;
- encourage seemingly eccentric lines of thought – even your wildest ideas might give rise to further ideas and even solutions;
- resist evaluating the ideas until later – the process of judgement may stifle your creativity;
- look for associations between your ideas – this may give rise to new patterns of thinking.

Most people use a mindmap or similar diagram to capture their ideas, and this method can also incorporate visual concepts. A brief description of the topic should be written out in the centre of the page so it can continually be referred to.

2 Finding connections

This method is essentially a more focused approach to brainstorming. It involves three main phases. First, write down a short description of the topic. Second, try to tease out the different aspects of the subject. Ways of doing this include:

- focusing on each key word or phrase of the topic description in turn to see what thoughts arise;
- addressing the six reporters' queries 'who?', 'what?', 'when?', 'where?', 'why?' and 'how?' to the topic;
- viewing the topic from a range of different perspectives, for example, the different sub-disciplines of your subject, different places, ages, protagonists, and so on.

The third phase is to review and select from the ideas you have produced.

3 Freewriting

This approach aims to get ideas flowing by making you write quickly and continuously about your topic. It particularly helps those with writer's block. First, find an undisturbed location and decide on a specific period of time to spend on the exercise. Now, write down your current theme and then start writing about it. Don't stop, just keep going, and write as speedily as you can. The idea is to capture a stream of consciousness. Don't worry about what you are writing or why, nor its neatness, grammatical correctness or spelling. If the text seems to drift off-subject don't be concerned – just keep writing (but try to return to the main theme if you can). Finally, after your allocated time is up, review what you have written and select the interesting points. Use these ideas within a further freewriting or brainstorming exercise.

4. Making random associations
This technique seeks to stimulate chaotic, unpredictable new thoughts about your topic. First, write down the topic. Now find five to ten random words (nouns are best). You could do this, for example, by flicking through a dictionary, a newspaper, a series of websites, or via an online random word generator. Now try to incorporate each word in a sentence about your topic. This forces you to think in spontaneous ways about it.

5. Going on a 'thought walk'
This is meant literally – going on a solo walk to focus on thinking. Perhaps surprisingly, many great thinkers have used this simple method, including Sigmund Freud. Several aspects of the approach may be valuable: • It gives you undisturbed time and space to think. • It seems that while part of your brain focuses on the repetitive motor action of walking, another part is released to think. • You may see random things or events on your walk that stimulate new thinking. There are other variations on this theme, such as mediation, walking a labyrinth or having a workout in the gym.

6. Keeping ideas notebooks, sketchbooks, mood boards and inspiration boards
The straightforward reason for keeping an ideas notebook or its equivalent is to prevent valuable ideas being forgotten. For written notes, a pocket or bag-sized book is best, so it can be carried with you for use at any time, for example, to note ideas that come when day-dreaming on public transport. Laptops, notepads and phones can also be used if preferred. You might also position a pen and pad near to your bedside to capture any ideas that come at night: inspiration at these times is easily forgotten.

PUTTING FORWARD A BALANCED AND UNBIASED ANALYSIS

In academic situations, the outcome of critical thinking should always be balanced. This means that due consideration must be given to all sides of a topic, before arriving at a personal viewpoint based on the evidence. 'Bias' is the opposite of such even-handedness and arises because a person's views are affected by such factors as:

• a specific past experience;
• their culture or ethnicity;
• their gender;
• having a strong political stance;
• looking at a small or skewed sample of sources;
• having a vested interest in a particular outcome.

Awareness, especially self-awareness, is important in minimising some of these sources of bias. This is not always easy to achieve. However, if you try to read widely around the topic, you may become aware of a greater variety of possible viewpoints on relevant issues, and some of these sources will also draw attention to bias in others. This will help you become more alert to this possibility in your own position. Discussing issues with others is another way of gaining a wider perspective.

When writing up your thesis, it is important to arrive at a position (**Ch 18**) and not sit on the fence. However, you must balance your discussion. You should mention the conclusions of others, but also provide well-argued reasons why you disagree. At the same time, you should always strive to be open-minded and receptive to the ideas of others. If you really feel there is not enough evidence to support *any* conclusion, be prepared to suspend judgement.

Think about opposing viewpoints

One way of ensuring balance is to take a 'devil's advocate' stance at some point in your deliberations. In this context, this means artificially taking a view you might not agree with, so that you can reveal the strengths and weaknesses of your preferred argument.

Language can help you to achieve balance. In particular, try to avoid 'absolutes': be careful with words that imply that there are no exceptions, for example: 'always', 'never', 'all' and 'every'. These words can only be used if you wish to imply 100 per cent certainty. Instead, it may be better to use the 'hedging' language typical of academic writing, such as 'this suggests', 'it may be' or 'it seems that' (**Ch 26**).

FALLACIES AND OTHER COMMON PITFALLS IN THINKING

The ability to dissect arguments is a key aspect of critical thinking. In some cases you will be trying to understand and counter a viewpoint while in others you will be trying to construct a coherent view of your own. In both instances you need to assess whether the argument is logical or whether it involves a fallacy – a breakdown in reasoning. A fallacy occurs where an argument initially seems to be valid, but is logically flawed, or is based on hidden assumptions that may not be true.

We can sometimes be bamboozled by a multitude of facts, complex arguments or strong rhetoric. You must look beyond the superficial and analyse the basic line of reasoning that is being used. Sometimes you will sense something is wrong and spot it immediately; at other times an error will only become apparent after close scrutiny. One of the best ways to detect fallacies is to study the basic types of fallacy, and then, by analogy, extend this understanding to the argument which you face.

Unfortunately, there are many different types of logical fallacies – one web source recognises over 70. Here we focus on some of those you are most likely to encounter (Table 17.3). Once tuned in to this way of thinking, you should observe that faulty logic and debating tricks are frequently used in areas such as advertising, politics and newspaper opinion columns. Analysing the methods being used in these presentations can be a useful way of developing your critical thinking skills.

Equally as important as an understanding of the characteristics of deeper thinking is an awareness of the pitfalls of shallow thinking. Apart from bias and fallacy, discussed above, here are some of the common bad habits and errors that we all make from time to time.

- Rushing to conclusions. In the context of research, this means basing a view on very little reading around the subject. Also included in this category might be situations such as relying on too few observations or experiments; or not carrying out the necessary statistical analysis of results.
- Generalising. This means drawing a conclusion from one (or few) cases. An awareness of other possibilities is important to avoid this mistake.
- Oversimplifying. This means arriving at a conclusion that does not take account of potential complexities or other possible answers.
- Personalising. This means drawing conclusions based solely or largely on your own experience or being subjective about an issue.
- Thinking in terms of stereotypes. Here, the danger is of thinking in terms of 'standardised' ideas, especially about groups of people. This 'received wisdom' may come about due to one's upbringing, gender, ethnicity and so on, and involves basing an opinion on superficial appearances, rather than the underlying facts.

Table 17.3 Some common examples of logical fallacies, bias and propaganda techniques found in arguments.

Type of fallacy or propaganda	Description	Example	How to counteract this approach
Ad hominem (Latin for 'to the man')	An attack is made on the character of the person putting forward an argument, rather than on the argument itself. This is particularly common in the media and politics	The President's moral behaviour is suspect, so his financial policies must also be dubious	Suggest that the person's character or circumstances are irrelevant
Ad populum (Latin for 'to the people')	The argument is supported on the basis that it is a popular viewpoint. Of course, this does not make it correct in itself	The majority of people support corporal punishment for vandals, so we should introduce boot camps	Watch out for bandwagon and peer pressure effects and ignore them when considering rights and wrongs
Appeal to authority	An argument is supported on the basis that an expert or authority agrees with the conclusion. Used in ads, where celebrity endorsement and testimonials are frequent	My professor, whom I admire greatly, believes in Smith's theory, so it must be right	Point out that the experts disagree and explain how and why. Focus on the key qualities of the item or argument
Appeal to ignorance	Without evidence for (or against) a case, it means the case must be false (or true)	You haven't an alibi, therefore you must be guilty	Point out that a conclusion either way may not be possible in the absence of evidence
Biased evidence	Selection of examples or evidence for or against a case	A writer who quotes those who support his/her view, but not those against	Read around the subject, including those with a different view and try to arrive at a balance.

	Description	Example	How to counter
Euphemisms and jargon	Use of phrasing to hide the true position or exaggerate an opponent's – stating things in mild or emotive language for effect. Use of technical words to sound authoritative	My job as vertical transportation operative means I am used to being in a responsible position (I'm a lift operator)	Watch for (unnecessary) adjectives and adverbs that may affect the way you consider the evidence
Repetition	Saying the same thing over and over again until people believe it	Common in politics, war propaganda and advertising – e.g. 'Beanz meanz Heinz'	Look out for repeated catch-phrases and lack of substantive argument
False dilemma	Offering a choice of alternatives when other options may be available	The patient can be treated with Drug A or Drug B. Drug B has side effects, so we should choose A.	Demonstrate that there are other options (e.g. Drug C)
Slippery slope	The notion that a step in a particular direction will start a chain of events leading to an undesirable outcome	If we let one property become a house of multiple occupancy, soon the whole street will be full of them	Point out that progress along the chain of events is not a foregone conclusion
Correlation used to imply cause	A correlation between two events (that is, they appear or disappear or rise and fall together) is taken to imply that one causes the other.	Whenever I wear this lucky scarf my football team wins	Point out that the two things are in no way connected or that there may be other factors causing the event
Straw man	A position is misrepresented in order to create a debating point that is easily accepted or rejected, when in fact the core issue has not been addressed	Many asylum seekers try to milk the benefits system, and it is wrong to milk the benefits system, so we should turn them all away	Point out the fallacy and focus on the core issue
Anecdotal evidence	Use of unrepresentative exceptions to contradict an argument based on statistical evidence	My Nan was a heavy smoker and she lived to be 95, so smoking won't harm me	Consider the overall weight of evidence rather than isolated examples

- Believing propaganda. This is false or incomplete information that supports a particular political or moral view.

- Making value judgements. These are statements that reflect the views and values of the speaker or writer rather than the objective reality of what is being assessed or considered. Value judgements often imply some sense of being pejorative (negative).

Examples of value judgements

In the example: 'Australian wines are the best – they are full bodied and smooth', the assumption is made that the listener/reader will share the view that a good wine needs to be full bodied and smooth – a value judgement. Similar assumptions may be inherent in descriptive phrases. For example, if a person is sympathetic to a cause they may refer to those who support it as members of a 'pressure group'; if they disagree with the cause, then its members become 'militants'; similarly 'conservationists' versus 'tree-huggers'; 'freedom fighters' versus 'insurgents'.

As with bias, many of these errors can be avoided by reading more widely around your subject – either to take account of a greater selection of views, the way they have been presented, or the methods used to analyse findings. You will also need to look beneath the surface of what you read. It is important to decide whether sources are dealing with facts or opinions; examine any assumptions made, including your own; and think about the motivation of writers. Rather than restating and describing your sources, focus on what they *mean* by what they write.

Being descriptive rather than analytical

This is regarded as a symptom of shallow thinking. Overly descriptive work relies too much on quotes, facts or statements. Being analytical, in contrast, involves explaining importance and context of information and showing an understanding of what it means or implies. Note that while some extensive description may be required at certain stages in a PhD thesis, this should only provide the foundation for making deeper critical analyses. Striking a balance between the simpler description and the more demanding analysis, synthesis and evaluation is an important skill – especially at the writing up stage.

17.1 Practise seeing different sides of an argument. Write down the supporting arguments for different sides of the issue, focusing on your least favoured option. This will help you see diverse aspects of a debate as a matter of course. Draw on the ideas and opinions of your peers and lecturers. Discussions with others can be very fruitful, revealing a range of interpretations that you might not have thought about yourself. You may find it useful to bounce ideas off others. Tutors can provide useful guidance once you have done some reading and are usually pleased to be asked for help.

17.2 When quoting evidence, use appropriate citations. This is important as it shows you have read relevant source material and helps you to avoid plagiarism (**Ch 20**). The conventions for citation vary among subjects, so consult course handbooks or other information and make sure you follow the instructions carefully, or you may lose marks.

17.3 Explore different types of fallacies and biased arguments. There are some very good websites that provide lists of different types of these with examples. Investigate these using 'fallacy' or 'logical fallacies' in a search engine. Not only are the results quite entertaining at times, but you will also find that your increased understanding improves your analytical and debating skills.

18

ARRIVING AT A POSITION AND SUPPORTING IT

How to sift fact and opinion and express your conclusions

As part of many research projects you will arrive at a position on a topic, and wish to express an opinion on it. This requires skills of research, thinking and argument, and an understanding of related concepts.

KEY TOPICS

→ Dealing with fact, opinion and truth

→ The nature of evidence and proof

→ Arriving at a position and backing it up

→ Putting forward your views

When analysing complex issues at PhD level, arriving at a personal viewpoint, or position, is rarely easy. It requires that you:

- read and understand sources;
- judge other arguments being put forward;
- check facts and assertions;
- arrive at a position;
- express your position clearly;
- support your view with appropriate evidence;
- review and reappraise your position in light of emerging publications and your developing understanding.

You may have to do this not only to arrive at an overall 'position' for your thesis, but also when considering narrower elements of the topic. Whatever the level, this is a multi-faceted activity, requiring elements of critical thinking, combined with skills of originality, argument, academic writing and referencing (**Chs 17, 20** and **26**). There can be no formula for arriving at a position, as each specific issue must be judged on its merits. However, understanding some concepts relevant to opinion-making should help you analyse what you read with greater clarity and thereby help you to form a view.

DEALING WITH FACT, OPINION AND TRUTH

When coming to terms with a wide diversity of viewpoints, you can easily become confused and lose sight of the differences between fact, opinion and truth.

Examples of fact, opinion and truth

The world record for the 100-metre sprint in athletics was set at 9.58 seconds on 17 August 2009. This is a fact. The record may change over time, but this statement will still be true. Some claim that many world records are created by athletes who have taken drugs to enhance their performance. This is an opinion. There is evidence to back up this position, but recent controversies have highlighted the problem of proof in these cases. Claims about drug misuse are open to conjecture, claim and counter-claim, not all of which can be true. Your duty is to identify the difference between fact and opinion and write with that knowledge. Do not avoid the controversy, but be clear about the facts, the truth and your opinion of the evidence.

A fact is a statement generally acknowledged as valid and knowledge is built from a body of facts. In the context of scholarly thinking, fact or knowledge is the basis for further theorising or discussion. Typically, you might find a fact in a textbook, encyclopaedia or website. Not all 'facts' are true – they may change with time as new information is uncovered, and some may be hotly disputed. In academic contexts, therefore, it is often important to establish the reliability of the source of a fact (**Ch 8**) and vital that you quote the source of your information (**Ch 20**).

In science, the concept of repeatability is important in relation to facts. Thus, it should be possible to repeat an observation or experiment that established a fact (**Ch 3**). This is one reason why scientists take such care to describe their materials and methods – results can sometimes depend on these factors. The unreliability of facts is often acknowledged: the error associated with a value is calculated or an estimate made of the probability of a hypothesis being wrong or right (**Ch 23**). This information should be taken into account when using facts in a discussion.

Objectivity and subjectivity

Concepts of truth and fact involve the notions of objectivity and subjectivity. *Objective* means based on a balanced consideration of the facts; *subjective* means based on one person's opinion (**Ch 23**). Understanding the distinction is important at PhD level. The key is to produce valid reasons for holding your opinion. Most academics aim for a detached, objective piece of writing, and your thesis will need to follow that notion especially when analysing results or dealing with emotive or controversial issues as in some Arts subjects. Additionally, this may be difficult at some stages because you may be impassioned by your subject and the thrust of your findings. Of course, it will important to state your own opinion at some point in the work, but it is important to couch this appropriately using objective language (**Chs 26–28**).

An opinion is a view about a matter which is not wholly confirmed by the current state of knowledge or on a topic that may be regarded as a matter of judgement. Thus, in many fields, for example, in arts and social sciences, there is often no 'right' or 'wrong' answer, simply a range of stances or viewpoints. It is therefore possible that your position may differ significantly from the viewpoints of noted authorities and possibly even that of your supervisor. When your thesis and the views expressed in it are examined, you will be assessed on your ability to argue your case and support it with evidence.

Truth is usually defined in relation to reality – our current state of knowledge. That is, something can be designated as true if it corresponds to known facts. However, the concept of truth involves a host of philosophical concepts (including perception, for example) which may complicate the issue. In debate, something is only true when all sides of the argument accept it. If a particular line of argument can be shown to lack credibility or to be in some way unacceptable, this will add weight to the counter-argument.

Always try to maintain a healthy, detached scepticism

However reliable a source of a piece of information seems to be, retain a degree of scepticism about the facts or ideas involved and question the logic of arguments. Also, try not to identify too strongly with a viewpoint, so you can be detached when assessing its merits and failings. In the research process, there is always the risk that you might pick out the material that supports your personal view without critical appraisal. It is important to be aware of such a tendency in your own approach.

THE NATURE OF EVIDENCE AND PROOF

The nature of evidence and proof differs according to discipline.

In the sciences, evidence will most likely be quantitative in nature, such as numerical or statistical summary data. This evidence will be the result of an observation or experiment. The data might have been obtained with the aim of testing some hypothesis about a situation (**Ch 3**). If statistics are used, it may be possible to assign a probability to whether the hypothesis is true or not. Even apparently 'on or off' qualitative results, as obtained, say, in molecular genetics, rely on assumptions and are capable of multiple interpretations.

Scientific Method and falsifiability

The notion of falsifiability is central to Scientific Method, which involves continually updating our understanding of the world through provisional notions of reality – hypotheses (**Ch 3**). Falsifiability means that, at least in theory, the evidence can be tested by observation or experiment. Thus, whether the Higg's boson exists is a falsifiable notion; however, the idea that extraterrestrial beings have visited Earth and erased all the evidence is not.

The word 'proof' often carries a connotation of certainty that is unsatisfactory in such contexts. Unsurprisingly, therefore, to most scientists, there is no such thing as proof: there is always a possibility, however remote, that an alternative explanation is true. In the Arts and Humanities, evidence is more likely to be qualitative in nature; that is, a description of an event, an interpretation or an opinion. Here, proof is still an elusive concept, because it involves the presentation of 'convincing' evidence (a matter of degree) and notions of persuasion. This explains why many conclusions are couched in tentative 'hedging' language (**Ch 26**).

Definitions: categories of evidence

- **Anecdotal evidence** – that which relies on the indirect experience of others, such as hearsay.
- **Circumstantial evidence** – indirect evidence.
- **Intuition** – personal feelings (hunches) obtained without the direct use of fact or reasoning.
- **Personal evidence** – obtained by one's own observations or experience.
- **Scientific evidence** – observations or data obtained or testable by experiment.

ARRIVING AT A POSITION AND BACKING IT UP

During the literature search phase for your thesis writing, you should take careful notes of information and other material you might like to quote at some stage (**Chs 7–9**). In addition, you should also be appraising the viewpoint of the writer(s). You will find yourself naturally attracted to some positions rather than others. This 'gut feeling' is a starting point for forming your own stance.

Before cementing your position, however, you should carry out an analysis of points for and against all the viewpoints you have encountered. When reviewing this, you should try to be as objective as possible. Does the evidence support your initial feelings? If not, then perhaps you should change your opinion. However, you should not necessarily be swayed simply by the extensive volume of literature in support of a particular viewpoint; it is the strength of the argument and the nature of the supporting evidence that should guide you.

Some other factors to take account of when trying to arrive at a position include:

- The guidance that you have received from your supervisor. Of course, you don't *have* to follow this, but there will usually be a very sound rationale behind his or her advice.

- The writings of noted authorities in the field. Again, you don't *have* to follow their viewpoint, but you should take account of the strong likelihood that it is likely to be carefully considered, based on research and defensible. In many instances, however, you may be faced with opposing positions.

- The views of your peers. This is not the most reliable of sources, but discussing the topic with other research students may assist you to form an opinion either by being swayed by an argument or by feeling the need to respond with an alternative view.

In scientific subjects, you may model Scientific Method by setting up an experiment specifically to test a hypothesis (**Chs 3** and **23**). The data you obtain will then lead you to a position related to the hypothesis. You must take care, however, to consider alternative explanations or reasons why your results might not be as clear-cut as they superficially appear to be. It is always valuable to support your conclusion with reference to an appropriate statistical test (**Ch 23**).

How convincing your argument is may depend on the evidence you use to support your position. Evidence comes in many forms: from statistical/numeric sources, from structured argument, from quotations, from experiments, or from observation. You should assess all potential evidence for relevance and value, and you must make sure you cite the source of the information in your own writing, otherwise you may be accused of plagiarism (**Ch 20**).

Above all, you should try to produce a *balanced* conclusion. This is one where you are open about counter-arguments and counter-evidence that does not, at least on the face of it, support your case. You must explain what others think or might think, then explain why you have arrived at the conclusion you have reached yourself.

Taking care with concepts of evidence and proof

- Provide evidence to support an assertions or statement of fact.
- Account for the nature and reliability of all evidence.
- Cite references to back up an assertion or statement of fact (**Ch 20**).
- Be clear when something is an opinion rather than a fact.
- Take care when using the noun 'proof' or the verb 'proves'.
- Use hedging language (**Ch 27**) to avoid implying certainty.

PUTTING FORWARD YOUR VIEWS

Argument through discussion, and its more formal partner debate, are vital parts of scholarship. A valid position on any subject should be capable of being defended. Similarly, you should feel able to attack a position with which you disagree. In some cases, the acts of defence and attack are artificial devices to explore a position.

The ground rules for this are as follows:

1 State your viewpoint. Of course, this requires that you have first arrived at a position on the topic, as discussed above. This view should be explained clearly, demonstrating, where necessary, the steps in logic you have taken to arrive at your view. A certain amount of background information may be important here.

2 Provide reasoning and evidence. As part of arriving at a view, you should have researched the topic (**Chs 4**, **7** and **8**) and this is your opportunity to summarise the key evidence.

3 Outline briefly the counter-arguments and your points against them. This forces you to identify and confront the potential weaknesses in your position, and is an essential part of arriving at a coherent viewpoint. If you have thought things through carefully, it should not be difficult to point out the flaws in other arguments, but remember again to use evidence to support this side of your case.

4 Conclude. This is where you summarise the key evidence for and against your position, the implications or consequences of taking this line of thought and ending perhaps with a final restatement of your case and why you feel it is valid.

 Keeping up attention and focus in your argument

When dealing with a complex issue, it is easy to become mired in detail. Avoid this by returning to your key theme from time to time. You can use 'reminding' wordings such as 'in relation to the theme of...' or 'this shows that...' which give you the excuse to repeat or summarise your position from time to time. Another approach is to 'number' your points (Firstly,...; then secondly,...; and finally,...) so readers will know where they are in your argument.

Various linguistic devices can be used to promote a point of view. General guidance on the structure, language and presentation of scholarly writing is provided in **Chapter 27**. Here, the focus is on persuasive writing technique, sometimes called rhetoric. These methods are important because a poorly scripted argument will fail to convince.

What's the value of understanding techniques for persuasion?

Not only will they help you structure your own case, these methods will help you to think about the way others' points are being made – particularly useful if you wish to counter their argument.

Table 18.1 outlines ten methods commonly used to persuade. However, it is easy to overdo some forms of persuasion, and if used wrongly they may even be the source of fallacies (**Ch 17**). Moreover, certain methods commonly found in politics, advertising and bar-room arguments are regarded as unacceptable in scholarly work. These include:

- use of emotive or pejorative wording;
- implication of certainty when this is unjustified;
- making opinion sound like fact;
- selective use of information;
- unjustified simplification and generalisation;
- use of exaggeration and melodrama;
- unsubstantiated anecdote or invented examples.

Some of these approaches may be associated with propaganda techniques, that is, providing strongly biased or partial information. Use of any these methods will almost certainly lead to strong questioning of your conclusions.

Practise your analytical powers by dissecting the arguments of politicians, pundits and external speakers

When watching a televised debate, news report or sports programme, listen carefully for the ways in which the participants' points are made – look out particularly for fallacies, methods of persuasion, or the incorrect use of evidence. Also, when attending seminars, pay attention to the techniques speakers use when presenting their views.

Table 18.1 Ten techniques for persuasion. These are phrased for a written argument as in a thesis where for 'reader' you might substitute 'external examiner', but they also apply for oral argument – the word 'reader' here could apply to listeners.

1 **Create a problem – and help solve it.** Convince your reader that there is an issue at stake and that your preferred solution is the best available. The more they identify with the problem or its consequences, the more they will be inclined to connect with your argument, and, potentially, to accept your answer. This method is much used in advertising.

2 **Create a consistent and logical route to your answer.** Start with an initial point that is easy for the reader to agree with, and then move step-by-step towards your conclusion, with each element moving on from the previous. Make the connections clear. It will be difficult to escape from your logic.

3 **Give reasons for agreeing.** Explain the advantages of agreement with your line of reasoning and the disadvantages of disagreement. This will reinforce your position in the mind of the reader. Help the reader imagine the consequences under different scenarios. Explain why things are likely to turn out as you predict.

4 **Provide evidence.** Back up your argument with relevant information that supports your case. Query the status of evidence that is used by those who oppose your view.

5 **Repeat your case in different words.** Restate your argument several times in the hope that it hits home. Use a range of different methods, such as direct statement, metaphor (see point 9) or anecdote (see point 10), or the repetition might antagonise the reader.

6 **Get your reader thinking your way.** Why not use rhetorical questions to do this? These are queries that you go on to answer for the reader. They are a good way to engage readers and can be used to lead them to your preferred answer.

7 **Deal with potential objections.** Lead the reader through any objections that they might come up with, then counter each of the objections. There will be only one path remaining: to agree with you.

The following methods are often used in debate, but should only be used with great caution in academic writing:

8 **Help the reader identify with your argument.** There are several methods for this. You could establish common ground and by extension a common goal; let the reader feel they are in on a secret; use humour; personalise the issue and its solution.

9 **Mix up the way you express your argument**. Employ metaphor, simile and analogy to restate your points in ways that will engage different sorts of reader.

10 **Illustrate your argument.** Tell a story. Lead the reader via an interesting anecdote. This will help them imagine the issue and the solution. Use visual images, if this suits the situation.

ACTION POINTS

18.1 Think further about the nature of opinion and evidence in your own subject. You can base this both on your undergraduate experiences and on your current reading. What types of views are expressed, and how? What types of supporting information are generally used? What can this tell you about the origins of facts in your discipline?

18.2 Reflect on the origin of your position on a specific issue. Think of a situation where you have had little problem in deciding where you stand. This could be a moral issue, a political issue or an academic debate. Why do you think the way to do? Think back to influences such as people, events or books. Why were you persuaded to have a particular viewpoint? How much is this supported by evidence, or is it, at least in part, intuitive? Would you have a problem in defending it in an academic scenario? What does this tell you about the way you should arrive at viewpoints for your thesis?

18.3 Look at a specific issue from all possible angles. Choose one in which you are not yet certain of your views. The idea is test whether your initial stance might be the result of unwitting bias (**Ch 17**) and whether consciously trying to see things in different ways changes or hardens your position. One way of doing this would be to imagine what the different 'stakeholders' in an issue would think or say. Even the act of thinking who these groups could be might open up possible 'takes' on the topic.

19

RESEARCH ETHICS AND SAFETY

How to conduct an appropriate, principled and safe investigation

For many research topics and methodologies, it is important to consider the ethical and safety aspects regarding your study. The precise details differ according to discipline and the nature of the investigation. This chapter outlines the principles and procedures that may apply to you as a PhD student.

KEY TOPICS

→ Ethical principles

→ Consent and confidentiality

→ Obtaining ethical approval

→ Safe research

The term 'ethics' in the research context refers to the principles, rules and standards of conduct that apply to investigations. Most disciplines have self-monitoring codes of ethical practice and your institution will operate its own internal research governance policy. The types of ethical requirements vary among disciplines and your study must comply with recognised practice in your field and your institution.

You must familiarise yourself with these codes and be able to bring that understanding to discussions with your supervisor. He or she will be responsible for ensuring that your research proposal complies with ethical practice in your institution, but you have an important part to play. Where necessary, your supervisor will help you prepare an application to conduct the research for submission to your institution's Ethics Committee. Note that there may be different committees and rules for clinical and non-clinical research.

ETHICAL PRINCIPLES

Any research project involving human beings should be characterised by protection of the human rights, dignity, health and safety of participants and researchers. This is achieved by observing three fundamental tenets:

- the research should do no harm;
- consent should be informed and voluntary;
- confidentiality should be respected throughout.

Research involving humans might require interactions with people of certain groupings – for example, people in their roles as patients, clients, pupils, parents or peers. The list is boundless. Whoever is involved and in whatever respect, these ethical principles must be recognised and followed in practice as well as spirit.

Ethical considerations may relate to non-human as well as human research activity. Important areas have included the use of animals in research, cloning, human embryo research, stem cell research, *in vitro* fertilisation, and nuclear research. In the UK, experiments involving animals are subject to Home Office approval. If this is required for your work, your supervisor will guide you through the procedures. Similarly, experiments involving genetic manipulation must comply with relevant legislation and you will be guided through relevant procedures if necessary.

CONSENT AND CONFIDENTIALITY

Participants may need to be informed in writing about certain aspects of your research. This is usually provided as a 'Participant Information Sheet', which generally includes the following information:

- outline of the purpose of the study;
- invitation and reason for being selected;
- explanation of the voluntary nature of participation and of the freedom of the subject to withdraw from the project at any time;
- explanation of the procedure to be followed in the research and the time commitment involved;
- advantages and disadvantages of participation;
- assurance of confidentiality and anonymity;
- information about outcomes;
- information about the funding source;
- names of lead researcher and assistants;
- information about any sponsorship or affiliation connected to the project;
- information about refunding of expenses, if applicable.

How ethical is your research?

Unethical approaches to research can be inadvertent and unintended. For example, vulnerable groups may feel pressured into participating although members of such groups may not express this to the researcher. Patients may feel that they will receive better treatment if they participate in a study and risk a poorer level of treatment if they don't. Consequently, your research design and consent forms must reflect your awareness of such potential perceptions. Cases of unethical research procedures are legion and, thus, the field of ethics is a complex one. If you have any doubts at all about the ethical dimension of your study then you should discuss these with your supervisor to ensure that neither you nor your subjects are compromised by the research activity.

Particularly in the clinical area, a 'template' is often adopted to frame the explanation for participants. However, in many instances this is often unsatisfactory because the language used, and the format and layout are often unclear to the non-specialist. Every effort should be made to inform participants about the project as concisely as possible in 'plain' English, that is, in language that can be easily assimilated and understood by people in all walks of life. In response to this information, participants are then requested to complete an 'Informed Consent Form' that requires their signature. In some instances, a debriefing form will also need to be completed once the data-gathering phase is concluded.

Human participants must be assured that their identities will be protected by the promise of anonymity. This means that the confidentiality of any representation of data whether in aggregated forms (for example, mean value) or as qualitative material that might be obtained from individuals (for example, through questionnaires, interviews or focus groups) is protected in any printed format. It is essential that written permission to quote informants be sought from them at the time of participation in the enquiry, with the proviso that identities will be protected when findings are reported.

Data protection

The storage and use of personal information is an ethical issue. In the UK, the Data Protection Act covers procedures that must be adopted. Consult your university's Data Protection Officer or relevant web pages for information and guidance on local procedures if you plan to store information either in paper files or electronically. Legislation apart, it is simply good practice to time-limit the period for which data will remain on your records – and to inform participants how their data will be stored, and when it will be deleted or destroyed.

OBTAINING ETHICAL APPROVAL

You should first read the guidance notes provided by your university's ethics committee or department. Consult your university's website for up-to-date and detailed information on approaches to research ethics. In addition to the ethical policy, there may be general guidance, information, discipline-specific advice, and links to useful websites.

Once you have satisfied yourself that you have made arrangements to cover the ethical dimensions of your research project, you will be in a position to frame your proposal for ethical approval. Institutions will vary in the formats required.

In general, you will need to provide information on:

- the title, purpose and duration of the project, and the location of the study;
- the methodological approach to be adopted, and information on how data will be stored securely;
- if appropriate, the way in which participants will be recruited, plus information as to age, gender and any inclusion/exclusion criteria;
- measures taken to ensure that all ethical dimensions are covered in compliance with the appropriate research code of practice in your institution, including confidentiality in reporting results;
- if appropriate, identification of the involvement of any funding body.

When preparing your research proposal (**Ch 3**), and subsequent revisions, you should make due allowance for the time taken to obtain ethical approval (your supervisor can advise on anticipated delays). Make sure that you carry out some relevant work, such as a literature review, while you are waiting.

Consult appropriate texts and websites related to ethics

If you wish to know more about this area, potential starting points are Sana (2000) and Shamoo and Resnik (2009), but also consult the library catalogue or ask at your library for holdings specific to your discipline. Websites for the learned societies in your discipline will include obtain up-to-date information about ethical aspects that may impact on your research study.

SAFE RESEARCH

It is a fundamental tenet of research activity in the spirit of international codes of practice that the health and safety of all those involved in research activity as participants or researchers should be a priority at all times. Thus, all research approved by the appropriate ethics committee must follow passed protocols exactly. Any modification to the original proposal has to be referred back to the ethics committee. For the purposes of postgraduate research proposals, although the student is acting as the 'Principal Investigator', the actual Principal Investigator responsibility remains with the Supervisor.

Those researching in laboratory- or field-based subjects will be familiar with the general regulations for safe research from their undergraduate days. Any local rules associated with lab or field work, even if familiar, will have safety as their primary concern, so you must pay attention to them. In some cases, as a postgraduate, however, you may be expected to take responsibility for acting safely. You may need to work with toxic chemicals, dangerous instruments, or in hazardous environments, so care is essential. At an initial meeting with your supervisor, you will be introduced to relevant safety measures and legislation, told about the fire drill and shown relevant hazard symbols (Figure 19.1).

In the lab, you will be expected to wear a lab coat – which should always be buttoned up – and, if you have long hair, asked to tie it back. Eye protection goggles may be necessary for some procedures, and those who normally wear contact lenses may be subject to special rules because vapours of corrosive laboratory chemicals may become trapped between the lens and the cornea of the eye. You should never eat or smoke in a lab. You should also keep your bench space tidy and quickly dispose of specimens or sharps as instructed.

Where hazardous materials or procedures are involved, you will be told about the COSHH risk assessment (see tip on the next page) and you have a duty to read this carefully.

 Explosive

 Oxidising agent

 Extremely or highly flammable

 Toxic or very toxic

 Corrosive

 Harmful or irritant

 Dangerous for the environment

Figure 19.1 Some of the main EU hazard symbols.

Following safety procedures

Your university will have a safety office and policies in place for potentially dangerous procedures or to cover risks like exposure to hazardous chemicals. Ignoring these would be regarded as a serious disciplinary offence. Completing paper work, such as Control of Chemicals Hazardous to Health (COSHH) forms, should be regarded as an opportunity to learn about the risks associated with your work, rather than a chore.

When working with chemicals or live organisms such as bacteria, take appropriate precautions:

- be aware of all possible modes of ingestion, including inhalation by nose or mouth, ingestion by mouth, absorption through exposed skill, inoculation through skin;
- take special care with procedures such as pipetting or transferring samples between vessels;
- note where eye washes and emergency showers are located in your lab and understand the appropriate procedures when you come into contact with chemicals;
- know what to do to contain or remove accidentally spilt chemicals (you will also probably need to report such events);
- make sure you know what type of fire extinguisher or fire blanket to use for the reagents being used, and where these are located;
- always wash your hands thoroughly after each lab.

Definition: COSHH

This stands for 'Control of Substances Hazardous to Health' – a UK regulation that came into force in 1999. It lays out the legal framework for risk assessment whenever hazardous chemicals, agents or procedures are used. Normally the person in charge of your lab work or field visit (your supervisor or a senior lab technician) will carry out a COSHH assessment, which should be displayed prominently and/or communicated to you.

For field visits, you will be advised about appropriate clothing. You should take special care to use appropriate footwear and be prepared for a change of weather conditions. If in a group, you should stay close to the main body of people; otherwise, try always to work with a partner, rather than alone. Any field work group should:

- take a first aid kit (and know how to use it, following basic first aid procedures);
- leave full details of where they are going and when they expect to return;
- consult a weather forecast before they leave, and if working on the sea-shore, find out about the state of the tides.

Modelling safe practice for others

Safety procedures are often common sense but how you observe them is part of your community responsibility. In the lab, as a PhD student, you will represent a role model for undergraduates and less experienced researchers. Hence it is important that you lead by setting a good example in your practice in the practical environment be it in the laboratory or in the field.

ACTION POINTS

19.1 Brainstorm the ethical dimensions of your research. Using this chapter as a guide, elaborate on these aspects and any others you should be taking into account – then research them fully. Where possible, discuss ethical dimensions of research with peers and academic staff. This will raise your awareness of issues that can arise and may also provide you with some benchmarks against which to judge your own study.

19.2 Familiarise yourself with the ethics guidelines that govern research activity in your specialist field. Often the guidelines are provided in the literature of your professional association. Look also at 'Materials and Methods' sections in relevant research papers to establish the norms for ethical behaviour your field of work. Use a search engine to identify any major cases that have raised ethical issues in the research context.

19.3 Address ethical and safety issues as soon as you can. If there are likely to be significant ethical and safety dimensions to your project, ask to meet up with your supervisor at an early stage to discuss these issues and how they should be handled.

20

CITING, REFERENCING AND AVOIDING PLAGIARISM

How to refer appropriately to the results and ideas of others

The ability to cite and quote sources correctly in your text and create an appropriately formatted reference list is essential for thesis and publication writing. This chapter outlines conventions and linguistic styles for achieving this.

KEY TOPICS

→ The rationale for correct citation and referencing

→ Avoiding plagiarism

→ Methods and styles of citation

→ Quotation techniques

→ Summarising and paraphrasing

→ An outline of referencing styles

With the advent of digital archiving and searching systems, today's researchers have, at their fingertips, a wide array of accessible material to support their learning and writing. Clearly, the ability to search, copy, paste and adapt that material has many advantages, but it also brings the risk of plagiarism closer. That risk can be ameliorated via the processes of citation, referencing, quotation and paraphrasing, when these are carried out in an appropriate way. This chapter outlines the principles behind these processes so that you can, from the outset, apply them correctly in your thesis and any publications.

Details of specific referencing styles

There are many referencing styles, each with very specific rules for layout and punctuation. Space precludes detailed descriptions here; instead the focus is on principles. The companion text McMillan and Weyers (2013) focuses on five of the main styles: American Psychological Association, Chicago, Harvard, Modern Languages Association and Vancouver, and should be consulted for guidance.

THE RATIONALE FOR CORRECT CITATION AND REFERENCING

Many citation and referencing systems exist and, over time, some have been modified to create an even wider array of similar and sometimes competing systems. When choosing and using one of these, the focus is often on the mechanics – the apparently complex and arcane layout and punctuation rules that cause so much angst to novice academic authors. However, there is more to following the conventions than slavish devotion to pressing the punctuation keys in the right places or sprinkling your writing indiscriminately with citations. The rationale behind the rules and conventions of citation and referencing can be approached via explanations of the key terms involved:

1 Plagiarism. Academic authors demonstrate their scholarship by writing and publishing in their own fields. They have the moral right to claim such work as their own property (this is sometimes referred to loosely rather than in the legal sense as 'intellectual property'). Hence, the academic community requires that academic authors, whether undergraduate, postgraduate or researcher, attribute the ownership of ideas, text and other forms of work to the original writers. There are two intertwined strands to avoiding plagiarism: the need to maintain your academic integrity, that is, your honesty, by giving correct attribution to sources; and the need to demonstrate your critical thinking skills (**Ch 17**), namely, your ability to analyse and synthesise new text from complex information.

2 Citation. In the academic environment, citation involves linking an idea within a new text to information or data derived from another source document and its author(s). This gives recognition to the original author by providing sufficient information from

the publication details so that the reader can locate the original document, if they wish. Integration of the ideas of others can be done:

- by direct quotation, that is, writing down what they wrote word for word; or
- by paraphrasing the idea in words that are different from those of the original author.

Whichever of these methods is adopted, the actual attribution in the text, namely, the publishing details, will follow the citation and referencing style required for your writing.

3 Referencing. There are two usages in the context of academic writing: providing information in the text about authorship of the original source material; and providing the publication details in some kind of footnote, reference list or bibliography in accordance with the citation and referencing style being followed. The rationale for this is:

- to protect the 'intellectual property' of the original author by acknowledging their contribution; and
- to provide readers with specific bibliographical information.

By structuring and presenting your views with appropriate attention to the published evidence, you enhance the quality of your research and acknowledge the contribution of others to the literature. Thus, learning how to cite and reference is essential to successful academic writing and will help you to achieve the highest of standards in your work.

AVOIDING PLAGIARISM

Academic literature is produced after extensive study of existing publications and developed through applied or theoretical research into the topic. The convention has developed that academics in their own writing cite the work of others to respect the original thinking and consequent ownership of that work – in effect, the intellectual property behind it. All academic authors are expected to follow this convention. To fail to do so is regarded as unethical. Institutions and the departments or schools within them have come to recognise the need to mark out their ethical position by having a formal code of practice on plagiarism, while some require students sign a disclaimer on their work to the effect that the work is entirely of their own making. A statement of this kind will be required at the start of your PhD thesis (**Ch 30**).

Definitions of terms

Some terms connected with referencing, citation and plagiarism are loosely used. Here are the definitions adopted for this text.

Citation (noun) – a quotation (a book, its author, or a passage from it) as an example or a proof; a mention as an example or illustration.

To cite (verb) – to use a phrase or sentence from a piece of writing or speech, especially in order to support or prove something.

Reference (noun) – a direction in a book to another passage or another book where information can be found; a book or passage referred to.

To reference (verb) – to mention a particular writer or piece of work; to create a list of all the books that are mentioned in a piece of academic writing.

Plagiarism (noun) – the process of taking another person's work, ideas, or words and using them as if they are your own.

To plagiarise (verb) – to take someone else's work, ideas, or words and use them as if they were your own.

Unfortunately, plagiarism occurs at all levels of study. Some notable cases have been reported where the use of search engines, for example, has exposed instances years after the plagiarism occurred. Whatever the circumstances, the negative consequences can be seriously damaging – shame, loss of professional status, loss of job, loss of marks, loss of degree and even expulsion from the institution. Thus, the pressure on academic authors not to plagiarise is significant.

Some people think (wrongly) that plagiarism can be averted by:

- creating a patchwork of quotations from original text; or
- substituting one or two words with synonyms; or
- rearranging the wording of the original text; or
- re-ordering the order of sentences; or
- mixing any of the above strategies.

These misconceptions can lead to unintended plagiarism where it appears that the writer has simply not understood the conventions and practices of engaging with the work of others within their own work.

However, there is a very thin line between unintended and deliberate plagiarism.

The right way to avoid plagiarism is to:

- cite the work of others when this is due;
- quote others' work where this is appropriate (within limits), with due citation;
- paraphrase the ideas or text of others, with due citation.

As can be seen, the key is appropriate citation. There can be no exceptions to this and you must preserve your academic integrity by following this academic convention.

METHODS AND STYLES OF CITATION

There are two fundamental ways of citing authors within the text, which are used according to your purpose.

1 Information-prominent citation. Here the text provides the idea or result first, and then provides the citation. This approach tends to be used when the statement being made is regarded as generally accepted in the field of study. For example:

> Providing enough copies of essential texts is a problem for university librarians and this can be a factor in students using the internet as their first research choice (Monaghan, 2012).

Alternatively, the statement may relate to literature that is less recent and which provides the foundation of a thread of research or reasoning. For example:

> Books have developed from handwritten texts illuminated by scribes to mass produced paperbacks that bring the printed word to all (Francis, 1991).

Note that these examples follow the Harvard style, in which the author's name and the date of publication are given in brackets.

2 Author-prominent citation. Author-prominent citation is used when the statement is more recent or contemporary or when the stress is on the ownership of the finding or idea, as when comparing two schools of thought. For example:

> O'Donnell (2010) surmised that the implications of downloading lengthy texts from the internet may infringe the intellectual property rights of authors. Smith (2011), on the other hand...

This example again follows the Harvard style, where the author's name is included as part of the sentence (in this case as the subject of the sentence); the date of publication is encased in round brackets and follows immediately after the name of the author.

How many citations do I need to include?

A whole string of citations does not add to the merit of writing if these are not germane to the purpose of discussion in the text. It is better to build up a cogent analysis of the existing literature identifying seminal works from which to build the framework of your analysis of the literature. From there you can then include citations that support your particular line of investigation or examine contrasting views or evidence with which you may or may not agree. If you look at a few articles in your own field, you will obtain a sense of the extent to which multiple references are the norm or whether only the more recent publications are cited. Following these practices will be important to you in the thesis writing process.

Conveying attitude in citation

When you select an idea to include in your work, it should be because of its relevance to your discussion. Therefore, to help direct your reader along a particular line of thought and to help build your discussion, your choice of verb reporting the authorship of the source material is important. This verb choice will be dictated by the function you are trying to perform using the source material as supporting evidence. Thus, for example, to demonstrate critical thinking (**Ch 17**), you may wish to introduce material to:

- provide factual information;
- present evidence that is non-controversial and universally accepted;
- express opinion;
- support or refute ideas or research within your own discussion;
- offer alternative viewpoints or approaches – either in agreement or contradictory.

Table 20.1 itemises some reasons that govern the decision to cite the work of others. These factors can be categorised according to whether they mark the beginning of a research theme – the 'received wisdom' in a particular field, or whether they take a positive or a negative view of existing literature, or whether they are outlining processes described in

Table 20.1 **Reasons for citing the work of others.** Source: This table is derived from *www.garfield.library.upenn.edu/papers/vladivostok.html* [Accessed 24 March 2012].

Rationale for citation	Positive context	Negative context	Processes involved
Indicating key reading to establish the context of work	Validating claims in earlier literature	Critiquing published literature reporting earlier research	Identifying methodology, equipment, etc.
Acknowledging the work of early investigators in a particular field	Acknowledging previous well-received work in a field	Identifying work that is not well-written, or related to existing literature	Authenticating data and classes of fact
Identifying original publications in which an idea or concept was first introduced	Identifying seminal literature	Rejecting the work or ideas of others (negative claims)	Alerting researchers to forthcoming work
Identifying the original publication describing an eponymic concept or terms such as Parkinson's Disease, the Peter Principle, Asperger's Syndrome or Boyle's Law	Acknowledging priority	Disputing the 'priority claims' of others, that is, questioning claims of 'ownership' of the instigation of a research theme or aspect within it or of ground-breaking achievements	Challenging the validity or merit of the work of others in respect of procedural methods or data interpretation

the literature. If there is a single 'golden rule', then it is that the citations should be relevant to the purpose of the author making the citations.

Whatever your purpose in citing the work of others, in order to make the citation, you will have to attribute the idea to the original author. However, how you report that work will reflect 'attitude' – that could be, how the content reflects the work of the original author as perceived in the academic world, or how you view the content. Within your discussion, it makes a considerable difference to interpretation if you report: *Brown contended that...* (meaning 'disputed in face of controversy') as opposed to: *Brown noted that...* (meaning 'made special mention of...') and both take the reader much further in their understanding of the case that has been compiled in the text than simply *Brown said that...* or *Brown stated that....* Table 20.2 provides some examples of positive and negative attitude verbs that are commonly used to report the work of others in academic texts.

Table 20.2 Attitude verbs used to report the work of others. This table derives from analysis of academic discourse across a range of disciplines. This is by no means comprehensive, but it reflects the diversity of expressions used in relation to citing the ideas and work of others. The shading in the table illustrates functions (column 3). The upper part of the table deals with positive connotations, while the lower part covers negative connotations.

Attitude verb in past tense	Definition in present tense	Function(s)
Positive connotation examples		
concurred with the view	be in accord	agreeing
supported the view	concur	agreeing
alleged	assert without proof	affirming
asserted	state firmly	affirming/declaring
averred	declare positively	affirming
declared	state emphatically	affirming/alleging
decreed	decide authoritatively	affirming/dictating
professed	claim forcefully	affirming/declaring
contended	dispute in face of controversy	alleging/maintaining
claimed	state to be true when open to question	alleging/maintaining
explained	make understandable	clarifying/simplifying
proclaimed	announce officially and publicly	clarifying
expounded the view	simplify by giving detail	clarifying/elucidating
reflected	make a statement of opinion	commenting/observing
affirmed	maintain to be true	confirming/validating
established	make of truth based on evidence	confirming
conjectured	infer from inconclusive evidence	conjecturing/surmising
guessed	form an opinion with little evidence	conjecturing/surmising
hypothesised	believe tentatively without evidence	conjecturing/theorising
inferred	conclude from evidence or facts	conjecturing/theorising
supposed	consider as a suggestion	conjecturing/suggesting
surmised	infer without sufficient evidence	conjecturing/guessing
defined something as...	state precise meaning	describing
characterised	categorise	describing
believed	accept as true or real	judging

Continued overleaf

Attitude verb in past tense	Definition in present tense	Function(s)
judged	form an opinion through reasoning	judging/evaluating
commented	explain judgementally	judging/interpreting
held the view	have an opinion	judging/opining
insisted	express an opinion strongly	judging strongly
noted	make special mention of...	judging/commenting
observed	understand through known facts	judging
opined that...	express a view	judging/stating belief
posited the view	put forward an idea for consideration	judging/offering opinion
stated	express particulars in words	judging/formulating
suggested	present for consideration	proposing/suggesting
advanced the view	bring to notice	proposing
proposed	put forward for consideration	proposing/proffering
Negative connotation examples		
warned	recommend caution	advising against
diverged	take different routes	differing
disagreed	to have a different opinion	disagreeing with
disputed	question on basis of poor evidence	disagreeing with
doubted	consider unlikely	disagreeing with
opposed	be resistant to an idea	disagreeing with
criticised	judge on basis of good and bad points	disapproving
disdained	regard with scorn	disapproving/ despise
questioned the view	express uncertainty	doubting/ disputing

Thus, your choice of reporting verb reflects your own attitude as well as that of the original author. This helps to construct your own argument and subliminally leads your reader through the analysis you are presenting. Table 20.2 also provides you with choices so that you do not 'wear out' particular verbs (and your reader/supervisor's patience) by repeatedly using the same wording.

Use of tense in reporting the work of others

Citation of the work of others has to be placed in a time frame. However, there is some inconsistency in practice in that some writers use the present tense to report the literature while others adopt a simple past tense. Those who favour the present tense might argue that the text is in front of the reader and therefore it is acceptable to use the present tense (*Brown contends that...*). However, other writers would state that:

- the research work has already been done;
- a view has already been presented for consideration by the academic world.

Hence, they reason that the simple past tense should be used (*Brown observed that...*).

You should ensure that you are consistent in the tense that you use, but note that the present tense is used regardless of time-frame to describe habitual conditions, for example, '*traditionalists argue that...*'.

Secondary citation in reporting the work of others

Secondary referencing occurs when a writer cites a source that they have not read themselves. This could be because the original is out of print or unavailable to them for other reasons. In this case, the item that is cited is the text that they read personally. Formerly, secondary citation (secondary referencing) was rare and was discouraged or disallowed. This remains the policy in some of the more common referencing styles. However, with the ease of access to online literature, the incidence of secondary citation has become more prevalent and style guides are beginning to acknowledge that this is a fact of academic life. Figure 20.1 shows how to cite a secondary reference in the text following the Harvard style. However, note that the source that should be listed in the references is the text that the writer read, not the reference for the unread text. It is advisable to check the guidance given in your area since this can differ from one style to another.

An information-prominent secondary citation would be presented as:

One of the most powerful criticisms is that reading on-screen is, for many people, a painful activity (Owen, 2007 cited in Peel, 2010).

An author-prominent secondary citation would be presented as:

Owen (2007 cited in Peel, 2010) considered that 'one of the most powerful criticisms of reading on-screen is that, for many people, this is a painful activity'.

Figure 20.1 **Two examples of secondary referencing in the Harvard style.**
These examples use the form of words 'cited in' but it would be equally acceptable to use the form 'quoted in' where material had been quoted. Note that secondary referencing can be used in paraphrased citations as well as in direct quotations.

QUOTATION TECHNIQUES

Quoting text directly from source material has a place in academic writing in many disciplines, whereas, in others, it is uncommon. If used, it is best to be used sparingly since it would be very easy to drift inadvertently into plagiarism because too great a proportion of your thesis relies on direct extracts from others' work.

Before you decide to quote from the literature you have sourced, you should give considered thought as to why you want to include the exact words used by the original author. Some questions to contemplate include:

- Will this quotation strengthen my discussion?
- Will the extract place special emphasis on the author's findings or viewpoint?
- Will the extract present a point that could be counter-argued?
- Will the words used make the author's point in a particularly powerful way that would be weakened if paraphrased?

Only if your response to any of these questions is 'yes', should you seriously consider including a quotation.

To quote correctly, you will need to assemble the following:

- the exact words from the text (sometimes described as '*verbatim* text');
- page number(s) or, in the case of journals, volume and page number;
- the publication details. Since different citation styles require different information, you might need all or only some of the following:
  - author(s)
  - date of publication
  - edition
  - editor(s)
  - title (of book, chapter or article)
  - journal title (if applicable)
  - place of publication
  - publisher.

These details in the main should become a routine part of your note-making practice (**Ch 8**).

When is quotation plagiarism?

As a 'rule of thumb' in many disciplines, if more than 10 per cent of a piece of work, article or book chapter is devoted to quotation, this is regarded is a form of plagiarism. The heavy reliance on the literature as a source of words, shows limited original thinking without real analysis or discussion of the issues and may even imply lack of understanding. However, it should be noted that in some disciplines, for example, English literature, more extensive quotation may be expected and thus does not constitute plagiarism, unless it has not been correctly attributed to its author.

Characteristics of quotations

The layout of quotations can differ from one discipline to another, but there are some key guidelines that can help you follow the general rules appropriately. Check the conventions in your particular discipline or subject area. In general, quotations may be laid out in one of the following formats:

- Long quotes consist of 30 or more words (some propose 40 words) of prose or two lines or more of poetry and should:
  - be indented by five character spaces from the left-hand margin
  - not include quotation marks at the beginning and end (only use quotation marks within the original text where these have been used in the original text)
  - be printed in single line spacing (although some styles require double-line spacing)
  - be followed by the author(s) surname, year of publication and page number separated by a full colon (:) or date of publication followed by page number printed as p. xx, depending on the preferred citation convention.

- Short quotes consist of fewer than 30 words and should:
  - be integrated within the sentence
  - include the author(s) name within the sentence where it often performs the role of the subject of the sentence. In this case, the date of publication would be in round brackets (...) immediately after the author name; and
  - give the page reference in round brackets (...) at the end of the quotation in the form p. xx.

These two methods are shown in Figure 20.2. Note that there are minor variations about punctuation across citation styles, so it is important to consult the relevant guidance source to check for any deviations from the 'official' style.

Quotations are commonly found 'dangling', under the title of the chapter or in the text, that is, without introduction or context so that the reader has no indication of the significance or relevance of the words quoted. Expecting your readers to make the connections for themselves is not indicative of well-explained logic and discussion. Thus, you should ensure throughout your writing that any quotation used in the text has a purpose and clear connection to the context in which it is found.

An essential prerequisite for monitoring demographic trends is efficient garnering of population data which means that the population census is essential to this process. Thus, while early records were relatively primitive in nature, more recent records that have been derived from computerised census data identify the relationship between birth rate and death rate as factors in population growth. This is described as the demographic transition model and is explained by Kay and Campbell (2011) as comprising

... four stages: high birth rate with fluctuating but high death rate; high birth rate with falling death rate; falling birth rate and falling death rate; and low birth rate with low death rate.

(Kay and Campbell, 2011:23)

More recent studies have attempted to interrogate the demographic transition model in order to identify socio-economic and ethnicity patterns from the birth-rate:death-rate data.

(a) Long quotation. This 'indentation' method is used where the quote is 30+ words or three lines of text. Note the positioning of the citation.

Simpson (1953) claimed that one factor affecting the demographic transition model involved 'the changing roles of women as key contributors to the economy since these roles impact on their traditional child-bearing roles' (p.63).

(b) Short quotation. This 'in text' method is used where the quote is less than 30 words or three lines of text. Note the positioning of the citation and that the quotation forms a part of the sentence, so the full stop is placed after the final quotation mark. This is different from the punctuation required in direct speech (the actual words said) in a novel or a newspaper report, for example.

Figure 20.2 Layouts for 'long' and 'short' quotations.

What forms of quotation marks should be used?

Single or double quote marks

Approaches to the use of quotation marks, which are sometimes called 'inverted commas', differ according to whether the text follows British English or American English.

- **British English**: Single quotation marks are used around the text to mark the exact words spoken or written. Any quote-within-the-quote is placed in double quotation marks.

- **American English**: Double quotation marks are used around the text to mark the exact words spoken or written. Any quote-within-the-quote is placed in single quotation marks.

Note that these conventions apply in most cases but there are some disciplines which do not follow them. Consult your supervisor if the required style differs from these.

'Curly' ('round') quotes or 'straight' quotes

Curly quotes are the inverted comma symbols that were found traditionally on typewriters. In word processors, these are sometimes referred to as 'smart quotes'. The single ones look like: **'this'** and double ones look like **"this"**. They resemble miniature digits 6 or 66 before the quotation words and digits 9 or 99 after the quotation.

Straight quotes are the inverted comma symbols that are often used by word processors as a single downward stroke. The single ones look like **this: '** and double ones look like **this: "**. There is no difference in form between the straight quotes before and after the quotation.

Ideally, 'curly' and 'straight' styles of quotation marks should not be mixed within the same document.

SUMMARISING AND PARAPHRASING

While quotation must exactly replicate the words in the original work of an author, the central concept of both summarising and paraphrasing is that writers use their own words rather than those of the original author, except in the following situations:

- where, within the paraphrase or summary, a direct quotation from the source document is used; or

- where there is use of same or similar wording to state aspects that are common knowledge, for example, dates, well-known facts or anything regarded as published in the public domain in information/ reference sources such as dictionaries or encyclopaedias; or
- where 'shared', subject-specific language has been reproduced from the original.

In both summarising and paraphrasing the final text will be shorter than the original text. The point is to distil the essence of meaning from the original but with important differences.

1 Summarising: while recognising that technical terms or 'shared language' can be retained, the aim is to use your own words in writing (but giving less detail than in a paraphrase) to

- give the general idea
- state the main points briefly
- include only the views of the original author.

2 Paraphrasing: while recognising that technical terms or 'shared language' can be retained, the aim is to use your own words in writing (but giving more detail than in a summary) to

- explain the key idea(s)
- clarify their meaning
- include only the views of the original author.

The differences between these two approaches to restating the work of others are modelled in Figure 20.3. As well as indicating variation in content, the examples demonstrate visually the relative difference in length. Paraphrasing will reduce the original text but not as much as a summary which will be significantly shorter than the original text or section.

When you decide to include the work of another in your text, you need to treat each citation as unique. As explained above, you will have evaluated the text and so have a reason for choosing to incorporate material from the literature. This will reflect the function that citation will perform within your text – supporting your viewpoint, critiquing other views and so on (see Table 20.2). This may also dictate whether you wish to introduce an idea in more general terms by summarising or elucidate a discussion in greater detail by paraphrasing.

Table 20.3 provides strategies for summarising and paraphrasing. The advantage of summarising and paraphrasing in these ways is that there is much less risk of plagiarism because you are using your own words and writing style to create the shorter version; you are also demonstrating your ability to engage with the material and reach conclusions that demonstrate your critical thinking skills **(Ch 17)**. In addition, as you become more practised and at ease with the process, you will be able to summarise or paraphrase by omitting some of the steps. These approaches will also help you to achieve a deeper understanding of the text and allow you to exploit the ideas more effectively in your own analysis.

A. Original text (51 words)

E-books are a function of the internet era and make access to otherwise unattainable material possible to wider audiences. The globalisation of literature means that individual authors can present their work to a wider audience without incurring abortive publication costs. This facility constitutes a considerable threat to publishers of traditional books. [51 words]

Source: Watt, W. (2011) *The demise of the book*. Cambridge: The Printing Press (page 13)

B. Summarised text (19 words)

With the advent of e-books, individual authors are faced with new approaches to publication of their work (Watt, 2011).

C. Paraphrased text (40 words)

Watt (2011) notes that there is concern amongst publishers of hard-copy printed books that the advent of e-books marks the end of their monopoly of the literature market since authors can publish directly from the internet thus avoiding publishing costs.

Figure 20.3 Examples of summarised and paraphrased text. Examples A and B follow the Harvard Style; B follows information-prominent style and C follows author-prominent citation.

Table 20.3(a) Strategies for integrating the work of others in your text.
McMillan and Weyers (2013) provide real-text examples of using these
approaches.

A strategy for summarising
Step 1: Identify the main idea or theme
• Read the topic and terminator paragraphs to identify the main ideas of the text.
• Read the topic sentences of the intervening paragraphs allocating a defining term to each paragraph to identify and note the main topic, point, argument or counter-argument presented within the paragraph. Write these terms as a list of words; this list will give you an overview of the content of the whole text.
• Highlight points of particular relevance to your reason for citing this source material.
• Go back and read the whole text (or the section most relevant to your own purpose).
Step 2: Write out your own version of the text
• Leave the text and do something else for a spell.
• Then return to the task and without looking at your notes and using your own words, try to write down your recollection of the main theme(s) and complementary points.
• Check your version with your earlier notes; add in anything that you have omitted.
Step 3: Reduce the word length
• Using your 'own word' version, remove unnecessary words or change word order or syntax to create shorter sentences or phrases.
Step 4: Create the summary
• Start by signposting the author, identify the main theme and key points, link these to the discussion in your own text. The summary can extend to a number of sentences. Either author-prominent or information-prominent formats may be used.

Table 20.3(b) **Strategies for integrating the work of others in your text.**

Three different strategies for paraphrasing	
1. Underlining approach Reduces content in three different steps to achieve the paraphrase.	**Step 1:** On a copy of the text, underline phrases and words that can be removed, either because they are verbose, or because they do not suit your purpose. **Step 2:** Eliminate those words, leaving the 'bare' relevant text. **Step 3:** Reword the remaining text and the ideas within.
2. Reporters' questions Allows deconstruction of the original text and gives a strategy for engaging with the original meaning and intention of the text.	**Step 1:** Read the original text. **Step 2:** Underline key points of interest. **Step 3:** Turn over original, and answer the reporters' questions in relation to the text. These are who?, what?, when?, where?, why? and how? **Step 4:** Use the key elements identified in step 3 to reconfigure the text to your purpose.
3. Theme re-grouping approach Allows deconstruction of the text by identifying its key themes and then rewording and reordering these.	**Step 1:** Paragraph by paragraph, identify the theme and key point of each and note these down (you may wish to number these, but this in not essential). **Step 2:** With reference to your purpose, select and reorder the themes, and points (you might use a different coloured pen to do this). **Step 3:** Write the paraphrase in your own words using the key point listing as a framework. It is acceptable to use a certain amount of shared wording if this is essential use of jargon or standard phrases.

AN OUTLINE OF REFERENCING STYLES

As a postgraduate, you will meet a range of referencing styles during your literature searching and reading. Being aware of the conventions associated with these styles is important as they may differ from those with which you are familiar.

Referencing systems can be classified as follows. Note that there are many permutations of 'rules' or interpretations within each of these approaches:

1 Author name/date (sometimes called parenthetical) systems are used in the social sciences and humanities as well as the natural sciences. However, there are significant differences about layout and language related to these and you should consult the guidelines you have been given for your recommended style. For example:

   'Campbell and Hutton (2012) suggested that ...'

2 Numeric/footnote plus reference/bibliography list systems are used in scientific styles to give information in a numbered footnote about authorship on the same page as the citation first appears. Numbering may be full-size or superscript. For example:

   'In the view of Campbell and Hutton[15]...'

3 Author name/page number systems are used in some disciplines within the humanities and includes the Modern Languages Association – (MLA) style. For example:

   'In the view of Campbell and Hutton (133) observed that...'

4 Numeric systems (sometimes called numbered or scientific systems) are used most commonly in the Sciences. It would inadvisable to use a system like this unless you have been told to do so. The number relates to the number of the reference in the reference list. For example:

   'In the view of Campbell and Hutton (15)...'or 'In the view of Campbell and Hutton15...

Figure 20.4 shows typical components of a Reference List or Bibliographic entry (sometimes called 'Works cited'). The layout and punctuation differs from one style to another. In practice, authors and universities tend to adhere to styles that are the norm for their disciplines or the departments within their institutions or the publishers of academic journals in their subject area.

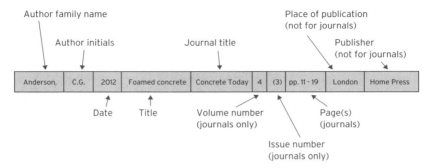

Figure 20.4 The main components of a reference as listed in a reference section (or bibliography or 'works cited' section). The precise details of order and punctuation will depend on the referencing style used.

Five commonly used referencing systems are illustrated in Table 20.4. This takes as an example a citation and reference to a journal article, but there are specific formats for other forms of publication, each differing according to the style adopted. Examples include: books, chapters in books, newspaper articles, e-journals, e-books and websites extending recently to blogs and wikis. You will find the specific details of the relevant styles in McMillan and Weyers (2013) or in the 'instructions to authors' section of journals.

Table 20.4 Five commonly used referencing styles. With each is shown the format of a citation and reference that would be used when referring to material from an article in a journal. For formats used with other types of source, see McMillan and Weyers (2013).

1 American Psychological Association (APA) style This is used in both sciences and social sciences. It follows a name/date style. Note that APA spacing for the Reference List should be double-line.
In publishing, for example, several notorious cases of plagiarism exist where the text and plot of a best seller have close similarities to the text and plot of another book by another author (Scribner, 2006).   Scribner, A. (2006). Authorship by proxy: the case of the non-original best-seller. *Journal of Professional Ethics* 2(3), 51–59.

Continued overleaf

2 Chicago Style This style is used in the scientific community and social sciences where a scientific approach has been followed. It follows a numeric/footnote style. Note that there are two options for laying out the Footnotes and the Reference List:

1. Footnotes are at the bottom of the page beneath a line across the page or as a list of endnotes at the end of the text with a full bibliography of all works cited at the end of the text.

2. Full citations in the footnotes or endnotes for the first mention and thereafter as concise notes; there is no bibliography.

In publishing, for example, there are several notorious cases where a best seller has been shown to be closely similar to another book by another author.[2]

Footnote or Endnote
2. Scribner, "Authorship by Proxy: the Case of the Non-original Best-seller," *Journal of Professional Ethics*, 2, no.3 (2006): 59.

Bibliography
Scribner, A. "Authorship by Proxy: the Case of the Non-original Best-seller." *Journal of Professional Ethics* 2 no.3 (2006):59.

3 Harvard Style which was not named after the US Harvard University but after John Harvard, an American clergyman, who bequeathed his library of books to Cambridge College, Massachusetts in 1637. This is one of the most commonly used styles and is accepted in disciplines across social and life sciences as well as in engineering. It follows the author/date style.

In publishing, for example, there are several notorious cases where a best seller has been shown to be closely similar to another book by another author (Scribner, 2006).

Scribner, A., 2006. Authorship by proxy: the case of the non-original best-seller. *Journal of Professional Ethics* 2(3), 51–59.

4 Modern Languages Association (MLA) Style as its name suggests is designed to suit disciplines in the humanities. It follows the author/page number style. Note URLs are no longer used but the medium is included at the end of the 'Works cited' (MLA term for Reference List). Also, double line-spacing is required for the reference list in this style.

In publishing, for example, there are several notorious cases where a best seller has been shown to be closely similar to another book by another author (Scribner 35).

Scribner, A. "Authorship by Proxy: the Case of the Non-original Best-seller."

Journal of Professional Ethics 2(3) (2006): 51–59. Print.

5 Vancouver Style is most commonly used in the medicine and related fields. It follows the numeric (scientific) style.

In publishing, for example, there are several notorious cases where a best seller has been shown to be closely similar to another book by another author. (1)

1. Scribner A. Authorship by proxy: the case of the non-original best-seller. *J Prof Ethics* 2006 Mar 3; 2(3): 51–59.

20.1 Find out about the citation and referencing style expected for your thesis work. Your supervisor should be able to guide you, or talk through the options, and the format may be specified in departmental or university rules. Once you know this, you can ensure that you format any citations and reference you use in draft text in the correct way, saving a lot of time and effort later on. At this stage you should consider whether using a referencing software package such as Endnote or Zotaro might be a useful strategy (**Ch 9**).

20.2 Examine your use of language when citing references. Use an early report or your project proposal. Do you use the same forms of wording repeatedly? Review the options mentioned in this chapter to see if you can expand your repertoire and provide more variety and accuracy in your writing.

20.3 Look self-critically at some of your writing to check whether your skills in summarising and paraphrasing could be improved. Do you feel you have mastered these techniques? If not, review the points in this chapter and test out some of the methods to see which might suit your way of working.

21

INTERPRETING AND PRESENTING DATA

How to understand and produce graphs, tables and basic statistics

PhD research often calls for detailed examination of results portrayed graphically and in tables. In certain disciplines you may need to present your own data using these means and then interpret what they signify. Often, this can only be done with the aid of relevant statistics.

KEY TOPICS

→ How to 'read' a graph

→ How graphs can mislead

→ Creating graphs

→ Creating tables

→ Important descriptive statistics

→ Concepts of hypothesis-testing statistics

There are many ways of presenting data sets and the methods chosen can affect your analysis or favour certain interpretations. A healthily critical approach is therefore essential when you are examining graphs, tables and statistics. Equally, when creating these items to condense and display your own information, your primary aim should always be to do this in a manner that is simple to understand and unbiased.

It is beyond the scope of this book to discuss all the possible modes of presentation and analysis; instead, this chapter provides a quick refresher on data interpretation and outlines the basic principles for constructing graphs and tables. The examples are simplified in order to demonstrate the processes rather than to illustrate advanced content.

Graph types

Some common forms are illustrated throughout this chapter, but a quick way of finding out about different options is to explore the forms available in a spreadsheet program like Microsoft Excel. Look at the 'Insert > Chart > Standard Types' menu, which illustrates sub-types and provides brief descriptions. This is also a good way of exploring ways of presenting your own data.

HOW TO 'READ' A GRAPH

The following elements are present in most graphs and charts (collectively known as 'figures'). Use them to work out what a specific graph means, referring to the example shown in Figure 21.1.

● The figure title and its caption. These should appear below the graph. Read them first to determine the overall context and gain information about what the graph shows. If the caption is detailed, you may need to revisit it later to aid your interpretation.

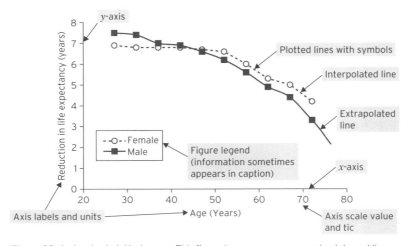

Figure 89 A standard plotted curve. This figure type uses *x-y* axes and points and lines to illustrate the relationship between two variables. *Source*: Data modified from Rogers, R.G. and Powell-Griner E., 1991. Life expectancies of cigarette smokers and non-smokers in the United States. *Soc. Sci. Med.*, 32, 1151–9.

Figure 21.1 The basic components of a graph.

Checklist for interpreting a graph

❑ Consider the context by reading the title, legend and main text.

❑ Recognise the type of graph.

❑ Examine what the axes show.

❑ Inspect the scale of the axes.

❑ Study the symbols and plotted curves.

❑ Evaluate what any error bars or statistics mean.

- The type of figure. With experience, you will come to recognise the basic chart types (Figure 21.2) and others common in your discipline. This will help you to orientate yourself. For example, a pie chart is usually used to show proportions of a total.

- The axes. Many forms of chart represent the relationship between two variables, called x and y for convenience. These are often presented between a pair of axes at right angles, with the horizontal x-axis often relating to the 'controlled' variable (for example, concentration or time) and the vertical y-axis often relating to the 'measured' variable (for example, income, weight (mass), or response). More than one measured variable may be plotted on the same graph, either using the same x-axis, or a second one (see Figure 21.2(b)). Some types of graph don't follow this pattern and if you are unfamiliar with the form being used, you may need to investigate further.

Plural terms

The following plurals are often misused or misunderstood:

Axis = singular;

Axes = plural;

Datum = singular;

Data = plural (hence, the 'data are presented in Figure 14').

- The axis scale and units. An axis label should state what the axis means and the units being used. Each axis should show clearly the range of values it covers through a series of cross-marks (tic, or tick, marks) with associated numbers to indicate the scale. To interpret these, you'll also need to know the units. Some axes do not start from zero, or incorporate a break in the scale; others may be non-linear (for example, a logarithmic axis is sometimes used to cover particularly wide ranges of numbers). Pay attention in these cases, because this could mean that the graph exaggerates or emphasises differences between values (see Figures 21.3(a) and (b)).

- The symbols and plotted curves. These help you to identify the different data sets being shown and the relationship between the points in each set. A legend or key may be included to make this clearer. Your interpretation may focus on differences in the relationships and, inevitably, on the plotted curves (also known as 'trend lines'). However, it is important to realise that the curves are usually hypothetical interpolations between measured values or, worse, extrapolations beyond them; and, because they may involve assumptions about trends in the data, they should be examined with care. Symbols may also include information about variability in the data collected (for example, error bars), which provide useful clues about the reliability of data and assumed trends.

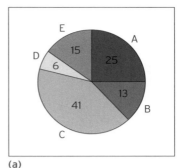

(a)

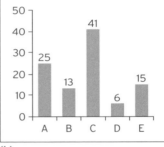

(b)

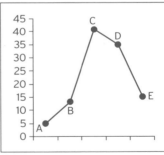

(c)

Figure 21.2 Common forms of graph. These are in addition to the standard plotted curve shown in Figure 21.1. (a) Pie chart, showing proportions of a total – here expressed as percentages. (b) Histogram, showing amounts in different categories. (c) Frequency polygon, showing distribution of counted data across a continuous range.

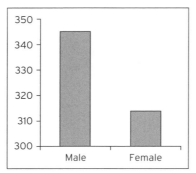 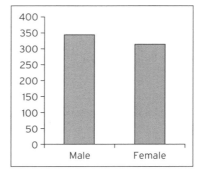

(a) Use of non-zero axis. In the chart on the left, it looks as if the differences between males and females are large; however, when the y-axis is zeroed, as on the right, the differences are much less noticeable.

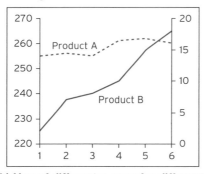 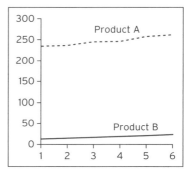

(b) Use of different y-axes for different curves. In the chart on the left it looks as if sales of product A (left-hand axis) are being caught up by those of product B (right-hand axis); however, when the same axis is used for both curves, then it can be seen that product B vastly outsells product A.

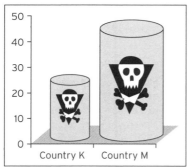 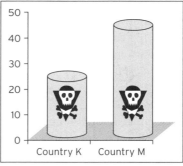

(c) Use of a two- or three-dimensional object to represent a linear scale. In the chart on the left, the barrel retains its shape in relation to the y-axis scale, so it makes it look as if country M produces much more toxic waste than country K. On the right, a truly linear representation is shown.

Figure 21.3 Three common examples of misleading graphs.

HOW GRAPHS CAN MISLEAD

You can learn a lot about data presentation by reviewing misleading graphs and learning why they might lead to incorrect interpretations. A selection of examples is shown in Figure 21.3. You should try to avoid confusing your audience by using these forms of misrepresentation when constructing your own figures.

Definitions: graphing

Interpolation: an assumed trend or relationship *between* available data points.

Extrapolation: an assumed trend or relationship *before* or *after* (below or above) available data points. Extrapolation is risky because the assumption may be made that a trend will continue when there may be little evidence that this will happen.

CREATING GRAPHS

What follows is naturally a generalisation, but this sequence will suit many circumstances.

1 Think carefully about what you want to plot and why, then choose an appropriate type of graph. Recognising the type of data you want to present is essential for this, and reviewing the common options shown in Figures 21.1 and 21.2 may help. If you are choosing a plotted curve, then you must decide which variable will appear on the *x*-axis and which on the *y*-axis. If you have selected an unfamiliar form of graph, you may wish to sketch out how this will appear for your data set. A spreadsheet can be a valuable tool when working through this phase.

2 Consider the range and units for the axes, where appropriate. What are the upper and lower limits of your data? Should you start each axis at zero, and, if not, will this act to distort the presentation (see Figure 21.3(a))? Will your axes be linear? Will they be in the same units as your measurements, or might you wish to work out ratios, percentages or other transformations before graphing the data? Once you have settled on these aspects, you can write the descriptive label for the axis, which should first state what is

presented and then, usually in parentheses ( ) or after a solidus (/), the units used. Other forms of graph, such as a pie chart, may require a descriptive label for each segment, or you may prefer to use a legend or key.

3 Choose elements of presentation. For example, if you are using a pie chart, select colours or shading for the segments. If your graph has axes, decide how frequently you wish the tics to appear: too many and the axis will seem crowded, too few and it becomes less easy to work out the approximate values of data points. Decide which symbols will be used for which data sets, and if presenting several graphs in sequence, try to be consistent on this. If measures of location (Table 21.1) are plotted, consider whether you wish to add error bars to show the variability in the data.

Adding trend lines to graphs

If you are drawing a graph, you will need to take special care when adding a curve, because any trend line you add indicates that you have assumed an underlying relationship between the variables. If the points carry no (rare) or very little error, then you may be justified in drawing a straight line or curve between each point. If, however, the points do carry error, then the curve should take an 'average' line between them. Since most plotted relationships are complex, then this probably should be a smooth curve rather than a straight line.

4 Write the figure caption. Your aim should be to ensure that the figure is 'self-contained' and that its essence can be understood without reference to detail normally given elsewhere, such as the material and methods section of a scientific report. Items to include here are:

– the figure number and title

– what the symbols and error bars mean (a legend or key within the figure may or may not be acceptable – check)

– if appropriate, how the plotted curve was chosen

– any brief details about the data (for example, differences in the treatments) that will help your reader understand the figure better without having to refer to another section.

The title and caption should always appear below the figure.

CREATING TABLES

A good table presents data in a compact, readily assimilated format. In general, you should not include the same data in a chart and a table. You might decide to use a table rather than a chart if:

- graphic presentation is not suitable for some or all of the data (for instance, when some are qualitative);
- there are too many data sets or variables to include in a chart;
- your audience might be interested in the precise values of some of your data;
- you wish to place large amounts of your data on record, for instance within an appendix to a report.

Think about and draw a rough design for your table before constructing a final version. Key elements include:

- The title and caption. Your table must have these as a guide to the content, just like a figure. Note that the numbering scheme for tables is independent from that of graphs. Titles and captions should always appear above the table.
- Appropriate arrangement and headings. Each vertical column should display a particular type of data, and the descriptive headings should reflect these contents, giving the units where data are quantitative. Each row might show different instances of these types of data. Rows and columns should be arranged in a way that helps the reader to compare them if this is desirable.
- Rulings. The default in word-processing programs such as Microsoft Word is to add boxed lines to tables; however, the modern style is to minimise these, often restricting their use to horizontal lines only.
- Data values. These should be presented to an appropriate number of significant figures. An indication of errors, if included, should be given in parentheses, and the heading should make it clear what statistic is being quoted.
- Footnotes. These can be used to explain abbreviations or give details of specific cases.

Figure 21.4 illustrates some important components of a well-designed table.

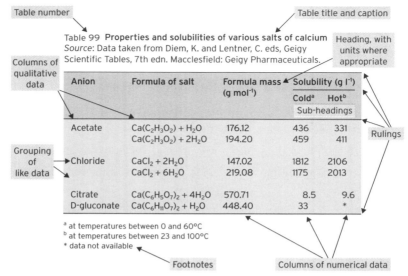

Figure 21.4 **The basic components of a table.** Note that shading is included here to emphasise the heading and data sections and would not usually be present.

 Definitions: data

Quantitative data: data that can be expressed in numbers, such as length, height or price.

Qualitative data: data that are descriptive and non-numerical, such as colour, place of manufacture, or name.

IMPORTANT DESCRIPTIVE STATISTICS

Descriptive statistics are used to simplify a complex data set, to summarise the distribution of data within the data set and to provide estimates of values of the population frequency distribution. Two aspects that are often quoted are:

- a measure of location – this is an estimate of the 'centre' of the frequency distribution;
- a measure of dispersion – this is an estimate of the spread of data within the frequency distribution.

Definition: frequency distribution

This is a description of the frequency of occurrence of values of a variable. You may be interested in the actual distribution in the sample you have taken, and you might use a frequency polygon (Figure 21.2(c)) to represent this. You might also be interested in the underlying population frequency distribution. This is often theoretical in nature and a smooth curve representing a model function might be used to represent it.

Different measures of location and dispersion are outlined in Table 21.1 and many of these values can be obtained simply, using a spreadsheet or statistical program. More complex descriptive statistics such as standard error (describing the precision of a mean), or quantifying the shape of frequency distributions, are outside the scope of this text and a specialist text should be consulted.

CONCEPTS OF HYPOTHESIS-TESTING STATISTICS

Hypothesis testing in a statistical context is used to compare the properties of a data set with other samples or to compare the data set with some theory about it.

Error and variability exist in all data sets (see box below), which means that it is impossible to be 100 per cent certain about differences between sets. Are the differences 'genuine' and due to a true

Sources of random error and variability

The following are reasons why the values and hence the descriptive statistics of samples of data may vary.

- **Sampling error**, due to the selection of a small number of individuals from a larger, variable population.

- **Measurement error**, due to the method of measurement of the variable.

- **Rounding error**, due to an attempt to use an appropriate number of significant figures, but often compounded in calculations.

- **Human error**, due to inaccurate writing or copying of data, mixing up of samples, and so on.

- **Error from unknown sources**, or unappreciated effects of sampling.

Table 21.1 Descriptive statistics and their uses

Measure	Statistic	How to calculate*	Uses, advantages and disadvantages
Location	Mean	The sum of all the data values divided by the number of values, n.	The most commonly used measure. It takes account of all the values in the data set, but can be influenced by the presence of outliers and is not representative of the whole body of data if this is asymmetric. Units are the same as the data.
	Median	The mid-point of the data values when they are ranked in numerical order. For odd-sized data sets, it is the value of the middle datum, while for even-sized data sets, it is the mean of the two central values.	May represent the location of the majority of the data better than the mean if the data set is asymmetric or there are outliers. Units are the same as the data.
	Mode	The most common value in the data set.	Easily found and unaffected by outliers; however, especially when the data set is small, it may be susceptible to 'random' variation in the distribution of values. Units are the same as the data.
Dispersion	Range	The difference between the largest and the smallest values in the data set.	Easy to determine, but its value is greatly affected by outliers and the size of the data set. Units are the the same as the data.
	Semi-interquartile range	The difference between the first and third quartiles, which are the median values for the data ranked below and above the median value of the whole data set.	Less easy to calculate than the range, but less affected by outliers and the size of the data set. Suitable to match with the median as a measure of location. Units are the same as the data.
	Variance	The sum of the squares of the difference between each data value and the mean, divided by $n - 1$.	Measures the average difference from the mean for all the data values. Good for data sets that are symmetrical about the mean. Units are the square of those of the data.
	Standard deviation	The positive square root of the variance.	A measure of the average difference from the mean for all the data values. Good for data sets symmetrical about the mean. Units are the same as the data, so preferable to the variance.
	Coefficient of variation	The standard deviation multiplied by 100 and divided by the mean.	A dimensionless (%) measure of variability relative to location. Allows the relative dispersion of data sets to be compared.

* Note that these statistics are often expressed as mathematical formulae and are usually best calculated using a calculator or spreadsheet package.

dissimilarity between the samples, perhaps because of a treatment you have administered to one of them, or are the differences you observe just the result of random errors? Hypothesis testing works by trying to put a probability on these alternatives.

The norm is to set up a 'null hypothesis' (NH) that says that the samples are the same or that they conform to some theoretical description. By making certain assumptions about the data, calculating a hypothesis-testing statistic, and looking up tables of probability (or calculating), you can find the probability P of the NH being true. The lower P, the less likely you are to accept it in favour of the hypothesis that the differences were 'real' and due to your treatment or a genuine difference between the samples. Conventionally, if $P < 0.05$, then the NH is rejected.

Parametric and non-parametric statistical tests

The former make the assumption that the data are distributed according to a particular mathematical function, usually the so-called 'Normal' function; the latter make no assumptions of this kind, but are less powerful in distinguishing between samples that differ marginally.

Hypothesis-testing statistics differ in their assumptions about the data and what they set out to test. Some common ones and their uses are:

- t-test – for comparing two means;
- x^2 (chi squared) test – for comparing observed against expected values;
- analysis of variance (ANOVA) – for comparing several means.

Precise details can be found in specialist texts.

ACTION POINTS

21.1 Look at the chart options within Microsoft Excel.
Knowing your way round this program, or a similar spreadsheet tool available to you, and finding out what it offers will help you to choose the most appropriate chart and presentation for your purposes. Where the output does not meet the expectations at the highest level in your discipline, you will need to learn how to manipulate chart formats to suit.

21.2 Find out how tables are normally presented in your discipline. This may vary, for example in the use of cell borders and lines, and you will probably be expected to adopt the style evident in text and journal articles in your area. If in doubt over a specific example, ask a colleague or your supervisor.

21.3 Research further on relevant statistics for your discipline. Many people come to study at higher degree level with perfectly sound knowledge of data handling. However, for some, their new study will take them to areas outside their 'comfort zone' and one such area might be statistical analysis. If you are in this position, then, when scoping your research and your approach to your study, identify the nature of data handling that might be required. If you need to go beyond simple descriptive statistics which would probably be within most people's competence at this level, then it might be wise to factor in time for an intensive course on basic statistics. This will not necessarily equip you with a highly sophisticated level of ability in statistics but it should be enough to allow you to know what kinds of questions can be answered by interrogation of data and, perhaps with help, to apply the means to achieve this.

22

ASPECTS OF QUALITATIVE RESEARCH

How to obtain and analyse non-numerical information

Qualitative research methods are commonplace in a wide range of arts, social sciences and scientific research work. This chapter explores the rationale for obtaining descriptive data, outlines some of the main techniques used to obtain them, and suggests appropriate ways of analysing and presenting such data.

KEY TOPICS

→ Theoretical perspectives

→ Key features of qualitative research

→ Qualitative research methods

→ Conducting face-to-face research

→ Coding and analysing data

Qualitative research methods are those investigative approaches whose outcomes are summarised as textual information, in contrast with quantitative methods where results are usually summarised numerically (**Ch 23**). Qualitative approaches have wide application and are especially useful when examining complex information that needs to be disentangled in order to make sense of it. Typically, this might entail scrutinising:

- opinions, feelings, and values (for example, in Political Science, Social Policy, Philosophy);

- participant interpretations and responses (for example, in Sociology, Psychology);

- behavioural patterns (for example, in Ethnography, Anthropology, Geography);

- processes and patterns (for example, in Education, Economics, Biology);

- case studies including critical incidents (for example, in Nursing, Education).

Although you may have used some of these methods at an earlier stage in your studies, at PhD level it is essential to have a thorough understanding of the theoretical base from which qualitative study methods have grown.

THEORETICAL PERSPECTIVES

In qualitative research, there is recognition that interpretation is conducted according to a set of values belonging to the researcher. However, a range of theoretical perspectives apply to evaluating information of this type. A good starting point when scoping your study would be examination of four commonly used observational approaches.

- Field research. This approach to qualitative research involves the collection, analysis and description of data from natural environments beyond the laboratory. The method requires methodical and detailed note-making that is then coded before it can be analysed and the phenomena described. Field work research is used in many disciplines and can be part of the process of some of the approaches listed below. The nature of collecting, coding, analysing and describing will differ according to discipline and context.

- Ethnography. This is based on participant observation and is a form of field research. In this approach, groups or organisations are observed in their natural contexts over a relatively short period. Members of such groupings share common experiences whether by virtue of social context, location or practices and it is the behaviours manifested in their mutual experience that make them of interest to the researcher.

- Grounded theory. This is 'real life' research that is 'grounded' on observation in group contexts. The process does not begin with a hypothesis (**Ch 3**) but starts with general questions that may be further refined and that can lead to the creation of more questions as ideas develop over time. The data generated are analysed and tentatively linked to theoretical concepts, new or existing. Later in the process core aspects and relationships between these and their associated theoretical underpinning are identified.

- Phenomenology. This is an observational technique that involves longer-term, detailed study of smaller groups of people. Several schools of thought exist regarding this approach but the common focus is on philosophical thinking about the essential questions of how to define being and knowledge. In its practical application the phenomena studied relate to participants' subjective interpretations of experiences and the world surrounding them, sometimes called their 'lived experience'. The phenomenologist tries to reach a better understanding of these experiences.

These four approaches have their origins in the Sciences, Anthropology, Sociology and Philosophy respectively. It is beyond the scope of this book to examine the theoretical underpinnings of qualitative enquiry in detail, but you may find it useful in making your decision about the best 'fit' for your study to consult one of the seminal works on aspects of qualitative research. Frequently recommended texts are: Cohen *et al.* (2007), Denzin and Lincoln (2005), Robson (2011) and Strauss and Corbin (2007).

Learning about qualitative research theory

Your supervisor may suggest a well-established approach to your research, following common practice in your discipline. In this case, writing about the research methodology can be done at the outset in a well-defined methods section. In other instances, the qualitative research approach to be adopted may not become clear until the research is under way and so it may be necessary to delay writing up the theoretical methodology. This does *not* mean that researching and developing an understanding of the qualitative research options should be delayed: reaching a deep understanding of these complex thought-processes can be lengthy and sometimes difficult.

KEY FEATURES OF QUALITATIVE RESEARCH

Qualitative research is generally exploratory in nature. It is especially important in the social sciences, where its aim is often to understand the complex reasons for human behaviour. Different approaches can be adopted.

- Case studies. (For example, 'Student X described her experience on her first day at university as…'.)

- Interviews. (For example, 'Interviewee A explained that, after seeing the video, his reaction was... This could be interpreted as...'.)
- Focus groups. (For example, 'One group member stated that her experience of peer marking was...'.)

Qualitative research generally involves individuals or small samples, in contrast to the large randomly selected samples favoured in quantitative research (**Ch 23**). These small samples may be carefully selected, and they may not be representative of the population as a whole, but that is not always an issue, because in many cases the value of qualitative research derives from the authentic and case-specific detail that it can encompass. The information obtained is potentially richer and deeper than that described in numbers and statistics, and can take advantage of the many subtle ways of using language to express opinions, experiences and feelings. On the other hand, these properties may mean that it is less easy to compare different responses and arrive at generalised conclusions.

Qualitative and quantitative research methods (**Ch 23**) are not mutually exclusive and may be used in the same investigation. For example, mixed types of data may be obtained as in a survey eliciting free-text responses and expressions of opinion on a Likert scale.

Avoiding survey questions that lead or restrict the answers

If you conduct qualitative research appropriately, the participants providing information are less likely to be 'led' by the questions asked than they may be with the quantitative approach. For example, a free-text question in a survey that neutrally asks for the participant's opinion of a political leader does not lead or restrict the respondent in the same way as a Likert-scale question that asks them to grade a leader on his or her response to a specific political issue (**Ch 23**). When sequencing interview questions, care needs to be taken to ensure that an early question does not place a particular idea or concept in the respondent's mind, thereby affecting their response to a later question. Therefore, you should try to move your questions or prompts from the general to the specific; for example, by asking participants for their opinions on a wide issue without prompting, then, later, asking them to comment on specific aspects of interest to you.

Bias in qualitative research

Qualitative research, by its very nature, implies a degree of bias. However, maintaining objectivity is as important in the conduct of the research as it is in reporting findings. It is important, therefore, to recognise the tensions that can arise between objectivity and bias. This is particularly relevant when selecting cases to study, aspects to report and language to describe observations. Observer preconceptions, value systems and cultural influences also need to be taken into account. Examination of the theoretical bases for this type of research (see above) can help to tease out these issues to achieve an objective appraisal of your research problem.

QUALITATIVE RESEARCH METHODS

This section describes techniques used in the most common types of investigation. If your discipline favours a different or modified technique, then consult relevant texts such as those suggested earlier in this chapter.

Observation and description

This category includes a wide range of approaches where the investigator will examine an artefact, person or location and describe it in words. A narrative (outline of developments through time) might also fall into this classification. Examples of suitable topics include:

- primary source material such as that found in an historical document;
- a biological habitat;
- a patient's symptoms;
- a drawing, painting or installation;
- the acculturation process among immigrants.

The specific detailed features to be reported will depend on your discipline and research area. Discussing these with your supervisor is advisable before proceeding too far with your research. Although description is sometimes categorised as a 'lower-level' academic thought process, the interpretations and generalisations that follow involve higher-level skills (**Ch 17**). For example, a detailed description you produce may be referred to when you are drawing conclusions about a wider topic.

Sometimes your purpose may involve comparing several sources of information. A useful technique when doing this is to create a table or grid where the columns represent the different sources and entries in the rows summarise the specific features of interest. In some cases, this matrix could be adapted for use in your thesis, but it would also be useful when writing a summary of the key features of the sources.

Example of a matrix approach to comparative description

The introduction to a student's thesis might involve comparing the health systems of several countries. Having carried out background reading and scan-read through selected documents, he or she might be able to come up with a list of key aspects to compare (for example, the nature of health care provision, the source of funding, the entitlement to free health care, private health care provision, or the nature of specialist care). This list could form the basis of a matrix (grid) comparing the different aspects, following a more detailed reading of the documents. In drawing up such a table, you should bear in mind that similarities may be just as important as differences.

Observations can generate large amounts of data. As with references and other source materials (**Ch 9**), you will need a well-organised system for filing data, constructing databases and recording your analyses. This is best decided upon before starting the research or perhaps immediately following a pilot or initial research exercise.

Use photography or scans to record complex information

Photos might be valuable for a field study, for example, by acting as a prompt when you start to write up. Another use could be recording notes made by a focus group on a whiteboard. Scans might assist when collating large numbers of documents. If photographing people, you may need to seek ethical approval (**Ch 19**) and possibly create a suitable permissions form.

Surveys and questionnaires

Both qualitative and quantitative approaches may be used in surveys and questionnaires (**Ch 23**). The main qualitative research technique is to ask an 'open' question, such as 'What do you think about the proposed phonic reading system?' or 'Do you have any further comments about local policing?' These questions tend to produce a variety of responses from a blank response to very detailed answers. Responses to open questions can be useful to enrich a report with authentic quotes illustrating representative points of view or opposing, polarised viewpoints. In some instances, this apparently qualitative material can be converted into quantitative information. Quantitative summaries (**Ch 23**) may be useful for establishing some of the background to research findings. Pilot studies (see below) are useful for working out what types of information might be valuable.

Value of pilot studies

In qualitative research, a pilot study is usually a preliminary study conducted on a small scale. This will:

- give you a chance to work through your approach to identify inconsistencies or weaknesses;
- help you decide which background demographic information will be required to correlate with participant responses;
- help you decide how you will analyse the results, and whether you need to adjust the approach because of this.

Not only does this save time in later face-to-face interview or focus group meetings, but it can help to identify possible discussion threads for these meetings and analytical approaches to the results.

Interview-based case studies

Qualitative research often draws on individuals' experiences of events, processes and systems. These can be reported as case studies. In one ideal sense, such investigations might be carried out without preconception by allowing the participant to provide a completely unstructured and uninterrupted stream of thought, with conclusions drawn following examination of the information obtained. In practice, you will use a body of prior knowledge and experience to structure an interview through a series of prompting questions. If you use a similar template for each case study, comparisons will be possible, so it is important to think this through beforehand. You also need to think carefully about how you are going to gather and record this information, for example, by audio- or video-recording, remembering that this might require transcription into printed format.

Case studies are sometimes presented in your final text in a self-contained text-box. If these are numbered, you can refer to them in the thesis text using the same conventions as figures and tables (**Ch 21**). There are layout rules for presenting quotes from sources in an academic document (**Ch 20**) and these should be adhered to consistently. Consult your supervisor if uncertain.

 Action Research

Academic departments often encourage students to undertake studies grounded in 'local' issues. In such instances 'Action Research' approaches are popular. These are particularly common in the 'caring' disciplines such as Nursing, Social Work and Teaching. The focus is directed on the context of the researcher's practice and a problem or situation within it which requires better understanding and, possibly, identification of some change to resolve or improve that situation or practice. This approach requires planning of the research approach, perhaps through data collection or observation; analysis and reflection through reference to theory; and, ultimately, a recommendation for action.

Focus groups

These are small discussion groups (four to six members are considered ideal), where participants are asked to comment on an issue or, for business purposes, a product or marketing tool. Focus groups allow you to take account of several viewpoints at a time, and to observe the outcomes of open and dynamic discussion among focus group members. Potential pitfalls include biasing any comments by leading the discussion yourself, or the tendency for focus group members to conform to a middle view if they fear exposing a minority opinion.

As focus group moderator, you should have thought through a list of discussion topics or questions related to your research interest. You should also intervene in the discussion to prompt new topics or bring the discussion back to the point, because a recognised danger is that the group drifts substantially 'off message'. Again, you need to think ahead about how you intend to record the information; good focus group practice involves the use of a scribe who is not a member of the group. Alternatively, you can let the group itself summarise its thoughts (see below).

Ethical and data protection dimensions for qualitative research

There are both ethical and data protection dimensions to interviews, focus groups and case studies derived from them. It is important that you read the material in **Chapter 19** and follow your university's rules and regulations carefully, as detailed in your institution's ethical guidelines. You may be required to:

- tell participants about the purpose of your study;
- obtain signed clearance from participants to use the information they provide in your research, especially where this may be reported externally;
- store participants' personal data appropriately and for a limited time only;
- gain agreement of participants *before* recording their input and give guarantees about confidentiality and destruction of recorded audio/video material after transcription.

If children are involved, you may need special clearance (the nature of which may be region-dependent). Your supervisor should be able to advise on this.

CONDUCTING FACE-TO-FACE RESEARCH

It is important to select your interviewees or focus group participants carefully, since this could bias the results. Choose participants according to a defined set of criteria, having discussed what these might be with your supervisor beforehand. For example, you might wish to interview people involved at all stages in a business process (shop-floor, administrative, management, marketing and customer); or a balanced set of students of both sexes representing different levels of study. You will need to provide details of the selection criteria in your thesis methods section (**Ch 28**). Record relevant participant details (either obtained beforehand as part of the selection process or by asking participants to complete a short questionnaire at the start of the meeting).

Before your planned interview or focus group activity, ensure that conditions are suitable for the type of research activity you intend to conduct. Make sure the meeting room is in a convenient and quiet location. Offer refreshments where appropriate. For lengthy sessions, include a comfort break. Think carefully about the seating arrangements, as this could contribute significantly to the success of your interview or focus group. It is important to consider a layout where people feel comfortable with each other since this could contribute significantly to the success of your interview or focus group. Figure 22.1 illustrates a good seating arrangement for individual interviews.

For focus groups, interactions among participants are said to be better if a 'closed circle' arrangement is used (Figure 22.2). In Figure 22.2(a), the scribe (S) and the moderator/researcher (M) are seated within the group whereas in Figure 22.2(b), the moderator/researcher and the scribe are positioned outside the focus group circle. It might be helpful to provide a whiteboard (W) or flipchart so that one participant from the group can act as a recorder (R). The whiteboard addition is shown in Figure 22.2(b), but could also be offered as a facility in the layout depicted in Figure 22.2(a).

One common denominator of the circle arrangement is that all members of the group can have full view of and make eye contact with all other participants. However, both layouts have advantages and disadvantages. One disadvantage of the Figure 22.2(a) format is that the researcher is part of the group and thus has the potential to influence group members by body language or by making interjections to the discussion. However, Krueger and Casey (2000) regard the integration of the moderator as a beneficial feature since their physical presence in the group allows them to observe interactions, interpret body language and prompt development of the discussion while not expressing a personal viewpoint.

Positioning the moderator and scribe outside the focus group as in Figure 22.2(b) allows the group to interact spontaneously without

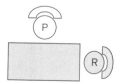

Figure 22.1 Suggested seating arrangement for one-to-one interviews. In those situations people often feel more comfortable sitting at right angles to each other, rather than sitting on opposite sides of a table or sitting side by side. Thus, in this example, researcher (R) sits at the shorter end of the table and participant (P) sits at the longer side.

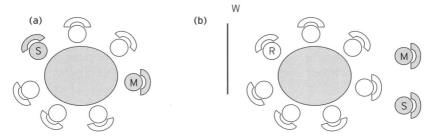

Figure 22.2 Two seating arrangements for a focus group. M = moderator; S = scribe; R = participant-recorder; W = whiteboard.

the intervention of the moderator. It is argued that this encourages the free flow of ideas and reduces influence from the moderator. A disadvantage is that it makes it less easy for the researcher to observe and interpret visual signals among the group members.

It is a good idea to write out an agenda for the interview and a list of question 'prompts'; if conducting a series of interviews, this may help when trying to ensure comparability. You may wish to start with a few questions to put the interviewee(s) at ease. These might stem from responses in a pilot study, if you have done one, and can serve to produce background information to 'situate' the case. The remainder of the question set should be defined by the aims of the project, smoothly moving from general topics to the specific.

Careful note-taking and fact-checking are important in interviews, focus groups and case studies. Most people find it difficult to act as both interviewer and scribe. In any case, good secretarial skills would be required to write down every spoken word. You could ask a friend to act as scribe for you to allow you to focus exclusively on the questions and moderating the session. However, it would be useful to discuss the note-taking strategy with your scribe beforehand to ensure that the data they record is what you require. This might even involve trying a 'dry run' to clarify exactly what both scribe and moderator/researcher expect from the approach.

The following tips may be useful during the meeting itself:

● Start by introducing yourself. Explain the purpose of the event and confirm the approximate length of time that you envisage the activity will take. If appropriate, invite the participants to introduce themselves to each other.

Consider using technology to support your interviews

With the permission of the participants, some researchers make audio- or video-recordings of the interview or focus group dialogue rather than take notes, preferring to stimulate a more natural discussion by simply observing the participants in the discussion. Some people do appear to relax more in these situations where there is no overt note-taking going on. If you opt to use recording methods, ensure that you:

■ know how to operate the technical equipment;

■ have practised using it beforehand;

■ have checked it out on the day before the session begins to ensure that you will be able to hear the recording clearly on replay;

■ have sufficient battery power and recording capacity for the whole period of the interview.

● Develop some means of identifying participants. When noting oral data, some researchers prefer to identify participants anonymously (for example, by giving them name tags or sticky label letters A, B, C, etc.), arguing that this emphasises anonymity from the outset. Other researchers feel that this approach is depersonalising and stultifies contributions. Therefore, they prefer to provide students with identifying labels or name tags on which are printed their first names. Either way, identifying contributors allows you to specify in your notes who said what and to link an individual's separate comments together.

● Take notes. Video or sound-record the discussion or ask a friend to act as scribe for you. Some researchers also encourage group participants to record their thoughts on a white board. If you decide to do this, you could photograph the notes as part of the record of the discussion.

● Use 'question probes' to encourage participants to develop the discussion further. For example, you might ask, 'Could you expand on that point a little further?' or 'What do you mean by x?' One of the strengths of interactive qualitative research lies in the flexibility it offers to explore areas that might be rich in the research context but which might not have been anticipated in the question bank created by the researcher/moderator. Therefore, make sure that your programme allows participants some scope to comment freely but within the time schedule. Otherwise, your interventions should only be made to ensure that you keep to the schedule and that the participant(s) do not digress significantly from the subject – be aware of the danger of 'leading' the group. If a digression does occur, then use your question cues as a means of re-focussing the discussion along the lines of your planned prompts.

- Stick to the pre-arranged time. You may want to run other interpersonal research activities and if you earn a reputation for taking up more time than you stated, these or other participants may decline to be involved further in your research.

- Thank the participants for their time and contributions at the end of the session. This is, of course, a matter of good manners: if you fail to observe the courtesy of thanking your participants, they or others in the target category may be less enthusiastic about assisting your research in future.

- Confirm details. After you have written up the interview, it is good practice to check the details you have recorded with the interviewee. For focus groups this might best be accomplished during the event by a staged approach where checks are made before moving on or by asking supplementary questions to clarify details.

CODING AND ANALYSING DATA

In analysing and presenting qualitative data, a key aim is to represent the material in a balanced and rational way. Do not be tempted to select only examples, answers or quotes that support your view. One way to prevent this tendency is to 'code' your data. To do this, you need to identify themes or patterns before you begin and allocate a code to each one. As you continue to process the data, other themes, patterns and behaviours may become apparent; similarly assign a code to these. Note also that while certain of your coding categories may expand, other anticipated categories may prove to be less significant.

Examples of studies where coding can be a valuable technique

Coding can be valuable in diverse investigations across many subjects, including, for example: recording subject behaviour on interview, describing animal mating behaviour, analysis of questionnaire responses, recording patterns of plants across an ecosystem transect.

Analysing your data will depend on format, content and time available to do this. In one approach, the process can be divided into two stages. In the first stage, go through the recorded data highlighting coded items and noting the code in the margin if appropriate. At the next stage, prepare record cards or a table to note:

- the code and sub-code for what you are recording (according to the key you have decided upon);
- details of the source's identity (could be, for example, a respondent or location);
- description of the source (could be, for example, a verbatim transcript, paraphrased transcript, comments, numerical information, photograph details).

This can be used to analyse a transcript or record, by entering the relevant information as you go through the data. For transcripts and records this process can be time-consuming and it is probably better to go through all the data for one code at a time and repeat for the next code and so on. Trying to transcribe all the codes for one transcript or record in a single sweep could be extremely time-consuming and complex, leading to error.

Once you have coded your transcript, record or raw data, you will be in a better position to judge the distribution of the data and thereby create a more balanced summary of your findings; this will also help you to identify 'outlier' events as such, where these occur. In some cases, the analysis may be aided by a basic summary of the codings and sub-codings using appropriate descriptive statistics (**Ch 21**), which may be more easily calculated if the codes are first entered on a spreadsheet. In other instances, it will be sufficient to unpack the coding and sub-coding elements as compatible or linked themes or groups that reflect the disparate nature of the data. This will enable you to write a tight and well-balanced report of your findings. Note that you should not discount those categories which transpired to be less significant than you had anticipated, but should consider why this is the case. Where you have used quantitative data collection to obtain parallel or analogous information, compare these findings with the qualitative data looking for inconsistencies as well as confirmations.

Looking for non-verbal information

Responses other than words may be relevant to your investigation, such as facial expressions, eye contact, voice tone and body language. If so, you may be able to develop a coding system for these, and include some record of them in your notes. This information could be important in your interpretation and reportage of the data.

ACTION POINTS

22.1 Seek out and try to learn from 'model' approaches to your topic. Investigate theoretical foundations for qualitative research applications by consulting your library or some of the sources suggested in this chapter. Whether you are writing a description, conducting a focus group or carrying out a case study, you should be able to find, perhaps with the help of your supervisor, a published study carried out in a similar way. Identify and examine the theoretical approach that has been applied. Consider whether this could be adopted for your own investigation. Also, study the ways the results have been analysed and presented to see if these might be suitable for your own findings.

22.2 Plan a set of question 'prompts' and possible 'question probes' for interviews and focus groups. If your investigation involves either of these approaches, it will be worthwhile setting out a sequence of question prompts as the framework for your face-to-face meeting. If you also note your reasons for asking the question, this will ensure that you garner material that is germane to your research project rather than a lot of interesting but possibly less relevant data.

22.3 Investigate potential methods of recording interview and focus group interaction. Think about the equipment and related facilities that might be available to you personally or ask about what you might be able to borrow from your supervisor or department. Test it so that you have a clear idea of how it should be used and that you can operate it competently.

23

ASPECTS OF QUANTITATIVE RESEARCH

How to obtain and analyse
numerical data

Quantitative research methods are commonplace in the sciences,
but are also relevant to some non-science subjects. This chapter
explores the rationale for obtaining numerical data and presents
some of the main techniques used to obtain them. It also outlines the
most appropriate ways of analysing and presenting these data.

KEY TOPICS

→ Key features of quantitative research

→ Quantitative research methods

→ Analysing and presenting your results

Quantitative research methods are defined as investigative approaches
resulting in numerical data, in contrast to those methods resulting
in qualitative textual information. Quantitative research is especially
valuable when:

- obtaining measurements (for example, in Biochemistry and
  Physiology);

- estimating error (for example, in Physics and Engineering);

- comparing information and opinions (for example, Sociology and
  Psychology);

- testing hypotheses (for example, in most investigative science
  disciplines).

The ideal in this type of research is for the investigator to be detached
and impartial to the results of the study.

Quantitative and qualitative research methods are not mutually
exclusive and may be used in the same investigation. For example, a

full description of a sampling environment may be vital to make sense of numerical data obtained within it.

KEY FEATURES OF QUANTITATIVE RESEARCH

Quantitative research is generally 'conclusive' in nature. It is especially important in the sciences, where its aim may be to provide a reliable value for a measurement or to test a hypothesis. A number of approaches can be adopted.

- experiments – for example, 'Treatment A resulted in a statistically significant increase in weight gain compared with the control';
- measurements – for example, 'The average insect wing length was 3.40 mm with a standard error of 0.14 mm, $n = 24$';
- surveys and questionnaires – for example, 'Over 45 per cent of respondents agreed with this statement'.

In quantitative research, your aim would usually be to base results on large unbiased samples. Large sample size is important to ensure that measurements based on the sample are representative of the population as a whole, and to improve your chances of arriving at a statistically significant conclusion. However, time or resource limitations on your research may limit the sample size you can use in practice.

Population and sample

Although these terms are used frequently in normal language, they have special meanings in quantitative research and statistics.

Population – the whole group of items that might be part of a study: for example, all men in the UK; all individuals of a species of bivalve mollusc on a particular beach; all Birmingham householders who use gas as a heating fuel.

Sample – a sub-set of individuals from a specific population, for example, the 28 men whose blood sugar level was measured and compared with that of 34 who had taken drug X for five weeks beforehand; the 50 bivalves collected from beach A, measured and compared with a similar sample from beach B; the 45 householders selected for telephone interview about their satisfaction with the service provided by their energy supplier.

Bias in quantitative research

Obtaining numbers to describe your results reduces subjectivity and allows comparisons between data sets. The inherent objectivity of quantitative research relies, however, on an unbiased approach to data collection. Some critics of the quantitative approach claim that experiments, surveys and the like are rarely entirely free of observer bias, even if this is unintentional.

 Objectivity versus subjectivity

Objectivity is the ability to arrive at a detached, unprejudiced viewpoint, based on the evidence and without the influence of feelings or emotion (the object = the thing observed).

Subjectivity is the ability to arrive at a viewpoint that takes account of personal impressions, feelings and interpretations (the subject = the observer).

Bias can be defined as a partial or one-sided view or description of events. Although the aim is usually to reduce bias as far as possible, it can arise because of subconscious decision(s) of the experimenter, which can mean that individuals selected for observation or experiment do not represent the population, or that values or measurements associated with them are skewed in a particular way.

Numerical results can be analysed with statistical techniques (**Ch 21**). These allow you to compare sets of observations or treatments, to test hypotheses and to allocate levels of probability (chance) of your conclusions being right or wrong. These are powerful tools and lie at the heart of much scientific scholarship.

However, just because you can measure something, or can compare data sets, this does not mean your conclusions are certain or relevant. For example, many scientists accept the conclusions of their studies on the basis that there could be a 5 per cent chance of their being wrong, so, on average, this will be the case 1 in 20 times (**Ch 21**). Moreover, even when a hypothesis is accepted as correct, the results may apply only to the very artificial experimental or observational environment. Statistical significance should not be confused with significance in the sense of 'importance' or 'value'.

The concept of proof

The word 'proof' should be used cautiously when applied to quantitative research – the term implies 100 per cent certainty, whereas this is very rarely justified owing to the ambiguity inherent in statistical analysis and experimental design. When writing up your thesis and associated papers, 'hedging' language (**Ch 27**) such as 'this indicates that...' or 'this appears to show that...' is therefore preferable to 'absolute' or categorical phrases such as 'it is always the case that...' or 'this proves that...'.

QUANTITATIVE RESEARCH METHODS

This section describes methods used in the most common types of investigation. If your discipline favours a different or modified method, then consult relevant texts.

Experiments

An experiment is a contrived or designed situation where the experimenter attempts to isolate the effects of changing one variable in the system or process, and then compares the results with the condition where no change has occurred. The aim behind many experiments is to establish causality – that is, to establish that a change in factor A causes a change in variable B. Experiments can also help elucidate in more detail *how* A causes B (see tip later in this chapter on correlation and causality).

Experiments are at the core of the 'scientific method', in which an experiment is set up that will allow a hypothesis to be accepted or rejected (**Ch 3**). Much of the progress in the modern world has been made through scientific advances based on experiments. Nevertheless, it is useful to recognise some limitations and difficulties:

- The situations required to allow manipulation of relevant variables are potentially artificial. Indeed, they may be so contrived as to be unnatural, making any conclusions of dubious value.
- It may be impossible to change one variable only in any treatment. Inevitably, other aspects change simultaneously. These are known as confounding variables. For example, if you attempt to change

temperature, you may also change humidity. Adding 'control' treatments are the way in which experimenters attempt to rule out the effects of confounding variables.

- Uncertainty in conclusions. Sampling and other errors can be taken into account in statistical analysis, but the results must always be expressed with a degree of uncertainty (**Ch 21**).

- Subjectivity or bias. There may be an unwitting element of subjectivity or bias in the choice of treatments; the choice of conditions (sometimes selected to accentuate effects of a particular treatment); and in some cases, in the recording of results.

Concept of 'the control'

A control is an additional treatment that attempts to test the effects of changing a potentially confounding variable. Suppose it is known that Drug A is acidic in nature and that the formulation available for testing also contains a synthesis by-product (impurity), Chemical B. A suitable experimental design might include the following treatments:

1 No treatment (usually involving a placebo, or pill without any added chemicals).

2 Drug A (administered as a pill).

3 Control for effects of pH (a placebo pill with the same pH or buffering capacity as the Drug A pill).

4 Control for the effect of Chemical B (a pill containing similar amounts of Chemical B as in the Drug A pill, but without any Drug A).

If the results show an effect in treatment 2, but not in 3 and 4, then the confounding variables can be ruled out; if there are also effects in 3 or 4, then the confounding variables may well be important.

The range of possible experimental designs is infinite, so it is impossible to provide specific guidance. The best path is perhaps to compare approaches used in recent publications in your area and take the guidance of your supervisor. Nevertheless, when designing an experiment, the following tips may be useful.

- Consider the likely method of statistical analysis from the start, as this may influence the experimental design. For example, it is possible to estimate an appropriate number of replicates to use to demonstrate a certain percentage difference between two treatments if a preliminary indication of the variability among the replicates is available. Another reason for considering statistical tests beforehand is that they may require assumptions about your data, which you can ensure by using, for example, a truly random sampling procedure.

- Keep your initial experiments simple. It is better to use a design that will provide a conclusive answer to a simple question than to over-complicate matters, run into logistical problems in setting up the experiment and collecting data, and end up with inconclusive results.

- Use experimental design to reduce the effects of confounding variables. Examples might be the 'Latin square' type of design that ensures that replicates of the same treatment appear only in one row and one column, so that any spatially changing variables are evened out among the treatments.

- Learn from 'trial runs'. These can help you work out where there will be difficulties in procedure and layout, use of instruments, and other important limitations on your experimental design. Be aware, however, that you could spend too much time working out what to do and how to do it – all experimentation involves a certain amount of compromise.

- Keep ethical and safety issues in mind. Think these through before you start work and try to bear the safety of participants and researchers in mind when focusing on collecting data (**Ch 19**).

The conduct of experiments is discussed further in **Chapter 24**.

Measurements and error determination

A measurement is an estimate of some dimension of an object or event as a ratio of a standard unit. It therefore consists of both a number and the symbol for the unit, for example: 0.5 metres; 1.6 litres; 39 kilograms.

The units chosen for most scientific studies are those of the Système Internationale or SI, a metre–kilogram–second scheme with defined symbols for units and prefixes for small and large numbers that differ by multiples of 1000 (10^3). Table 23.1 provides some examples of commonly used dimensions and their official symbols, while Table 23.2 provides a list of prefixes.

All measurements contain error, which can be of two types: accuracy or precision. In practice, measurements are often assumed to be accurate and the more important thing to estimate is the precision.

Table 23.1 Some examples of SI units. For the prefixes normally used in association with these units see Table 23.2.

Quantity	Si unit (and symbol)
Base units	
Length	metre (m)
Mass	kilogram (kg)
Time	second (s)
Temperature	kelvin (K)
Amount of substance	mole (mol)
Electric current	ampere (A)
Luminous intensity	candela (cd)
Supplementary units	
Plane angle	radian (rad)
Solid angle	steradian (sr)
Some examples of compound units	
Energy	joule (J) = m^2 kg s^{-1} = N m
Force	newton (N) = m kg s^{-2} = J m^{-1}
Pressure	pascal (Pa) = kg m^{-1} s^{-2} = N m^{-2}
Power	watt (W) = m^2 kg s^{-3} = J s^{-1}
Electric charge	coulomb (C) = A s
Illumination	lux (lx) = cd sr m^{-2}

Table 23.2 SI prefixes. Note that after the first row, small number prefixes have the ending 'o', while large number prefixes have the ending 'a'.

Small numbers			Large numbers		
Value	Prefix	Symbol	Value	Prefix	Symbol
10^{-3}	milli	m	10^{3}	kilo	k
10^{-6}	micro	μ	10^{6}	mega	M
10^{-9}	nano	n	10^{9}	giga	G
10^{-12}	pico	p	10^{12}	tera	T
10^{-15}	femto	f	10^{15}	peta	P
10^{-18}	atto	a	10^{18}	exa	E
10^{-21}	zepto	z	10^{21}	zeta	Z
10^{-24}	yocto	y	10^{24}	yotta	Y

There are two main ways of estimating precision:

- By providing a range that relates to the observer's or instrument's ability to discriminate between readings. For example, if measuring length with a ruler, you might write 104 ± 0.5 mm because you were using the scale divisions on the ruler to estimate to the nearest mm; that is, the dividing points between adjacent values below and above 104 are at 103.5 and 104.5 mm.

- By providing an estimated error that is based on repeated measurements of the same quantity. For quantifying measurement error alone, this would be obtained from several independent attempts at measurement, for example, five independent values obtained from the same weighing machine of someone's weight (mass). In many scientific studies, this error is taken to be included in the overall sampling error obtained from replicates.

When reporting measurement data, you should use appropriate measures of location and dispersion to describe them. These are outlined in Table 21.1.

Accuracy and precision

Accuracy is the closeness of a measured or estimated value to its true value. Example: a balance would be said to be inaccurate if, instead of giving you a value for a standard 1 kg weight as 1 kg, it consistently gave a value of 1.02 kg. All measurements of similar weights from the instrument would thus be approximately +2 per cent wrong.

Precision is the closeness of repeated measurements to each other. For example, if you weighed a specimen several times on the same balance and got very different results each time, then the instrument would be said to be imprecise. A mean of 1.000 kg might be considered to be accurate, but if the standard deviation of the measurements was 0.25 kg, this would be considered rather imprecise.

Correlation

This is a way of describing the relationship between two measured variables, for example, the number of cigarettes smoked per day and life expectancy. A variable is well correlated with another if their values alter together, either in a positive fashion, or in a negative fashion. This is illustrated in Figure 23.1. A statistic called the correlation coefficient can be used to express the strength or degree of linear correlation

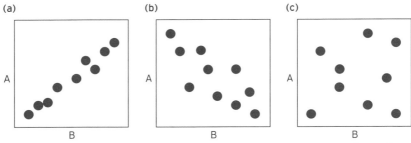

Figure 23.1 Examples of correlation. Each dot represents an experimental subject measured for variables A and B. (a) The two variables have a strong positive correlation; that is, if one variable increases, so does the other. (b) The two variables are negatively correlated; that is, if one variable increases, the other decreases, but in the case illustrated, the points are more widely scattered, so the correlation is less strong than in the first example. (c) The two variables have no strong correlation: that is, they show no discernable relationship.

between two variables. This takes values between –1 and 1; the closer its value is to these extremes, the higher the degree of correlation, and the closer to zero, the lower. The sign indicates whether the correlation is positive or negative. The coefficient can be used in a statistical test to find out whether the correlation is significantly different from zero.

Correlation and causality

Vital to an understanding of quantitative research is an awareness that correlation does not necessarily imply causality. If A is well correlated with B, this alone is not enough evidence to state that A causes B. It could be something related to A, or even, due to coincidence, something unrelated to A. So, if people with high blood pressure are more likely to have heart attacks, this alone does not show that high blood pressure is a cause of heart attacks, although if there were no relationship between the two, you might be inclined to rule out this possibility. The only way to become more certain is to gather more evidence.

Surveys and questionnaires

These are valuable tools for gaining quantitative information from respondents (although it must be remembered that these tools can also provide qualitative data). Respondents can be a representative sample (for example, members of demographic C2 chosen at random or using a sampling protocol) or a population (all staff members within a school). Before designing a survey, you should consider what demographic information you might need to associate with other responses and how you intend to report the results (**Ch 21**) as this may influence the questions asked and the way you write them.

Ethics and data protection

Ethical aspects of qualitative and quantitative research apply particularly to surveys and questionnaires (**Ch 19**). It is important that you read this material and follow local rules and university regulations.

Questions fall into one of two categories, closed or open. There are several types of closed question.

- Categorical. Here, you can only select one of the options, for example: 'Gender: M/F'; or 'Do you agree with the above statement? – Yes/No/Don't know (delete as appropriate)'. Results are best expressed as percentages of responses in each category.

- Numerical. These request a numerical answer, for example 'What is your age in years?' These can be summarised by appropriate statistics of location and dispersion (**Ch 21**).

- Multiple-choice questions (MCQs). These are useful when there are mutually exclusive options to select. This type of question will be familiar from assessments at school and university. The answers given can be summarised easily as percentages of respondents selecting each option.

- Multiple response questions. These are like MCQs, only respondents are allowed to choose more than one answer. The answers can also be summarised as percentages selecting each option, but note that the total number of options selected may be larger than your sample size. In fact, the average number of options selected may be an interesting supplementary piece of data to report.

- Ranking (ordinal) questions. These ask you to place possible answers in an order; for example, 'Place the items in the following list in order of preference, writing 1 for your most preferred option, 2 for the next and so on, down to 5 for your least preferred option'. You can present the results as the most common selection at each rank or as percentages of respondents choosing each rank for a specific item (perhaps as a histogram). A 'mean rank' is another possible way of expressing the data, but this should be interpreted cautiously.

- Likert-scale questions. These are useful for assessing people's opinions or feelings on a five-point scale. Typically, respondents are asked to react to a statement. An example would be:

'Smoking is dangerous for your health'. Which of the following best describes your feelings about the above statement? (Circle the appropriate number.)

1 Agree strongly

2 Agree

3 Neither agree nor disagree

4 Disagree

5 Disagree strongly

Some Likert-scale designs only use four categories, missing out 'neither agree nor disagree', to force respondents to indicate a preference on one side or the other.

The results of Likert-scale questions are often treated as ordinal data and non-parametric statistical tests are applied (**Ch 21**). Responses to Likert options may be combined, as in the example 'over 57 per cent either agreed or agreed strongly with the statement…'.

Likert scales

These are named after Rensis Likert, an American psychologist who pioneered the use of a five-point survey scale in 1932.

Open-answer survey questions require input from the respondent and are useful when you do not know all the possible answers, or you do not wish to lead the respondent. In a student survey, an example might be 'Why did you choose module P201?' or 'Please summarise your experience in the exam'. The text responses often provide valuable quotes for a report or case study, and this use would be classified as qualitative (**Ch 22**). It is possible, however, given a reasonably large sample, to code and/or categorise the answers and present them in a quantitative fashion, for example, in the form of a pie chart (**Ch 21**) showing the proportion of respondents giving each type of answer.

When conducting a questionnaire or survey consider the following tips.

- Make sure your instructions are clear and unambiguous. Not everyone in the sample will make the same assumptions as you. For example, if you write: 'Do you agree with this statement? Yes/No', unless given clear directions, some respondents may circle the answer they agree with, others may score out the one they disagree with, and some may provide other marks that you will find difficult to interpret. A score might look like a tick, for example. Look at the wording of others to see how they have tackled any issues that might occur.

- Try out the question set with a friend or family member before using it on real subjects. This may reveal problems with the wording that you may not have appreciated, and is therefore best done with someone relatively unfamiliar with your topic, but who is willing to provide you with informal feedback.

- When explaining how your survey was conducted, supply appropriate details. These should include:
  - Sampling methods. How were the respondents contacted or chosen? What ethical procedures were followed?

- Details of respondents. You should provide a summary of demographics (gender, age, background of those responding). This information can be derived from specific questions, often placed at the start of the survey. However, observe good research practice by ensuring that the privacy and anonymity of your respondents are protected (**Ch 14**).
- Questionnaire design. The principles and rationale behind the design should be discussed and a copy of the questionnaire provided, perhaps in an appendix.
- Procedure. How was the survey administered?

- Correct your respondents' grammar and spelling errors. When reporting responses, this is generally acceptable practice, because it is true to the spirit of what was written and helps the reader focus on the main points made. You should add a note to the 'Material and Methods' section to explain that you have done this. Clearly, however, this would be inappropriate if your study were about language and the inaccuracies in the responses were the main focus of the research.

Observe six basic rules of surveys

1 **Keep your survey as short as possible.** Use the minimum number of questions required to obtain the information you need

2 **Only ask a question if you have a clear idea of how you will use the information obtained.**

3 **Make sure your questions are unambiguous.**

4 **In deciding the order of questions, try to move from the general to the specific.** There will then be less chance of early questions influencing responses to later ones.

5 **Make sure you obtain appropriate demographic information.** This will allow you to describe your sample accurately and to draw correlations.

6 **Always pilot your survey before releasing it.** That way you will iron out potential misunderstandings.

Technology has come to the aid of the researcher with the introduction of survey software often available under licence to academic institutions. Such software allows postgraduates the facility to compile and distribute survey questionnaires electronically to an identified population. The results can be collated and interrogated electronically and a report produced in hard copy. Such technology can offer considerable time-saving in data collection and analysis.

ANALYSING AND PRESENTING YOUR RESULTS

Rarely are results of observations, surveys or experiments reported without subsequent analysis. Indeed, your ability to analyse and present your results will be examined thoroughly in the course of your *viva* exam.

- Adequate description of your methods is vital. One goal of quantitative research is to produce repeatable results from which general conclusions can be drawn. This normally means that a 'Materials and Methods' section contains enough information to allow a competent peer to repeat your work (**Ch 28**).

- Descriptions should use clear unambiguous language, and qualitative terms used should be defined if possible. For example, the colour of a specimen might be described with reference to a standard colour chart.

- Repetition is vital. Simple measurements should be repeated if possible, so that a figure indicating their accuracy (dispersion, **Ch 21**) can be provided.

- Figures and tables should be used appropriately. When describing results, appropriate use should be made of figures and tables and these should be constructed according to the usual discipline conventions (**Ch 21**).

- The results of experiments should be analysed using statistical tests (**Ch 21**).

ACTION POINTS

23.1 Plan out a survey or experiment, or the procedures necessary for a measurement. Aim to identify the different steps in the process and, in particular, resource constraints. In the case of a survey, the latter might include the respondents' time; in an experiment, the availability of test subjects or equipment; and for measurements, the number of replicate readings it is possible to carry out.

23.2 List potential forms of bias in your research. Being aware of these will help you to avoid them. Discuss your list with your supervisor to see whether you have missed anything, and to explore methods of avoiding the most important sources of bias in your work.

23.3 Find out about the statistical tests that can be carried out using the specific software available to you. Will you be able to accomplish your aims using tests within a spreadsheet program like Excel, or will you need more sophisticated software? What 'learning curve' is required to understand and master these tests? To help overcome potential difficulties, try out the software functions using dummy values, before using them with real data.

24

EXPERIMENTS AND FIELD STUDIES

How to design and conduct laboratory and field investigations

Many research projects, particularly in the sciences, involve laboratory and/or fieldwork. These situations provide opportunities to observe specimens, carry out experiments and take relevant measurements. Good design and working practices are essential to ensure the validity of your results.

KEY TOPICS

→ Designing experiments

→ Sampling

→ Preparation for research activity

→ Appropriate conduct in the lab and field

→ Carrying out instructions and noting results

In many disciplines, research activity is undertaken in the laboratory ('lab') and/or field. You are likely to have experienced lab and field sessions and project work as an undergraduate, so will know what to expect. At PhD level, the rigour with which you carry out this work must be of the highest possible standard: essentially, your methods and results should be of publishable quality. While precise methods will always depend on your discipline and the nature of the investigation, the content of this chapter should help to provide a sound foundation for this work.

DESIGNING EXPERIMENTS

In many experiments, the aim is to provide evidence for causality (**Ch 23**). If x causes y, we expect, repeatably, to find that a change in x results in a change in y. Hence, the ideal experiment of this kind involves measurement of y, the dependent (measured) variable, at one or more values of x, the independent variable, and subsequent demonstration of some relationship between them. Experiments therefore involve comparisons of the results of treatments – changes in the independent variable as applied to an experimental subject. The change is engineered by the experimenter under controlled conditions. Subjects given the same treatment are known as replicates (they may be called plots). A block is a grouping of replicates or plots. The blocks are contained in a field, that is, the whole area (or time) available for the experiment.

Terminology of experiments

Many of the terms used for experimentation originated from the statistical analysis of agricultural experiments, but are now used widely in science.

Table 24.1 outlines the important stages in designing an experiment.

Controlling variables in experiments

Interpretation of experiments is seldom clear-cut because uncontrolled variables always change when treatments are given.

● Confounding variables increase or decrease systematically as the independent variable increases or decreases. Their effects are known as systematic variation.

● Nuisance variables are uncontrolled variables that cause differences in the value of y independently of the value of x, resulting in random variation.

Confounding variables can be disentangled from those caused directly by treatments by incorporating appropriate controls in the experiment. A control is really just another treatment where a potentially confounding variable is adjusted so that its effects, if any, can be measured and taken into account (**Ch 23**). There are often many potential controls for any experiment. The consequence of systematic variation is that you can never be certain that the treatment, and the treatment alone, has caused an observed result. By careful design, you can, however, 'minimise the uncertainty' involved in your conclusion. Methods available include:

● ensuring, through experimental design, that the independent variable is the only major factor that changes in any treatment;

● incorporating appropriate controls to show that potential confounding variables have little or no effect;

Table 24.1 Five key stages in the design of an experiment. Tips are provided for each phase.

1 Preliminaries
• Read background material and decide on a subject area to investigate. • Formulate a simple hypothesis to test. It is preferable to have a clear answer to one question than to be uncertain about several questions. • Decide which dependent variable you are going to measure and how: is it relevant to the problem? Can you measure it accurately, precisely and without bias? • Think about and plan the statistical analysis of your results. Will this affect your design?

2 Designing
• Find out the limitations on your resources. • Choose treatments that alter the minimum of confounding variables. • Incorporate as many effective controls as possible. • Keep the number of replicates as high as is feasible. • Ensure that the same number of replicates is present in each treatment. • Use effective randomisation and blocking arrangements.

3 Planning
• List all the materials you will need. Order any chemicals and make up solutions; identify, grow, collect or breed the experimental subjects you require; check equipment is available. • Organise space and/or time in which to do the experiment. • Account for the time taken to apply treatments and record results. Make out a timesheet if things will be hectic.

4 Carrying out the experiment
• Record the results and make careful notes of everything you do. Make additional observations to those planned if interesting things happen. • Repeat experiment if time and resources allow.

5 Analysing
• Graph data as soon as possible (during the experiment, if you can). This will allow you to visualise what has happened and make adjustments to the design (for example, timing of measurements). • Carry out the planned statistical analysis. • Jot down conclusions and new hypotheses arising from the experiment.

- selecting experimental subjects randomly to cancel out systematic variation arising from biased selection;

- matching or pairing individuals among treatments so that differences in response due to their initial status are eliminated;

- arranging subjects and treatments randomly so that responses to systematic differences in conditions do not influence the results;
- ensuring that experimental conditions are uniform so that responses to systematic differences in conditions are minimised.

To reduce and assess the consequences of nuisance variables, you can:

- incorporate replicates to allow random variation to be quantified;
- choose subjects that are as similar as possible;
- control random fluctuations in environmental conditions.

 Constraints on experimental design

In most experiments, you will find that there are resource constraints on the design. For example, limits may be set by availability of subjects, cost of treatment, availability or cost of a chemical or bench space. Logistics may be a factor (for example, time taken to record or analyse data). Your equipment or facilities may affect design because you cannot regulate conditions as well as you might desire. You may have to accept a great deal of initial variability if your subjects are collected from the wild.

Use of replicates

Replicate results show how variable the response is within treatments. They allow you to compare the differences among treatments in the context of the variability within treatments – you can do this via statistical tests such as analysis of variance (**Ch 21**). Larger sample sizes tend to increase the precision of estimates of parameters and increase the chance of showing a significant difference between treatments, if one exists. For statistical reasons, it is often best to keep the number of replicates similar among treatments.

 Can subsamples act as replicates?

The short answer is 'no'. Subsamples are derived from the same original specimen, and this could mean readings or specimens. Statistically speaking, the degree of independence of replicates is highly important: subsamples are not wholly independent. They can tell you about variability in the measurement method but not in the quantity being measured.

Randomisation of treatments

The two aspects of randomisation you must consider are:

- positioning of treatments within experimental blocks;
- allocation of treatments to the experimental subjects.

For relatively simple experiments, you can adopt a completely randomised design: here, the position and treatment assigned to any subject are defined randomly. A completely randomised layout has the advantage of simplicity but cannot show how confounding variables alter in space or time. This information can be obtained if you use a blocked design in which the degree of randomisation is restricted. Here, the experimental space or time is divided into blocks, each of which accommodates the complete set of treatments. When analysed appropriately, the results for the blocks can be compared to test for differences in the confounding variables and these effects can be separated out from the effects of the treatments.

A Latin square is an example of a method of placing treatments so that they appear in a balanced fashion within a square block or field. Treatments appear once in each column and row (see Figure 24.1), so the effects of confounding variables can be 'cancelled out' in two directions at right angles to each other.

Figure 24.1 Examples of Latin square arrangements for three and four treatments. Letters indicate treatments; the number of possible arrangements for each size of square increases greatly as the size increases.

Pairing and matching subjects

The paired comparison is a special case of blocking used to reduce systematic variation when there are two treatments. Examples of its use are:

- 'Before and after' comparison. Here, the pairing removes variability arising from the initial state of the subjects, for example, weight gain of mice on a diet, where the weight gain may depend on the initial weight.

- Application of a treatment and control to parts of the same subject or to closely related subjects. This allows comparison without complications arising from different origin of subjects, for example, drug or placebo given to sibling rats, virus-containing or control solution swabbed on left or right halves of a leaf.

- Application of treatment and control under shared conditions. This allows comparison without complications arising from different environments of subjects, for example, rats in a cage, plants in a pot.

Multifactorial experiments

These involve applying two or more treatments to the experimental subjects in a predetermined way that allow interactions among the treatments can be analysed by specialised statistics. They are economical on resources because of 'hidden replication' – when two or more treatments are given to a subject, the result acts statistically as a replicate for each treatment.

Matched samples represent a restriction on randomisation where you make a balanced selection of subjects for treatments on the basis of some attribute or attributes that may influence results, for example, age, sex, prior history. The effect of matching should be to 'cancel out' the unwanted source(s) of variation. Disadvantages include the subjective element in choice of character(s) to be balanced, inexact matching of quantitative characteristics, the time matching takes and possible wastage of unmatched subjects.

When analysed statistically, both paired comparisons and matched samples can show up differences between treatments that might otherwise be rejected on the basis of a fully randomised design, but note that the statistical analysis may be different.

Repetition of experiments

Even if your experiment is well designed and analysed, only limited conclusions can be made. Firstly, what you can say is valid for a particular place and time, with a particular investigator, experimental subject and method of applying treatments. Secondly, if your results were significant at the 5 per cent level of probability (**Ch 21**), there is still an approximately 1 in 20 chance that the results did arise by chance. To guard against these possibilities, it is important that experiments are repeated. Also, it makes sense to repeat work so that you can have full confidence in your conclusions. Many scientists recommend that experiments are done three times in total.

SAMPLING

When carrying out research, it is rare to be able to observe or measure every individual or location in the population or space in which you are interested. In practice, statistics obtained from a subset (or sample) are used to estimate relevant parameters for the total population or area. Samples consist of data values for a particular variable (for example, sodium ion concentration), each recorded from an individual sampling unit (for example, a core sample) in a sample of n units (for example, $n = 50$ cores) taken from the population or area under investigation (for example, a particular geographical location). The term 'replicate' can be applied either to the measurement or the actual sampling unit. When estimating population or location parameters from sample statistics, the sample size is important, larger sample sizes allowing greater statistical confidence. However, the optimum sample size is normally a balance between statistical and practical considerations.

Sampling is used in fieldwork where natural populations are to be observed under undisturbed conditions; however, the same principles apply in a laboratory context.

At the outset, it is important to provide a complete description of the biological population or area being sampled. Failure to do this will make your results difficult to interpret or to compare with other observations, including your own. You should take great care to minimise selection bias, or population parameters inferred from your samples will be unrealistic and this may invalidate your work and its conclusions.

Definitions

Population – all those individuals or locations within a specified time or space about which inferences are to be made, specified according to some biological definition (perhaps related to life history, growth stage, or sex), and normally investigated at a particular location and time.

Parameter – a numerical constant or mathematical function used to describe a particular population or location (for example, the mean height of 18-year-old females).

Statistic – an estimate of a parameter obtained from a sample (for example, the height of 18-year-old females based on those in your keep-fit class).

Choosing a relevant population: factors to specify

These should include:

- exact geographical location;
- type of habitat or geology;
- date and time of sampling;
- age, sex, physiological condition and health of sampled organisms;
- other details relevant to your work, for example, an index of pollution, geological background.

This information might apply to all members of the population or form a matrix of data associated with all samples. Do not include data for which the appropriate population specification is unavailable.

Deciding on a sampling strategy

A sampling strategy should allow you to obtain reliable and useful information about your particular population(s) or area(s), while using your resources efficiently. Selecting a sample involves the formulation of rules and methods (the sampling protocol) by which some members of the population or locations are included in the sample. The chosen sample is then measured using defined procedures to obtain relevant data. Finally, the information so obtained is processed to calculate appropriate statistics. Truly representative samples should be:

- taken at random, or in a manner that ensures that all members of the population or all parts of an area have an equal chance of being selected;

- large enough to provide sufficient precision in estimation of population characteristics;
- unbiased by the sampling procedure or equipment.

You should decide on a sampling protocol before any investigation proceeds. The main aspects to be determined are: the position of samples; the size and shape of the sampling area; and the number of sampling units in each sample. Before this can be done, however, information is required about the likely distribution of organisms or other factor of interest. This can be even (homogeneous), patchy (contagious), stratified (homogeneous within sub-areas) or present as a gradient (Figure 24.2). You might decide which type applies from a pilot study, published research or by analogy with other systems.

When choosing a sampling strategy, the chief options are:

- point sampling, where samples are taken at specific co-ordinate locations;
- quadrat sampling, where samples are obtained within a 2-dimensional area;
- transect sampling, where samples are taken along a linear track.

Table 24.2 outlines relevant matters to take into account. Regarding sampling position, Figure 24.2(b) illustrates representative strategies mentioned in this table.

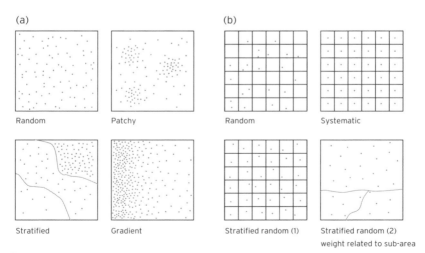

(a)

Random   Patchy

Stratified   Gradient

(b)

Random   Systematic

Stratified random (1)   Stratified random (2)
weight related to sub-area

Figure 24.2 Examples (a) types of distribution and (b) methods of sampling.
In (a) the dots represent individuals, while in (b) they represent sampling positions.

Table 24.2 Issues to be considered when creating a sampling strategy.

The shape and dimensions of the sampling area

- Quadrats are usually circular or square. A circular quadrat has the advantage that its position can be marked as a single (central) point and the area defined by use of a tape measure, whereas a square quadrat may require marking at each corner. Transects are generally used when it is difficult to move through the site to positions.

- When the distribution is truly random, then all quadrat sizes are equally effective for estimating population parameters (assuming the total number of individuals sampled is equal). If the distribution is patchy, a smaller quadrat size may be more effective than a larger one: too large an area might obscure the true nature of the clumped distribution. If the distribution is stratified or graded, then the sampling area is generally less important than sampling position. However, the size of the organisms must be considered: it is obvious that you would require different-sized quadrats for trees in a forest than for daisies on a lawn.

- Small sample areas have the advantage that more small samples can usually be taken for the same amount of labour. This may result in increased precision and many small areas will cover a wider range of the habitat than few large ones, so the catch can be more representative. However, sampling error at the edge of quadrats is proportionally greater as sample area diminishes. To avoid such effects, you need to establish a protocol for dealing with items that overlap the edge of the quadrats.

Position of sampling

- In simple random sampling, the coordinates for sampling points are chosen using random numbers. Every organism in the population or location thus has an equal chance of selection, but the area may not be covered evenly. This method works best if the distribution of organisms or factors is homogeneous.

- Systematic sampling involves using some form of pattern or grid to select samples. The advantage is simplicity, but the disadvantage is potential bias if the pattern coincides with some periodic distribution of the population or factor.

- Stratified random sampling ensures that each part of the area is represented. The area is divided into sub-areas within which random sampling is carried out.

Number of sampling units per sample

- When small numbers of sampling units are present, values of sample statistics will be susceptible to the effects of random variation – especially true if the underlying spatial distribution is patchy. You may then be unable to demonstrate statistically that there are differences between populations or areas. On the other hand, measuring very large numbers of replicates may represent an impractical workload.

- If you do not wish to sample the whole of a quadrat, perhaps because the density of sampling units is too high, you can employ sub-sampling by studying a defined part of the quadrat ('two-stage sampling').

Sampling in time

If your samples are taken at different times, this can present problems, especially those related to logistics. Also, if examining a phenomenon that fluctuates regularly (for example, with a period governed by day and night, or high and low tide), then the frequency of sampling has to be determined with that periodicity in mind.

PREPARATION FOR RESEARCH ACTIVITY

If you want to gain the most from your research activity, good preparation is essential. Often lab procedures and field observations are tightly scheduled and you should be prepared to be 'up and running' almost from the start. You should:

- know the theoretical background to the methods you will be using;
- be familiar with any instructions or protocols you've been given or have developed;
- have a detailed plan for what you will be doing, if necessary with minute-by-minute instructions;
- make sure you have the appropriate equipment ready to take to carry out your work;
- be ready to record the results or observations, for example, by preparing a table ready to write down data values.

If the methods you are using are new to you, then it may be helpful to discuss them with your supervisor or another student, postdoc or technician familiar with what is involved. If you are trying to replicate materials and methods from a research paper, there may be minor aspects of the procedures that are vital for success. Try to identify and copy these.

Reserving shared equipment or facilities

In planning your work, make sure you have identified points in the research process when you may need to reserve specialist equipment or facilities and so ensure that it is available when you need it.

APPROPRIATE CONDUCT IN THE LAB AND FIELD

It is easy to become complacent about safety, especially as accidents are thankfully rare. However, the rules associated with lab or fieldwork (**Ch 19**) will have your safety as their primary concern, so you must pay attention to them. You may have to work with toxic chemicals, dangerous instruments or in hazardous environments, so care is essential. It will be assumed you are familiar from undergraduate days with basic safety measures and legislation, about the fire drill and relevant hazard symbols. Ensure you attend training events if this is not the case.

 Giving priority to safety

Safety rules are common sense and should be part of your normal practice. However, be sure that you keep safety as a priority and do not become slap-dash just because you've become familiar with the procedures or working environment.

CARRYING OUT INSTRUCTIONS AND NOTING RESULTS

Often, you will need to follow procedures as indicated from a series of instructions, or detailed in the Materials and Methods section of a research paper. Always read instructions right through before starting as this may help you organise your activities. You may wish to highlight key points or lay out tables ready to record your data. The language of instructions will be very precise and should be followed to the letter or number – for example, success will often depend on the precision with which you measure out reagents, carry out timing or control temperature.

 Use 'dead' time effectively

During lab experiments, there may be delays between parts of your work as reactions develop, or as instruments complete a process. Use this time to look ahead to what you will be doing next, to create tables or graphs ready for recording your results, to jot down ideas for your conclusions or to read related literature.

Being able to record accurately what you see and measure is a vital skill in the sciences. The following key tips may help for recording your observations.

- Don't rely on your memory – write down everything.
- Never write on scraps of paper (you'll lose them) – use a proper lab notebook.
- Always date each page and provide full details of the specimen or experiment.
- If you are recording numbers, use an appropriate number of significant figures to take account of the precision (or, perhaps more strictly, the lack of precision) of your method.
- If drawing diagrams, make sure these have a descriptive title and are well labelled.
- In the field, be prepared for bad weather – buy a special wet-weather notebook or take a clear plastic bag to enclose your notebook, and use a pencil as this will write on damp paper.
- Draw any graphs or tables according to the normal scientific conventions (**Ch 21**).

Always try to write up your work when it is fresh in your mind. You may be tired after a lengthy session in the lab or field, but if you delay for too long you may forget useful details.

ACTION POINTS

24.1 Read up about your methods before you start work. Having a deeper understanding of what you are doing and why it will help you to work safely, make sure you do not waste resources through mistakes in procedure and ensure you obtain more accurate results. For these reasons don't be tempted to skip this stage and move directly to the procedure itself.

24.2 Think in advance about statistical analysis. Work out how you will analyse your data – this may dictate some aspects of the experimental layout or sampling protocol. If you have some idea of the variability of the data, this may help you to work out how many replicates will be required to demonstrate a significant difference between treatments or samples.

24.3 Create a checklist of potential safety issues. Take into account the safety information provided in the relevant lab handbooks, lab notices and your supervisor's advice. Rehearse safety scenarios: imagine what you would do in different situations, such as if there were a fire, if a lab colleague swallowed a toxic chemical, or if someone cut themselves. This will make you more aware of the dangers of the lab or field environment and might help you react faster if needed.

WRITING UP
YOUR RESEARCH

25

LINKS BETWEEN RESEARCH, WRITING AND SPEAKING

How to gain from the interactions between investigation, communication and thought

The act of research stimulates new ideas; the process of writing up these thoughts refines and generates further thinking; speaking about your research and writing promotes yet more ideas. This chapter prompts an understanding of the processes and outcomes involved in this cycle.

KEY TOPICS

→ Recognising key features of academic discourse
→ How research informs what you write
→ How writing helps thinking
→ How speaking helps thinking, writing and research
→ Placing your academic writing in context

That your research activity will inform your writing might be regarded as self-evident for, without the research, there would be no writing. Less apparent is that both the acts of writing and speaking about your work contribute beneficially to thinking and, hence, the research process and the academic discourse that supports it.

RECOGNISING KEY FEATURES OF ACADEMIC DISCOURSE

Academic discourse is the term used to describe the ways of thinking about and explaining concepts by means of objective and systematic analysis and argument. To achieve this in both speech and writing in academia in general, particular forms of words are used and further styled to meet the needs of specific disciplines. Thus, learning about, understanding and using appropriate discourse models is vital for PhD study since these models inform researching, writing and speaking within these communities, creating a shared medium of communication that is readily absorbed and understood.

Characteristics of discipline discourse

To a certain extent, academic discourse concerns appropriate use of vocabulary and grammar – the 'mechanics' of writing – but it is about much more than this at the subject and discipline level, including: characteristic patterns of logic and reasoning (Chs 17 and 18); standard methods of quotation and citation (Ch 20); acceptable and unacceptable forms of expression, such as analogy and abbreviation (Ch 26); distinctive discourse markers (Ch 27) and deployment of statistics, figures and tables (Ch 21).

Without an awareness and assimilation of the appropriate style of communication, no postgraduate can function effectively. These discipline discourses are the building blocks of thought that go beyond simple description. They help define and refine ideas, create new ways of looking at a problem and extend those that have already been introduced. Thus, thinking, writing and professional discussion are part of a virtuous circle of research that benefits all three activities but are predicated on developing a mastery of the relevant discourse.

HOW RESEARCH INFORMS WHAT YOU WRITE

As a starting point, imagine that you have some formative ideas about your area of study, based on your initial researches and proposal (Chs 3 and 4), but have yet to refine the detail. Conventionally, this would mean delving yet deeper into the literature covering your area of interest. This would allow you to establish a context for your later thinking, and in the sciences, a platform for setting up observations and experiments (Ch 24).

A review of the established literature (the 'classic' articles and books) in your field of study might have started with a few sources recommended by your supervisor or those that are mentioned in a review of the subject by a noted figure in the area. If the area is completely new to you, an advanced undergraduate textbook might also be suitable. From this reading, you should have gained:

- an understanding of the scope of the subject;
- the key concepts;
- any jargon, key terms and commonly used word 'strings';
- the theoretical background;
- the orthodoxy, or established viewpoint; or, where there is disagreement, the major schools of thought.

Displacement activities versus writing

The synergy between research and writing can, at some stages and for some students, lead to a tension. For example, there is the potential for convincing yourself that the work of the laboratory, Action Research activities or research reading require just one more trial, one more interview or one more article to ensure completeness. In reality, this is often a kind of displacement activity that is undertaken to avoid getting to grips with the thesis write-up or completing the progress report or paper. Recognising this tendency is valuable and one of the best ways of overcoming it is to ensure you write and speak about your research as soon and as often as possible.

Your deeper reading should involve a thorough search of the current literature that has appeared in recent journals and review volumes. You could source this material by browsing in your library, engaging with subject-specific search engines and conducting an online searches using key words related to the topic of interest, or again, by consulting your supervisor or specialist librarian (Ch 7). An analysis of this reading might provide an indication of:

- the research workers who are currently active;
- new trends in thinking in your area;
- the main areas of present-day activity;
- areas of unresolved debate or difference;
- any new methodological approaches being applied.

Often, your first readings in an area are highly influential on your later thinking. Your research reading might reveal a sub-topic or niche area that interests you, or an area which is not currently understood, but which you feel might be advanced by your efforts. Moreover, none of this research reading will be wasted effort because any reading you do has the potential to contribute to your expanding understanding of the field.

Research reading is valuable in another respect that relates to your writing. It introduces you to the discourse conventions of your subject. This inevitably influences your own writing, although your assimilation of the use of language and ways of explaining and arguing particular to your discipline may be subliminal over time rather than a conscious and deliberate attempt to emulate others writing in your field.

How you engage with the material you read will reflect on your writing in that you will be making notes, recording observations of your own thoughts and those of others, all of which will involve constructing writing. You will be processing thoughts about the research and to some extent experimenting with and rehearsing explanations, use of terms and expressions that will influence the writing that will ultimately appear in your thesis.

In the sciences, this processing of thought and language in the research process often happens through the practical activities of record-keeping relating to carrying out experiments, or making observations, and involves analysis of the data obtained. The thinking that arises from analysis of results as well as from reading related literature feeds into new avenues of research and/or experimentation. Thus, carrying out trial experiments or observations lets you know what is feasible, relevant or practical and can inform your later and final research and conclusions.

Extracting meaning from complex data sets

Often, the meaning behind data will be masked by the volume of numbers or the complexity of the information. The way you write up the results and the conclusions you draw from them will develop as your analysis progresses. Thus, condensing quantitative data into descriptive statistics and graphical and tabular summaries can assist in its interpretation (**Ch 21**); hypothesis-testing using statistical methods can allow you to place probabilities on provisional theories about your results. Data analysis also has value in topics based on qualitative information. This can be categorised and evaluated through the use of tables, comparative grids and coding (**Ch 22**). Such exercises force you to think of similarities and differences and even writing the headings for columns and rows can make you think more analytically about a topic.

HOW WRITING HELPS THINKING

Writing is clearly a process that involves various aspects of thinking. You need to decide what to write, recall the appropriate subject-specific vocabulary to express this, create a logical pattern to the words, sentences and paragraphs following the conventions of language and analysis, and ensure that what you have written conveys the intended sense and meaning.

Scholarly writing follows particular conventions (**Ch 26**). These involve aspects of structure, language and citation. The act of putting your thoughts into words in a scholarly manner has many beneficial outcomes, including:

- establishing a coherence to your thoughts, through the need to create a logical written narrative within a formalised structure;
- formulating your ideas more precisely through the requirement to choose appropriate vocabulary to describe and explain them;
- expanding on ideas through the need to explore consequences, make comparisons, analyse alternative hypotheses, and ensure balance in discussion;
- putting your ideas into the overall research context by referring to the work of others;
- thinking more deeply about your work by formulating an introduction to it and laying down the conclusions you have made;
- providing a detailed examination of results (for example, inspection of evidence, statistical analysis) that may reveal hitherto unexpected features and conclusions;
- sparking new ideas by focussing your thoughts during the writing process itself.

The last of these potential outcomes is probably the most intriguing. Research about how original thought and inspiration come about has not identified particular mechanisms. Nevertheless, some activities allied to writing seem to assist in the generation of new ideas.

- Making notes. This can be as simple as jotting down quotes and key ideas from a source, and then elaborating them with your own secondary thoughts. Keeping a notebook beside you at all times can allow you to take advantage of opportunistic thoughts – you may

Keeping a research journal

This is an excellent way of forming links between your research and your writing for students in all disciplines. Some supervisors recommend keeping a daily or weekly diary that records progress, issues arising, questions to be addressed and points for discussion with the supervisor as well as ideas and concepts. This 'routine writing' can help to enhance fluency in writing and, again, stimulate thinking as you write. Furthermore, since the average three-year period of postgraduate research is a long time to keep ideas in your head, it makes great sense to jot down provisional conclusions and ideas as you go along.

be 'in the mood' or the muse may strike you at odd times and often when you least expect it. If you are ready to jot down these notions, then they won't be lost. Related to this is the note-making process that is part of research reading activity (**Ch 8**) and is probably one of the earliest engagements that the reader/writer has with transforming thought into words.

- Taking a disciplined approach to the content of your writing and its organisation. This applies to note-making, to planning, to drafting and to crafting text. For example, a brainstorming activity (**Ch 17**) and the organisational plan (**Ch 26**) for your writing that results from it might identify missing elements of an overall picture. It is sometimes only when a writer has an overview of a topic that he or she is able to identify where an argument, position or the evidence that supports it is incomplete, and what needs to be added to fill the missing space.

- Prompting associations. The act of writing seems to assist the mind to focus on an idea and to develop it. At its most extreme, this is seen in the method known as 'free-writing', where a writer in search of inspiration is advised to start and continue a defined period of rapid writing with the sole aim of generating new thoughts and ideas (**Ch 17**). Sometimes, the act of making associations can be spontaneous and can occur as part of the action of writing. Experts in the field of writing composition and discourse analysis call this process 'writing as thinking'.

- Reflecting and carrying out reflective writing. Analysing your own reactions to events or to your research readings can be a useful way of generating ideas. This can take you beyond simplistic surface responses to what you read or observe, and into a realm of deeper analysis.

- Editing and refining a piece of writing. This activity often prompts you to think more deeply about content and how you have expressed ideas. Indeed, a key postgraduate skill is the ability to analyse and critique your own writing (**Ch 30**). This becomes evident especially when condensing written text or working to a specified word limit, as this forces you to seek the essence of your idea before expressing it accurately in a minimum number of words.

Some or all of the above activities may prove valuable as you develop your thesis and the notions that lie behind it. It can be seen that writing and research interact, the one prompting the other. A corollary of this is that writing your thesis is not an event that starts at a single point of time. It is part of a continual process that begins with initial reading, note-making and the preliminary research proposal that arises from this. It continues as you analyse research material, observe or experiment and reaches a new intensive phase when you decide you are ready to assemble a thesis.

HOW SPEAKING HELPS THINKING, WRITING AND RESEARCH

The ability to speak is what distinguishes humans from other mammals; the ability to speak fluently and cogently about your research is what will mark you out as a promising PhD student. This ability cannot be achieved by sitting quietly pondering in a corner until you need to make a formal presentation or enter into less formal discussion with your supervisor. To express your thoughts cogently, they first need to be gathered and organised, and this usually means that they are recorded in some sort of written form, allowing you to:

- put ideas into words – even the thoughts that you did not know you had;
- put these thoughts into some kind of cogent order;
- rehearse the language used to express your thoughts;
- rehearse the argument or debate or audit of supporting evidence;
- describe findings without the aid of visual cues (in some cases); and
- revisit and reformulate thoughts.

All of this can be done without interruption and without criticism – it is essentially a solo activity that is the preliminary to speaking about your work. When you present your ideas orally – perhaps with the support of the printed word in PowerPoint or handout format – you are replaying the ideas from your initial written thoughts, since writing and speaking complement each other in refining thought and expression.

When you are writing text, you have more time to tease out and play with ideas, but there is no immediate feedback as in speaking situations, where you can see the body-language of your audience. For example, when talking, it is possible to judge whether people have a clear understanding (they will, smile, nod or reply 'yes' or 'I agree', or frown and indicate disagreement or lack of comprehension). If the latter, then you may have to rephrase things. This requires mastery of your topic and will reveal where your own understanding or expression are weak.

Reading your text aloud

When you have done a particularly complex piece of writing you should try reading it aloud to yourself in the first instance. You will readily identify errors of expression and inconsistency in logic. New thoughts may occur to you as you progress through the text; secondly, you should read it aloud to a friend or better still, try to explain your written text orally without reference to the text to that friend and ask them to interrupt you when they do not understand something. Again this will provide you with opportunities to amend the form or content of your writing – whichever applies.

There is a commonplace observation that you never understand a concept as well as when you have tried to explain it to someone or a group of people. Expressing your thoughts orally requires that you tease out the concepts and present them in clear (if sometimes colloquial) language. Opportunities to do this arise in several situations and modes. In terms of formal delivery, honing your written ideas into a style appropriate for presentation of a conference paper or poster will require you to adopt one style of academic discourse and your thinking about how to do this will influence structure and language. By contrast, in order to deliver similar content in a teaching situation, it will have to be considered from different perspectives involving different thought processes, possibly involving some simplification to meet the needs of that audience. In another situation, that of a progress committee interview, explaining your research will involve different thought processes and preparatory writing. In each instance, you have to think carefully about the best way to explain your ideas for the understanding of others.

Putting your ideas and results in their research context is a vital aspect of scholarly writing. This can be seen from inspection of many articles in the primary literature. You will find that the text is interspersed with references to the work of others. There are several reasons for this.

- It helps the author to avoid plagiarism by giving due credit to others (**Ch 20**).
- It allows precedence to be assigned to the originators of ideas.
- It can be used as a shorthand for explanations and detail by referring the reader to a source.
- It can reflect the strength of opinion – *pro* or *contra* – about a research theme.
- It demonstrates that the author of the current work is aware of the key research and those active in the field.
- It allows the author to place his or her work alongside its historical background.

The exploratory work of reviewing the literature is often reflected in research writing. For example, an Introduction (either to a thesis or a research paper) may consider the historical development of a subject. This can be used as a device to introduce key concepts and their originators, explain theoretical background, mention disagreements between past researchers and place the current work in a developmental timeline. The Methods or Methodology section may similarly refer to extant literature and demonstrate the linkage between that and your research and corresponding writing. The Discussion section will often include comparisons with previous results or findings. In these ways, the threads between research, thinking and writing can be drawn through your thesis, to create a cogent, interlinked whole.

ACTION POINTS

25.1 Find an opportunity to discuss your current research with a friend or family member. Afterwards, reflect on how well you explained things, what that reveals about your own understanding, and what new thoughts about your research have arisen from the experience.

25.2 Review your working practices to see whether you are capitalising on all your ideas. Do you ever feel you have 'lost' an idea because it has been forgotten because 'life got in the way'? Do you keep a notebook or computing device with you at all times to ensure this cannot happen? When you have a new idea, do you deliberately set down to explore subsidiary threads of thought and connections? Do you brainstorm ideas as soon as possible and store these notes appropriately? What methods might help to improve your productivity?

25.3 Create a 'system' for use when reading a new source. This might simply be a checklist or table of aspects of your study or thesis that you might use to prompt thought on the source's relevance and context in your research position (**Ch 18**). It could also be a 'map' of the subject, constructed like a mindmap. If these notes or diagrams are stored appropriately, they may assist greatly when you come to produce your final draft.

26

THE NATURE OF SCHOLARLY WRITING

How to produce formal writing at PhD level

An understanding of the requirements of academic writing for research purposes and the developmental process required to reach the standards required will help when starting the process of writing up your thesis.

KEY TOPICS

→ Fundamentals of good scholarly writing

→ The developmental process for scholarly writing

→ Your supervisor as your initial academic audience

Scholarly writing by implication is intended for academic audiences and needs to meet the standards judged essential when presenting work to specialist and wider academic communities. This does not mean that scholarly writing has to be complex in its structures or heavy in style or use of language. Its function is to convey ideas clearly, succinctly and effectively, so that readers can understand and absorb clean lines of thought, argument or discussion, presented in a logical manner.

To develop such a style of writing you need to understand its nature and what it requires of you as a developing writer.

FUNDAMENTALS OF GOOD SCHOLARLY WRITING

Scholarly writing is an expression of higher-order thinking (**Ch 17**). In terms of a PhD thesis, it explains the research journey and its outcomes and must fulfil the following criteria:

● Accuracy – reporting an accurate account of the research process and findings.

Find and adopt models of good writing

As you read the literature in your subject, you will note that some sources seem to be written better than others. A symptom of this is that you are able to comprehend the 'message' of the writing easily, even though it might involve complex ideas. In contrast, other sources will seem impenetrable, jargon-ridden and difficult to understand. Look more closely at the well-written sources to see if you can work out how the author(s) have achieved their clarity. Look also for the qualities of balance, objectivity and tentativeness. Use these sources as a model for your own writing.

- Clarity – writing in a style and format that are easily comprehended.
- Balance – providing a considered appraisal of the issue by building from the known to unknown (**Ch 18**).
- Originality – reporting research that introduces new knowledge to the field (**Ch 17**).
- Objectivity – avoiding bias (**Ch 18**).
- Principled methods – reporting work conducted following established methodologies based on ethical procedures for the collection of data (**Ch 19**).
- Referencing sources – affording recognition to other contributors in the research field by attributing their work following a recognised citation and referencing model (**Ch 20**).
- Tentativeness – acknowledging that findings are rarely definitive by explaining the uncertainties that exist in the research (**Chs 22** and **23**).

No single approach applies to all areas since how we write as scholars relates to the norms of subject discipline. However, three fundamental factors influence all postgraduate writing. These are:

- the precise writing task to be completed (genre);
- the intended readership (audience);
- the conventional tone and style of the text (register).

Genre

This term describes types of writing for particular contexts. As a postgraduate, you will find that, although writing your thesis is the end-goal of your research, writing in different genres will be a part of your postgraduate work.

Some typical examples are:

- Abstracts
- Case studies
- Critical incidents
- Data recording
- Essays
- Journal articles
- Lab reports
- Letters and emails

- Literature reviews
- Note-making
- Note-taking
- Ordinance transfer reports
- Postgraduate feedback
- PowerPoint slides

- Progress monitoring reports
- Proposal writing
- Reflective analyses
- Research notes
- Summaries
- Surveys
- Theses

Each genre requires a subtly different approach to the writing. This might mean level of detail, it could mean verb tense, and it might include vocabulary. It will be necessary to adopt these different forms of language as you write your thesis; others will be required for the administrative aspects of the research process. However, all writing contributes to your development as an academic author.

Find models for genre

When writing up your work in a particular genre for the first time, find a model you can follow. This might be one of your supervisor's papers, a section of a previous student's PhD thesis, or a publication from your field. Use this as a template for your own writing. This does *not* mean copying it, but rather adopting a similar style.

Audience

Your audience will include your academic peers in your discipline area, so you will need to use professional language in ways that are consistent with scholarly principles and expression. Thus, not only the language structures, but also the argot (jargon and idiom) of the discipline is key to writing for the expert audience. Each discipline and even sub-discipline or school of thought has its own jargon (shared language). In certain cases, the same word may mean different things in different subjects.

However, if your writing is too complex and jargon-rich then your reader may simply discard it as impenetrable. Conversely, if it is too down-to-earth, then it could appear simplistic and 'beneath' your target readership. The two examples below show, firstly, an overly complex piece of writing that would confuse many audiences and, secondly, a simpler text is that is clear, neutral and understandable by most audiences.

Example 1

These neophyte cognitive developers have innate resistance to the inculcation of cerebral processing in relation to technological ramifications of knowledge acquisition. Absence of verbal intercourse in cognitive fora aggravates their detachment from reality and reinforces isolationism.

Example 2

These new students have a natural fear of using technology in learning. Their silence in lectures adds to their isolation from the learning process.

The first version comprises 36 words while the second uses only 24 words. The difference in word count provides another good reason for simpler writing.

Register

Tenor or register in scholarly writing is important. Traditionally, writing in a formal tone is expected. Language should follow the rules of grammar, including sentence and paragraph structure, punctuation and spelling. For example, it would not be appropriate to use contractions or slang expression. Therefore, the sentence 'We ain't gonna spend too long banging on about this' would be entirely out of place in scholarly text and would perhaps be expressed more formally as 'Little time will be spent considering this point'.

This is an extreme example and modern approaches in some disciplines are less stringent with regard to some aspects of language use such as passive voice, first person singular/plural and a more conversational register. However, the academic world is often very conservative in its practices and, if in doubt, it is best to opt for the more formal option. Scholarly writing should never replicate spoken language.

Some students find that writing can present difficulties. This may simply be because they are unsure of the expectations, conventions and practices (**Chs 27** and **30**).

THE DEVELOPMENTAL PROCESS FOR SCHOLARLY WRITING

Table 26.1 contrasts the nature of undergraduate and postgraduate writing. As this table illustrates, the writing process for PhD level research probably requires new and higher-level skills than the type of work you have been carrying out until now. Essentially, as an undergraduate, your research and writing skills will have been driven by the demands of your coursework; as a postgraduate you will still have to conform to university regulations but within those confines you will have considerably more latitude in how you learn and to what end. While this may seem obvious, what may be less obvious is how differences in your approach to study will manifest itself in the nature of your academic writing.

Practical institutional guidance on the specifics of producing writing for thesis purposes is variable. The level of detail can vary widely and relate more to presentational features (**Ch 30**) and generalisations about aspects such as plagiarism (**Ch 20**). Therefore, in practice, new scholars can find it often difficult to identify sources of advice in respect of the structure, the writing style, the structuring of content and the thinking that should characterise writing related to the research process. Those new to formal academic writing often find that they have to 'second guess' the implicit 'rules of the game' with the postgraduate common room, office or laboratory providing fertile

Table 26.1 The contrasting nature of undergraduate and postgraduate writing.

Undergraduate writing	Postgraduate writing
Strict guidelines defined in handbook	Guidelines general and implicit rather than articulated; understanding and knowledge of these tends to be assumed
Short lead time and fixed deadline	Deadline in months and years
Relatively short but complete text	Intermittent writing episodes but with need to produce much longer integrated text
Essay or report format	'Traditional' thesis format or more innovative structure chosen by writer
Writing in response to set task, topic or question	Themes, topics and approaches identified by the writer
Limited literature search often based on secondary source material	Extensive literature search based on seminal works and cutting-edge research sources
Possible short answer formats in coursework and exams	Varied styles for publication, presentation and thesis
May be exclusively technical in content with minimal prose	Extensive prose explanations and analysis based on own and others' research
Feedback in grade format with additional individual written guidance in some cases on response to task rather than writing	Feedback intermittent; may focus on content in earlier stages with language issues highlighted – in detail or in general

grounds for the creation of folklore about the nature of writing at this level – often anecdotally based on the personal preferences of an individual supervisor or department.

Lack of explicit direction on writing the thesis may be attributable to different reasons. In one respect, at the outset, this may seem less relevant than setting up the research project. In another respect, because supervisors are successful academics they may be unaware of the writing difficulties that their postgraduate students may anticipate, unless they have themselves found writing problematic. Another view is that accessing the formal regulations and working out how to write the thesis is, in a sense, seen as an indicator of deeper thinking and of the initiative expected at this level.

Whatever your situation, your supervisor will be the person who will monitor your research work and the writing that relates to it. You will write in a variety of genres such as those listed earlier and your supervisor will be your first critical audience. Consequently, it is as well to be aware of the expectations that your supervisor will have of you.

YOUR SUPERVISOR AS YOUR INITIAL ACADEMIC AUDIENCE

When you were an undergraduate, your written coursework represented a 'private' dialogue between you and the academic who graded your work and provided some written feedback. Depending on the institution, there may have been an element of anonymity about this process. Hence, some students may not even know the identity of the person who assessed their work, let alone have a conversation about the strengths and weaknesses of their writing or the subject content.

At postgraduate level, this is not the case. The 'solo' nature of undergraduate writing alters because supervisors have a much more direct relationship with their research students and, consequently, with their writing. This is still a private dialogue, but is one that will eventually reach a wider audience. Hence, your supervisor will have a more influential impact on what and how you write based on certain assumptions. Table 26.2 shows how shifts in perception, assumption and expectation apply to the academic in these different roles. Thus, at the outset of your working relationship, it is as well to be aware of how your supervisor may view your writing.

However, scholars new to postgraduate study may be hesitant to ask for definitive guidance on writing from supervisors. This can be for a number of reasons such as a fear of looking stupid in the eyes of the supervisor because as postgraduates they feel that they should know about writing. However, more often, it is simply that students do not know until they have started writing what the questions might be. While

Table 26.2 Academic roles in relation to student writing. This shows the changing role of the academic as assessor or supervisor as you progress from undergraduate to postgraduate level.

As assessor of undergraduate assignments	As supervisor of postgraduate
Assumes good writing style and competence	Assumes competence and sophistication in writing style
Expects ability to self-correct with moderate guidance	Expects ability to self-correct with minimal guidance
Accepts simpler, less technical language	Expects use of more sophisticated language and technical terms
In some subjects, requires short pieces of writing rather than extended prose; accepts effects of limited exposure to conventions of academic writing	Aware that some students may never have had to write academic prose previously and recognises unfamiliarity with style, levels of formality, specialist language use in earlier stages of writing up
Places more focus on content and response to set task than on language or style	Expects facility with modifying language, for example, combining sentences for conciseness and improved information flow
May tolerate less coherent discourse [although not recommended]	Dislikes 'padding' expressions, clichés and circuitous explanations
Accepts use of first person sometimes but may advise avoidance in other assignments	Permits and may encourage selective use of first person depending on context or referencing style
Tolerates some measure of colloquial style [although not recommended]	Expects more formal, and hence less colloquial, register as norm for thesis and publication

acknowledging this, early discussion with your supervisor about the general principles of academic writing is recommended because this will help you develop your understanding of possible strategies and models that may be possible within your field.

ACTION POINTS

26.1 Check out guidance for submission of theses in your own institution. These may include guidance on writing, or directions to relevant guidance sources.

26.2 Discuss writing preferences with your supervisor. Clarify preferences in relation to language usage issues such as passive voice, use of contractions, abbreviations and specialist language. Having this conversation at an early point in your working relationship will save you inordinate amounts of time when you are writing. For example, having to rewrite an entire paper using passive voice and other features of formal register in accordance with your supervisor's preferences will be both time-consuming and irksome.

26.3 Ask a fellow student, friend or family member to read a sample of your writing. It might be better if they are not familiar with your subject. Ask them to comment on the style of your writing, whether it is easily understood, and whether they can appreciate the logic and sense of your text, even though they may need to take some facts or jargon for granted.

SCHOLARLY WRITING STYLE

How to construct effective academic text

Scholarly writing has its own style, with modifications for each discipline. Having a grasp of the organisation of this form of writing will help you to develop your own style and organise the text of your thesis appropriately.

KEY TOPICS

→ The organisation of the discourse of text

→ Functional aspects of written text

→ The organisation of paragraphs and sentences within text

→ Aspects of language used in academic writing

Research writing takes time to develop. Your final thesis will be your best writing, but it will be the product of a process consisting of many drafts, false starts and discarded work before it reaches the near perfect state of the final version. To help you embark on the process of developing your writing, this chapter explains some of the discursive language frameworks that underpin the construction of good academic text.

? Why is the composition of writing important?

Some people write well naturally, while others need to work at it. Scholarly writing places a premium on clear logical expression, which requires an underpinning structure. This, in turn, requires very high levels of skill in writing. An awareness of some of the technical aspects of academic writing will help you to improve these skills and construct your thesis to the expected standard.

THE ORGANISATION OF THE DISCOURSE OF TEXT

Working out how to organise and explain the huge body of ideas and information that you will derive from the literature and your own research can present a daunting challenge especially in the early stages of your postgraduate studies. However, writing your thesis can become a less formidable prospect if you have some insights into the structuring of academic text.

New writing challenges

Many disciplines at undergraduate level require little extensive writing, concentrating instead on data handling or truncated forms of writing such as short answers. Consequently, students can find themselves outside their writing 'comfort zone' at postgraduate level, because they will be expected to write extensively in ways of which they have little experience. As a result, many novice PhD researchers need to work hard at developing their writing. An awareness of the ways in which scholarly writing is achieved and of the associated skills is fundamental to successful thesis completion.

The research work of discourse analysts has contributed to a greater understanding of how language is constructed at sentence, paragraph and text levels for different genres, formats and disciplines. Analysis of scholarly writing has identified a basic model common to text in most academic disciplines, that is, one that identifies three fundamental elements: introduction, main body and conclusion. If we add to that format the principle of leading readers from general to specific points and after that back to general points, then an outline model of academic writing begins to emerge (Figure 27.1). This structure can be applied to the format of the full thesis, to the individual chapters and even to paragraphs. **Chapter 28** uses this model to construct the different chapters of a thesis. Here, the focus is on the different elements in discourse terms rather than in the specifics of the thesis.

Figure 27.2(a) shows the introductory element of Figure 27.1 as a scene-setting section covering:

- The general context of the text or topic – what the text is about, defining the parameters of the discussion within the wider field.
- The specific issue to be examined – what particular aspect will be

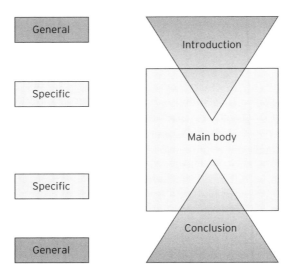

Figure 27.1 The basic structure of academic text. This diagram shows the fundamental structure of a typical piece of academic text working from the top to the bottom of the diagram. Note that each section in a chapter, for example, will comprise a number of paragraphs.

examined and possibly what will be excluded from that examination giving reasons for this choice.

- The 'statement of intent' – how the examination of the topic will be addressed in detail so that the reader is provided with a 'map' of the writer's thought process. With this insight into what to expect in the text, the reader can reflect on what they anticipate will be covered.

- The transition to the main body – how the writer prepares the reader for the specific detailed discussion of the topic.

The final section, (Figure 27.2(b)), draws the work to a conclusion by:

- restating the key theme of the work – outlining the main focus and purpose of the text;

- reviewing key issues raised in the main body of the text – reminding the reader of the main aspects explaining these in a concise way by using more technical/professional language;

- stating key conclusions derived from the main body of the discussion – an assertive stance on the conclusions reached within the text;

- placing conclusions in the wider context of the study – resituating the topic within the broader body of knowledge.

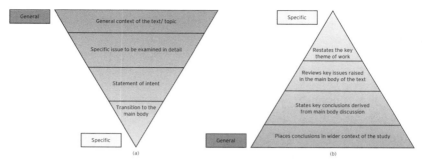

Figure 27.2 Typical structures (a) of introductory paragraphs; (b) of concluding paragraphs. The writer would usually cover these topics in order from the top to the bottom of the diagram.

There may seem to be a degree of repetition between the introductory and concluding sections. However, in practice, the difference is that the introductory section is expressed using simpler language formats and less specialised terms. By contrast, the concluding paragraphs use more sophisticated expression and terminology introduced in the main body. The latter will also refer to the results or arguments described in the main body whereas the introductory section mainly involves scene-setting.

The main body of the text should present a reasoned explanation of individual points following recognised steps of logic as part of the greater whole. However, different approaches are possible, using either inductive or deductive logic. These can be explained as follows:

● Inductive model of text structure – the writer begins by presenting the supporting information and concludes with the main point.

● Deductive model of text structure – the writer moves from the key idea and follows it with supporting information or evidence.

These models may be deployed according to customary discipline style. Some disciplines favour the inductive approach while others use the deductive approach. Sometimes also, there is no consistency within a discipline area with one academic differing in their preferences from a colleague in the same discipline. In other disciplines these approaches may be used as seen fit as a stylistic feature to vary the rhythm used in your writing.

Examples of inductive and deductive logic in writing

The sequences of statements shown here could represent the themes of sentences within a paragraph.

Inductive model – moving from examples to general principle(s)

1 Postgraduate students of nursing use action research in their doctoral studies.

2 Postgraduate students of education use action research in their doctoral studies.

3 Postgraduate students of social work use action research in their doctoral studies.

4 Therefore, all postgraduate students in the caring professions use action research in their doctoral studies.

Deductive model – moving from general principle(s) to particular instances

1 All postgraduate students in the caring professions use action research in their doctoral studies.

2 Person A is a postgraduate student of nursing.

3 Person B is a postgraduate student of social work.

4 Therefore, Persons A and B use action research in their doctoral studies.

FUNCTIONAL ASPECTS OF WRITTEN TEXT

Another dimension that academic writers need to consider involves taking into account what they are trying to do in relation to their text. For example, do they wish to describe, outline, analyse, compare or give definitions? These examples represent aspects of the text known in language terms as 'functions'. The functions most commonly used in scholarly writing and the typical discourse markers employed to achieve them are shown in Table 27.1.

Having a grasp of these functions can help when writing, especially when considering the purpose of the different sentences and paragraphs in your text. Sometimes this understanding comes subconsciously and naturally as you write, but at other times you will struggle with words. In such cases the question 'what am I trying to achieve here?' might help, and the answer might come from Table 27.1. For complex thought patterns,

Table 27.1 Important functions in scholarly writing with corresponding discourse markers.

Function	Discourse markers	
Adding	• additionally • again • also • and • and then • as well as • besides (this) • either ... or ... • equally • furthermore,	• in addition to • indeed, • in fact, • moreover, • neither...nor • not only (X) but also (Y) • or • too, • what is more,
Cause (outlining)	• as • as a result of • because • because of • due to • for the reason that	• for • inasmuch as • in response to • in that • since
Comparing	• by the same token • compared with • in like manner • in comparison with	• in the same way • likewise • similarly
Conditions (presenting)	• even if • if • given that • on condition that	• only if • providing that • unless
Contrasting and conceding	• although • besides • but • by way of contrast, • conversely • despite (this) • even though • however, • on the contrary, ... • on the other hand, ... • regardless (of this) • still ...	• in contrast, • in spite of (this) • instead, • naturally, • nevertheless, • nonetheless, • notwithstanding • of course, • though, • whereas ... • while ... • yet, ...

Continued overleaf

Effect (outlining)	• accordingly,	• so that
	• as a	• so
	• as a consequence	• so much so that
	• because of	• the consequence is that ... then
	• consequently,	• therefore
	• for that reason	• thus
	• hence	
Exemplifying	• as (evidence of)	• like
	• as an illustration,	• notably,
	• especially,	• particularly,
	• for example,	• such as
	• for instance,	• thus,
	• including	• to demonstrate this
	• in particular,	• to illustrate this
	• let us take (the case of ...)	
Giving alternatives	• again	• on the other hand
	• alternatively	• the alternative is
	• better still	
Inferring	• if not	• that implies
	• in (that) case	• then
	• otherwise	
Numbering	• at first,	• last,
	• firstly, secondly, etc.	• next,
	• finally,	• to begin with,
	• initially,	• then,
	• in the first place,	
Reasons (giving)	• as	• in order to
	• as a result of	• in response to
	• because	• since
	• due to	• so as to
	• in order that	• so that
Results (giving)	• accordingly,	• hence,
	• as a result,	• the consequence is that
	• consequently,	• then
	• for the reason that	• thus,
	• therefore,	
Reformulating	• in other words,	• to put it more simply,
	• rather,	• to paraphrase
	• that is to say,	

Summarising/ concluding	• finally, • eventually, • hence, • in all • in conclusion, • in short, • to sum up,	• in brief, • lastly, • to summarise • therefore, • thus, • to conclude,
Time sequencing	• after (a while) • afterwards • at first • at last • at the same time • before (that time) • eventually, • finally, • in the end,	• meanwhile, • next, • previously, • since (then) • so far • subsequently, • then • (up to) then
Transition (making)	• as far as ... is concerned, • as for • incidentally,	• now • to turn to • with (reference) to

pondering about the functions you are trying to perform might help you to disentangle the different elements of your position or argument. In addition to those listed in Table 27.1, the following functions are also found in academic texts: arguing; categorising; classifying; conceding; counter-arguing; defining; describing (appearance, function, operation, position, time); elaborating; enumerating; explaining; listing; opining (giving an opinion); reformulating; refuting; reporting; replacing; and sequencing.

THE ORGANISATION OF SENTENCES AND PARAGRAPHS WITHIN TEXT

Sentences in paragraphs

Understanding the role of some of types of sentence will help you to understand how these contribute to the paragraphs of which they are the building blocks. Table 27.2 lists some different types of sentence while Figure 27.3 illustrates their use in a representative paragraph.

Paragraphs in text

Paragraph formats vary according to the function that they are performing in the particular text. The example in Figure 27.3, for

Table 27.2 Some types of sentences used in paragraphs.

Type of sentence	Role in paragraph
Topic introducer sentence (TI)	Introduces the overall topic of the text (generally in the very first paragraph)
Topic sentence (TS)	Introduces a paragraph by identifying the topic of that paragraph
Developer sentence (DS)	Expands the topic by giving additional information
Modulator sentence (MS)	Acts as a linking sentence and is often introduced by a signpost word moving to another aspect of the topic within the same paragraph
Terminator or transition sentence (TERS)	Concludes the discussion of a topic within a paragraph, but can also be used to provide a link to the topic of the next paragraph

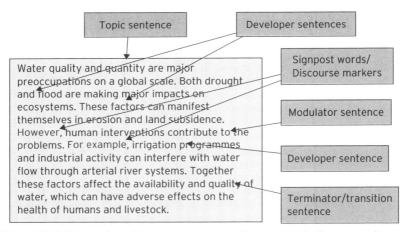

Figure 27.3 Illustration of how sentences make up a typical paragraph.

example, is a paragraph that is describing a situation; from a different perspective, it might be seen as reporting cause and effect. This suggests that the function of some paragraphs depends on their position in the text. Table 27.3 shows some different paragraph models. These are then exemplified in Table 27.4.

ASPECTS OF LANGUAGE USED IN ACADEMIC WRITING

Analysis of the organisation of text gives insights into the use of the language within academic writing, as discussed below.

Table 27.3 Outlines of paragraph models. These outlines can be compared with the texts modelling the structure in Table 27.4.

Describing paragraphs: appearance/position	Describing paragraphs: time sequence	Describing paragraphs: process (how it works)	Defining
Topic introducer	Method 1	Topic introducer	Topic sentence
Developer(s)	Event a + event b + event c	Developer 1	Example 1
Terminator	Method 2	Developer 2	Example 2
Tip: Move from top to bottom; left to right; centre to perimeter	By date order	Modulator	Example 3
		Developer 1a	Terminator sentence
		Developer 1b	Tip: Don't use a different form of the word being defined in order to define it
		Terminator sentence	

Classifying	Exemplifying	Generalising	Listing
Topic sentence	Topic sentence	**Method 1**	Topic sentence
Example 1	Example 1	Developer 1	Developer sentence
Example 2	Example 2	Developer 2	Modulator sentence
Terminator sentence identifying category	Restatement sentence or terminator sentence	Topic sentence (generalisation)	Terminator sentence
		Method 2	
		Generalisation	
		Developer 1	
		Developer 2	
		Restatement sentence	

Relating cause or effect (Method 1)	Relating cause or effect (Method 2)	Comparing	Contrasting
Topic introducer	Topic introducer	Topic introducer	Topic introducer
Topic sentence	Topic sentence	Topic sentence	Topic sentence
Developer 1	Developer 1 Theme A	Developer 1 Theme A	Developer 1 Theme A
Developer 2	Developer 2 Theme A	Developer 2 Theme A	Developer 1 Theme B
Modulator	Modulator (transfer to B)	Modulator (transfer to B)	Developer 2 Theme A
Developer 3	Developer 1 Theme B	Developer 1 Theme B	Developer 2 Theme B
Developer 4	Developer 2 Theme B	Developer 2 Theme B	Terminator
Terminator/restatement sentence	Terminator/restatement sentence	Terminator/restatement sentence	Restatement sentence

Table 27.4 **Paragraph models as text.** These texts can be compared with the outlines shown in Table 27.3.

Describing paragraphs: appearance/position	Describing paragraphs: time sequence	Describing paragraphs: process (how it works)	Defining
The Loch Ness monster is a beast of legend. It is depicted as a long snake-like amphibian showing three humps above the water line and a head that resembles the mythical dragon. Its length is unknown as it has never been seen in Loch Ness.	**Method 1** Total hip replacement requires post-operative physiotherapy. In addition, a follow-up visit may be offered at 6-weeks and again after 1 year to check the patient's mobility. **Method 2** Three major events influenced the creation of the European Community. Chronologically, these were the Second World War and the creation of the Council of Europe. The final event was the success of the European Coal and Steel Community.	Academics submit a proposal for an article to a journal. This is considered by an editorial committee and perhaps a peer reviewer. Once approval has been given the academic can begin writing. This will involve conducting a literature survey and reporting their own findings. When completed, the article is submitted for approval.	Scholarly writing requires particular skills that need to be developed. The writer must have a good understanding of language. A sound base of knowledge of the subject area and the specific topic is essential. A third requirement is that of patience for frequent re-drafting and editing will be necessary.
Classifying	**Exemplifying**	**Generalising**	**Listing**
International organisations can be divided into two broad categories: intergovernmental and non-governmental organisations (IGOs and NGOs). Further sub-division can be made, for example, into global	Historians look at authentic documents to investigate their topic. For example, they may look at old parish records or at reports from criminal courts to explore levels of crime in the 19th century.	**Method 1** Children learn to talk by listening. They also experiment by making 'baby' sounds. Children whose parents speak to them regularly are more likely to learn to speak quickly.	The biologist Linnaeus developed a taxonomy classifying plants. There are seven levels: kingdom, phylum, class, order, family, genus and species. These taxa were identified on the basis of the structure of the flower.

Relating cause or effect (Method 1)	Relating cause or effect (Method 2)	Method 2	
		and global organisations. These can then be divided by function, for example, defence, education, economy, health.	Linnaeus' principles have been used to classify other structures, for example, international organisations.
		Comparing	**Contrasting**
The existence of significant numbers of smokers in developed countries can be attributed to several causes. Smokers report that social pressures forced them to smoke. Others state that daily stress made them become smokers. Statistics imply that advertising plays a key role in the uptake of smoking. The cheapness and accessibility of cigarettes are also cited as causes. There appears to be no single factor that can account for the use of nicotine as a social drug.	Changes in attitudes towards smoking have had a number of effects. Smoking is recognised as socially unacceptable. Demands for protection from passive smoking have risen with the effect that smoking is no longer permitted in public buildings. Changes have also come about in relation to health issues and smoking. Health professionals are more willing to challenge smokers about their habit. Smokers are given more active encouragement to quit. The net result is a downturn in smoking-related illness.	Some research work has been done on the subject of water supply and quality. Problems exist in accessing water and in some countries bore wells are sunk to reach a supply. In other countries, dams, reservoirs and supply infrastructures have been created to ensure supplies. Where such initiatives have taken place, there have been unforeseen problems. The bore wells can be polluted by arsenic and reservoirs succumb to contamination. New ways of ensuring water supply must guarantee safe and clean water.	Electronic book readers are relatively new. Some people love them; others loathe them. Those who like them like the convenience. Others find them awkward to handle and use. Aficionados like their portability. The disaffected fear that their portability makes them an attractive target for thieves. Opinion thus far remains divided. This suggests that more time will be needed before bookshops become directly threatened and the electronic book becomes the only option.

(Row relating to Method 2 / Comparing)

Babies who speak early hear language from an early age. Parents who speak to their small babies can encourage this. Such claims are supported by anecdotal evidence.

Critiquing your own writing

Sometimes paragraphs expand to become overlong and people are unsure about how they can be split to make more reader-friendly text. In this situation, it can be useful to analyse long paragraphs in terms of function and then apply the paragraph models concept to indicate where separations can be inserted to achieve shorter, clearer paragraphs.

Collocations

This term used to describe words that are commonly used together. In the current context, two types are of interest:

- 'Clusters' comprising three-, four- or five-word groupings. Examples include: 'the extent to which'; 'is defined as'; 'it was found that'. Such groupings represent a kind of 'shorthand' that allows readers to process content more quickly because they can be used to link key information. Clusters are frequently used to show relationships to the research (location, procedure, quantification, description and topic), while others relate to the organisation of the text.

- Noun groupings. Strings of words – sometimes adjective + noun [dysfunctional + family (social work)]; other times verb + noun [eliminate + famine (epidemiology)] – that are commonly used together to express ideas that are particular to the theme or subject of study.

Certain cluster and noun groupings (sometimes called 'strings') are specific to disciplines while others are more prevalent in one than another. This indicates the importance of undertaking some intensive study of these 'cluster' expressions in your own discipline to identify commonly used devices, so that your writing adopts the discipline norms or 'mode of discourse'. This will eventually become a subconscious activity, but as a novice academic writer you may need to think things through as you write.

Discourse markers

As discussed above and shown in Table 27.1, discourse markers act as signpost words – the 'glue' that brings cohesion to text. These relate to functions and so bring a sense of logic to the text. The importance of using such terms in your own work is important because they help guide your reader through the complexity of extended writing and help to make linkages between the points you seek to make in your writing.

These features are only some of the conventions – often unspoken – that are expected to be observed in academic writing. Table 27.5 outlines some more simple rules that will help you to develop as an academic author and will save time at proofing stage because you will have avoided some basic errors of usage or expression.

Table 27.5 Conventions in language use and grammar in academic writing.

Absolute terms
In academic writing, it is important to be cautious about using absolute terms such as: *always and never*   *most and all*   *least and none* This does not mean that these words should never be used; simply that they should be used with caution, that is, when you are absolutely certain of your ground.
Acronyms
These are formed by taking the initial letters of a name of an organisation, a procedure or an apparatus and then using these letters instead of writing out the title in full. Thus, World Health Organisation becomes WHO. The convention is that the first time that you use a title with an acronym alternative, then you should write it in full with the acronym in brackets immediately after the full title. Thereafter within that document you can use the acronym. For example: The European Free Trade Association (EFTA) has close links with the European Community (EC). Both EFTA and the EC require new members to have membership of the Council of Europe as a prerequisite for admission to their organisations.
And and But
In academic writing, sentences should never begin with 'and' or 'but' – these are joining words used to unite two independent ideas within a sentence.
Clichés
Living languages change and develop over time. This means that some expressions come into such frequent usage that they lose their meaning; indeed, often they could be replaced with a much less long-winded expression. For example, *First and foremost* (firstly,. . .); *last but not least* (finally, . . .) This procedure is the gold standard of hip replacement methods. (This procedure is the best hip replacement method.)
Colloquialism
This use of language is regarded as informal and more common in spoken than in written language. Colloquialisms would generally not be used in academic writing. For example, the following would be inappropriate: 'Not to beat about the bush or mince my words, that is a load of rubbish!'

Continued overleaf

Contractions

In spoken English, contractions such as 'don't', 'can't', isn't, 'it's', 'I'd' and 'we'll' are often used. However, in academic written English, they should not be used.

Gender-free expression

Try to use gender-free expressions by using plurals. For example, instead of writing: 'Students asked each colleague to give his or her time to the project' the alternative plural construction would be preferred: 'Students asked colleagues to give their time to the project'.

'Hedging' language

Often in academic writing it is impossible to state categorically that something is or is not the case. There are verbs that allow you to 'hedge your bets' by not coming down on one side or another of an argument or for allowing you present a variety of different scenarios without committing yourself to any single position:

    seems that   *suggests that*   *looks as if*   *appears that*

This involves using a language construction that leaves the reader with the sense that the evidence presented is simply presenting a hypothetical, or imaginary, case. To emphasise this sense of 'hedging' the use of a special kind of verb called a modal is introduced. These verbs are called modal auxiliary ('helper') verbs:

    can/cannot   *may/may not*   *could/could not*   *might/might not*

These can be used with a variety of verbs to increase the sense of tentativeness. For example: 'These results suggest that there has been a decline in herring stocks in the North Sea.'

More tentatively, using the modal, this could be: 'These results could suggest that there has been a decline in herring stocks in the North Sea.'

Idiom and slang

These are usually colloquial and are used in different ways. For example, where:

- the language is used in such a way that the meaning is difficult to interpret because there is no apparent link between the words – to give someone short shrift;
- the literal sense is only partial in explaining the meaning – to strike while the iron is hot;
- the whole meaning can be guessed from the parts – as the crow flies.

Thus, idioms should be avoided in academic writing because they are sometimes unclear or simply in vogue for a short time. Their use in academic text might be perceived as inappropriate to the genre and register.

Impersonal language

Impersonal expression is encouraged in many disciplines and this means that the passive voice is the standard. In other disciplines, especially those which embrace reflective writing, then the active voice and use of the first person is expected. If you are unsure, speak with your supervisor about this.

Personal pronouns

Experiment with other language structures so that you avoid the personal pronouns – I/me, you, we/us and one. Generally, these are avoided in academic writing although there are instances in which they may be appropriate, for example, in reflective writing or writing about group research.

Rhetorical questions

Some writers use direct rhetorical questions as stylistic vehicle to introduce the topic addressed by the question. However, although this is a good strategy if you are making a speech, it does not have the same power in academic writing. Therefore: 'How do plants survive in dry weather?' becomes 'Understanding how plants survive in dry weather is important'.

Signposting

You can guide your reader through your text by using appropriate 'signpost' words from the discourse marker list (Table 27.1). For example, if you are presenting a point of contrast, then you would use 'however'; or if you are presenting a list of points, then you might use 'firstly,...'.

Pronouns that 'demonstrate' some reference to something already mentioned are 'this', 'these', 'that' and 'those'. In academic writing it is often better to back reference to the concept or thing being represented by such words. For example, rather than writing the following in relation to the plan of a new motorway: 'This will take ten years to complete' you should consider writing: 'This project will take ten years to complete'. This addition ensures clarity and precision.

Split infinitives

A commonly quoted split infinitive comes from the *Star Trek* television series where the Captain's Log records that the aim of the Star Ship Enterprise is 'to boldly go where no man has gone before'. Although this makes good television, its effect has outlived the television programme. This usage has evoked sometimes passionate debate ever since, because 'to boldly go' is a split infinitive. This means that an adverb (boldly) has split the infinitive (to go). It should read as 'to go boldly'. A split infinitive is regarded as poor English in some quarters and the tendency is to avoid this kind of structure in academic writing.

Tense

This grammatical term is used to describe how verbs are used to indicate the time of the action. In general, tenses can be divided into three categories – past, present and future. The tense you need to use will depend on the context of your work, for example, whether you are narrating a sequence of events in the past, whether you are discussing concepts or whether you are conjecturing about events in the future.

Voice: active or passive

The academic world is divided on whether the active or passive voice should be used in academic writing. The difference between these two forms is perhaps best shown in two examples:

1. Active voice: 'We deprived the plants of water for six days.'
2. Passive voice: 'The plants were deprived of water for six days.'

Choosing between active and passive voice

The passive voice focuses attention on the action rather than the actor and helps to maintain objectivity in this an impersonal style. Note that some referencing styles require the active as simpler and easier to understand (**Ch 20**). The rules are not hard and fast but many academics have strong views in favour of one or other. It is advisable to consult your supervisor to find out if they or your department have any stated preferences.

ACTION POINTS

27.1 Study your supervisor's publications. Read some of your supervisor's publications and try to identify how they present their reasoning – inductively or deductively. Look also at the publications of other experts in your field and try to identify the same thing. This could help you to understand how your supervisor may expect you to present your logic in writing; it may also suggest discipline practices in this respect.

27.2 Analyse your own writing. The more you write, the more you will develop your own personal style. Sometimes, however, writers overuse certain expressions – especially discourse markers – which can make their text seem repetitive and dull. You can use the list of discourse markers in Table 27.1 (a) to check your usage and (b) to expand your options for any overused cohesive terms.

27.3 Collect collocations and synonyms. Collecting your own 'glossary' as soon as you begin exploring the literature can be a helpful aid to developing your writing in your field. A collocation dictionary may help you to you may find alternatives to replace a verb or adjective that you may have overused in your writing. Synonyms (words similar in meaning) can be found by using a good thesaurus. A further way in which you can become more conversant with specialist terms and frequently used collocations in your field is to analyse published papers to identify some of the language structures and terms that are commonly used in this standard of writing.

28

ELEMENTS OF A THESIS

How to structure and write up the different sections

The model for PhD thesis structure differs across the disciplines, and especially across the 'arts–science divide', but there are some common or analogous components which adopt similar principles of content and presentation. The guidance offered in this chapter can be adapted to suit specific discipline requirements.

KEY TOPICS

→ Deciding on content

→ Structural options

→ Preliminary material

→ The main generic thesis elements

Different models of research lead to different models of thesis writing. There will therefore be a discipline practice with which you will be expected to conform. Matters of content and structure are linked, but usually your thesis content should drive the fine detail of its structure.

For many, a student–supervisor discussion about possible content and structure will occur after about two years of full-time equivalent study. At this point you will have a good idea of progress and what you plan to achieve in the remaining time at your disposal.

DECIDING ON CONTENT

In some cases, there will be a breakthrough event or a moment when the theme of your thesis becomes clear or self-evident. For example, if a trial method works, then this may open up a clear avenue of

Research thesis structures

At an early stage, compare the structures adopted by other students in your research group or department. A consistent model may be used, which you can adopt, or there may be variety, in which case you can decide which model might suit your research the best. Note that there tends to be greater flexibility in the Arts domains about how the work should be explained in the thesis.

research, leading to obvious content and structure. You might find a sudden understanding following a meeting, seminar or when reading a particular research paper. Often, making an intellectual connection between ideas or findings will lead you to inspiration.

Most PhD students are encouraged write draft material and notes as they proceed and may then accumulate so much work and so many ideas that they struggle to see how it might appear as a coherent, cohesive piece of writing. This is where your supervisor's experience and wisdom will be valuable. He or she should have a wider view of the subject area and know what is likely to be judged significant, and what not. Supervisors will have seen through the process of thesis design several or many times and can advise on that basis. Hence, when you are ready for this stage, arrange a meeting to discuss the options. Think through a number of possible scenarios beforehand so you can discuss these.

Trialling the thesis design

When you have a clear idea of how your thesis should be arranged, it is wise to map out the framework as far as you can before you meet with your supervisor. This gives you a starting point for your discussion. You should take this draft framework further than a listing of the common elements – introduction, literature review, methods and materials, results, discussion and conclusion. You will need to include specific sub-headings under each of these elements and this means thinking through the detail of what you intend to write and where. Only by doing this will you be able to recognise that some pieces of information or work need to precede others; some may need to be analysed and explained in greater or less detail; and some chapters may potentially be overloaded whilst others may be 'light' on content.

If your research has gone (is going) well, then you and your supervisor may be thinking already about how it might be published (**Ch 32**). In some disciplines, an entire thesis might be published and some of these have even become academic best-sellers. It is more likely, however, that specific areas of study (for example: work on a particular organism or chemical; analysis of a particular historical phenomenon, test of a specific hypothesis) will form 'potentially publishable units'. Imagining how this collection of units might look is one way of visualising a possible thesis structure, perhaps using the 'repeated chapter' model discussed below.

When should I stop researching and start writing?

There is no all-encompassing answer to this. There are, however, a number of ways of answering that question, any of which may be relevant:

- When you know more or less what the theme of the thesis will be (you can then start writing drafts with a purpose).
- When you have enough data of publishable standard for more than one publication (this means your work will have reached the required standard).
- When you are running out of time (you will need about four to six months to write up, longer if writing is difficult for you).
- You should start writing draft material from day one (that is, do not partition the research and writing processes).

STRUCTURAL OPTIONS

The structural norms for PhD theses differ among disciplines and while some elements will be dictated by university rules, there is usually an element of flexibility, allowing you to choose a structure that fits with your research process and outcomes. Generally speaking, the discipline 'standard' will differ across Arts and Sciences. Table 28.1 shows possible listings that show essential elements for both although all may not apply in all cases.

Table 28.1 Sections found in representative Arts and Sciences theses

Arts	Sciences
• Title	• Title
• Preliminary material	• Preliminary material
• Abstract or Summary	• Abstract or Summary
• Introduction	• Introduction
• Literature review	• Methods
• Methodology	• Results
• [Investigation]	• Discussion
• Discussion	• Conclusions
• Conclusions	• References
• References	• Appendices
• Glossary	
• Appendices	

From Table 28.1, it can be seen that sections/chapters may carry different names: for example, 'Materials and Methods' is common in the sciences; 'Analysis' may be preferred to 'Results'. Sometimes sections may be combined (the literature review being part of the introduction or the conclusions appearing as a final part of the Discussion, for example). Whatever the sections or chapters are called, the elements described in Table 28.1 can be seen as generic content of any thesis although some might straddle more than one section.

For a thesis composed of work in different areas or using divergent approaches, the following model is an option:

- Preliminary material
- Abstract or Summary
- General Introduction
- General Methods (or General Materials and Methods)

Then, the elements in brackets, repeated as often as necessary:

- Chapter x
  - Introduction
  - Method (or Materials and Methods)
  - Results
  - Discussion
- General Discussion
- Conclusions
- References

This model allows very specific approaches and their methods to be outlined closer to the relevant results and discussion. Again, some elements may carry different names or be combined. Note the use of a General Introduction and General Discussion before and after the chapters. These introduce and discuss the thesis as a whole, whereas the Chapter Introductions and discussions deal primarily with the theme of each specific chapter. In some cases there will only be one Materials and Methods section before the first results chapter (i.e. where these are essentially common to all parts of the thesis).

One advantage of using this type of design is that any figures and tables can be made independent among chapters, by adopting a numbering system relative to each chapter (e.g. Figure 3.4 is the fourth figure in Chapter 3). This means that you can add figures and tables to a chapter without disrupting the numbering system for the whole thesis. It also means you can write the chapters in any order, avoiding a tedious renumbering exercise.

How long should a thesis chapter be?

Many academics would say that a thesis chapter should be equivalent in length to a research paper (and in some countries the postgraduate thesis consists solely of published work). In planning your thesis structure, it might therefore be helpful to think about 'virtual' papers you might aim to publish.

In general, the institution will dictate the content, and sometimes presentation of the preliminary material (see below), but you will have some freedom to decide options for presenting your methods, results and discussion. The style of citation and the reference section usually need to follow discipline norms or department/university regulations (**Ch 20**).

Some disciplines, especially those that are relatively new, such as Computing, Art, Design and professional subjects such as Teaching and Nursing, have adopted different models of thesis structure that fit with the prevailing methods of research. In these cases, always follow your supervisor's guidance in the first place, and try to source other theses in your area to see how they are constructed (these can be consulted within the library). However, the ultimate decision about structure of the thesis remains yours – providing it follows the necessary 'standards'. Adopting a more novel approach as long as it is within the regulations may be a real factor in asserting your doctoral qualities. Therefore, you should be prepared to construct a design with which you are happy and be able to defend your decision in the *viva*.

Check the thesis rules at an early stage

Access your university's PhD regulations at an early stage and print and file the section on structure and presentation. You may wish to create folders and files for mandatory sections so that you can draft these as you go along. For example, a note of people who help you could be added to a draft of the acknowledgement section (**Ch 30**).

The following sections discuss content and approaches for each of the elements outlined above. In each case, this is necessarily a general outline as disciplines and writers may have different expectations and wishes respectively. Before committing words to paper or getting too far down a particular avenue, always discuss your plan with your supervisor and/or progress monitoring committee and respond to any feedback received.

The thesis title

The first version of the title of your thesis is usually created at an early stage in the research process, perhaps when writing your research proposal (**Ch 4**). However, as your work proceeds you may find that this draft title no longer reflects the content of your thesis. The general principle is that the title should be a concise yet informative description of what the study or research was about. It might help to think about key words first, before framing the title, that is, those that you would expect another researcher to input into a database search program when trying to find out about work like your own. The convention is not to write 'An investigation of...' or 'Studies on...', as this is assumed. In the Sciences, thesis titles would normally encompass wider topics than those of research papers and might be more analogous to those of research reviews. In the Arts, the possibilities are wider ranging, but you still may find that the original title of your thesis is honed to a much simpler wording by the end of the writing process.

The title page usually includes the title, the volume number (if more than one), the author's full name and qualifications, the name of the degree for which the thesis is submitted, the department (school or centre) and university, the date of submission (usually just month and year).

There are many technical parts of a thesis that need to be included before the text proper, depending on institutional rules, theses may include the following components, sometimes with different titles and possibly in a different order, according to local regulations.

● Library declaration and deposit agreement. This indicates your permission to allow the library to release you work for other academics to read.

● The table of contents. This is a sequential list of the sections or chapters of the thesis, with page numbers. Clearly, this can only be completed properly after the thesis is written, although a 'shell' document can be constructed ahead of this without the final page information. If there is more than one volume the full contents table should be given in volume one, with relevant part contents for subsequent volumes.

● List of figures and tables. This is exactly what the title implies, with numbering and page numbers. The aim is to allow an examiner or reader find a specific piece of information quickly.

● Acknowledgements. This is a list of all those who have helped and supported you and to whom you wish to pay tribute. It may include thanks to a funding body.

● Declaration. This is effectively a statement that the thesis is all your own work, except where indicated. These normally follow institutional formats. Figure 28.1 provides an example.

'Following the acknowledgements, if any, there shall be: a signed declaration, that the candidate is the author of the thesis; that, unless otherwise stated, all references cited have been consulted by the candidate; that the work of which the thesis is a record has been done by the candidate, and that it has not been previously accepted for a higher degree: provided that if the thesis is based upon joint research, the nature and extent of the candidate's individual contribution shall be defined'

Figure 28.1 An example of a typical regulation for the thesis declaration.
Taken from The University of Dundee Code of Practice for Supervised Postgraduate Research (2006). Available at: *http://www.somis.dundee.ac.uk/ calendar/senate/hdtheses.htm* [Accessed 29 August 2012].

- An indication of the status of any related work. This might include that from a linked prior thesis (for example for a master's degree) or published work, which would normally need to be clearly identified.

- Abbreviations. This is a comprehensive list of the shortened forms used in the thesis. Normal practice is to introduce the abbreviation at the first point of use, but if a reader sees a later use but has forgotten the meaning, it can be found in this section. The abbreviations with expanded versions are listed in strict alphabetical order.

THE MAIN GENERIC THESIS ELEMENTS

The material under the following sub-headings details the content and organisation of the main components of a thesis. They are necessarily generalisations. To accommodate the wider differences in practice, they have been divided into parts for 'sciences' and 'non-sciences' where relevant, but there may be overlap in some subjects.

Abstract (or Summary)

This is an outline of the thesis often about 300 words in length, but this may vary according to discipline or regulations. This is usually quite difficult to write because of the length restriction. It should cover: the aims of the investigation or research, the methods, the findings and the conclusion. The language should be general rather than technical, if possible. The Abstract should allow a reader to comprehend the original contribution(s) to knowledge and understanding made in the thesis.

Trialling the abstract

Many times over the period of your PhD studies you will be asked what your dissertation is about. The answer could be one word – for example, 'feet' – or it could be a lengthy exposé on the damage caused to feet by the use of ill-fitting shoes. Neither explanation is going to be appropriate for your abstract. However, once your research is under way you could try writing down an explanation of your study in no more than, say, 55 words. This should include information about topic, purpose, method, findings and (anticipated) conclusion. This is an excellent way of arriving at a clear understanding of where you are going and why. This draft may also help you find the clarity needed for a good (expanded) abstract when you write the final version.

Introduction

The aim of the introduction should be to provide a rationale for your work. Thus, it needs to include background information leading to a description of the issue under investigation and the reason for the study. For a thesis it would normally incorporate a review of past work (the literature) in the area, leading to the aims of your own work.

Possible topics to be addressed in an introduction might include:

- general and current importance of the (wide) research area;
- a brief description of the structure of the thesis;
- a review of the wider subject area and the context of your particular field, including its potential importance;
- a review of recent findings in your (narrow) field;
- a description of the hypothesis or hypotheses you intend to test (sciences);
- identification of the 'gap' in knowledge or understanding that suggests the need for investigation that will be addressed by this study and described in the thesis;
- comments on novel aspects of experimental design, materials, or methods; in some cases it may outline the content of the work.

Literature Review

In the Sciences, reviewing and appraising the literature may be a component feature of the Introduction. However, in some disciplines including those in the Arts, reviewing the literature might require an independent chapter. In some instances, the review of literature might fit more appropriately within separate chapters with only a general mention of seminal work in the literature provided in the introduction chapter of the thesis.

When should a thesis consist of more than one volume?

The basic answer is when it is longer than the extent allowed by the bindery – about 300 pages or so. A second volume might also be a useful option when large amounts of raw data or photos need to be included. Note that in some institutions, permission must be sought for submission of a thesis running into more than one volume. In such cases, the author has to provide justification for this extended submission.

Finalising your introduction

The introduction is the first detailed explanation of the context and purpose of your study. It sets the scene and whets the appetite of the reader; it helps your examiner to understand the context and possibly how you intend to 'unpack' the problem. Furthermore, it will be the section that the examiner may read as a reminder of the content prior to your *viva*. That said, while your introduction is of considerable significance, it can only reflect the content of the full work. This means that you should not 'worry away' at achieving a perfect introduction until you have completed all the other chapters. Until you have finished the conclusion, you should see your introduction as 'work in progress'. Only when everything else is written, should you re-read your introduction and remodel it so that it does, indeed, reflect the content of the full work.

Methods (or Materials and Methods) (or Methodology)

Sciences

In these disciplines, your aim is to describe what you did in sufficient detail to allow a competent lab worker in your field to carry out exactly the same research as you did. This is a key part of any scientific communication, because the essence of all science lies in its repeatability (**Chs 3** and **23**). There is no need to go into unnecessary detail. For example, a competent technician would be able to work out how much of a specified chemical to use to make a solution of defined concentration, and to use a stirrer bar to dissolve the solution. However, the precise supplier, purity and concentration of the chemical might be crucial to the results, and should, therefore, be specified. Structure the Materials and Methods into sections in the order in which they are presented in the thesis (which may not be the order in which they were done). For example, you might start with how the experimental material was obtained. Crucial at this point is an adequate description of its origins and nature (in life sciences, for example, this would include the binomial Latin name plus authority of any organisms studied). You might then move on to describe how each experiment was carried out. Finally, you might have a section on data analysis (and presentation).

This section should be written in past tense, for example, 'The drying board was positioned at an angle of 45°'; 'The leaves were dried out overnight'.

Do not:

- separate materials from methods (unless otherwise instructed): as you describe what you did, incorporate information about what you did it with;

- include any results: there are rare occasions when (say) a calibration might be included, but in general, experiments which validate your methods should come in the first section of the results.

Non-sciences
A methods or methodology section in arts-related subjects can relate to both the theoretical approaches that underpin the research activity and the way in which the research was conducted. The former part may require an in-depth scrutiny of theoretical, often qualitative, approaches to research (**Ch 22**) and explanation of why one particular approach is best suited to your study over other options. It follows, therefore, that the description of the conduct of the research will derive from these theoretical parameters. Increasingly, diverse approaches are being used in research in the Arts and Social Sciences which may mean that this chapter is a lengthy one.

Results (or Findings)
Sciences
The Results section should consist of a clear sequential description of your findings. The exact sequence need not be the order in which you did the thinking or carried out the experiments, but it should be logical. You need to 'lead the reader' through the figures, pointing out the main points. Refer to them in sequence, numbered strictly in the order of first mention. For example, 'Figure 1 shows that treatment x had a greater effect on z than treatment y'.

Construct the figures and tables before you start writing the results

As a result of the dynamic nature of results analysis, figure and table numbers and numbering may change frequently because you are creating new representations or even feeding in new results as you complete a chapter. When this process is complete, lay them out in the order you wish to describe them, and this will dictate their numbering.

Data should be simplified and presented clearly (see **Ch 21**). Include information about statistical hypothesis tests (for example values of P, the probability of getting your result by chance).

Do not:

- repeat data in more than one form, unless this is crucial to your conclusions;
- give all the replicate data;
- include discursive material: put this in the Discussion section. If you find it difficult not to discuss the results, consider using the Results and Discussion option (see below).

Always do the statistical tests before you start writing up the results. These analyses could materially alter your perspective on the data and affect the subsequent discussion dramatically.

Non-sciences

In these disciplines, a section labelled 'Results' or 'Findings' may not exist, although this does not mean that there are no findings in the thesis. Much will depend on the discipline, the thesis topic and also, perhaps, on the regulations, but the findings may suitably be introduced in the main body of the thesis where analysis of the issues and the related literature may be divided into individual chapters. Gradually, as the dimensions of the research problem are examined and the data are introduced to amplify understanding, the 'finding' element will be revealed. For those conducting research in the Arts and Social Sciences, this allows a valuable flexibility to compartmentalise analyses and their corresponding findings.

Do I need to write my thesis in the sequence that the chapters will appear?

Writing is a dynamic process and you can write the sections whenever you feel that you can. This means that you can jump around in the sequence (is it really 'order'?). This can be helpful because there will be moments when you just do not feel like writing about a particular aspect of the study or you may find that you don't feel like writing at all. At such times, choose an area where you felt that you can write fluently and accurately with a good chance of being productive. For scientists, one such area might be the Methods and Materials section; this more descriptive writing may be easier to construct. Conversely, those in Arts subjects may find that their Methodology section presents a challenge in the writing process that is best left to a more auspicious moment. Instead, starting at the literature review might induce more fluent writing.

Discussion

Sciences

Here, you should state the significance of your results. This is an important section, because it shows that you understand what you have done. The Discussion should be critical, that is, mentioning both good and bad points about your study. Be prepared to reject your original hypothesis, but state what others you might now adopt in its place. Be aware that you cannot 'prove' anything in science (**Ch 3**) and that there will always be an alternative (low probability) explanation, which should be discussed. You may also wish to:

- state the main conclusions;
- compare your results with other published data;
- indicate what future studies might be undertaken;
- mention the significance of the work in a wider context.

Do not:

- extend the Discussion too much; it can easily degenerate into waffle;
- simply repeat the Results section; you should be analysing your results rather than describing them.

Non-sciences

As with the above explanation of the positioning of results/findings in these disciplines, it can follow that the 'discussion' is subsumed in each of the sections/chapters that comprise the main body of the text. However, there may also be a separate chapter that brings together these discussion points and relates them to the conclusions reached regarding the study.

Conclusions

This is not always a separate section and may be combined with the discussion (see above). An option to consider is to state your main conclusions in a numbered list or logical sequence of paragraphs. Conclusions can provide the stimulus for discussion of your thesis in the *viva* and so you should have some clear notion of further directions that could be followed arising from your study or provide indicators of recommendations that you might make for further action and change (see also **Ch 31**). These should appear within the Discussion/ Conclusion chapter of the thesis.

Cohesion in your thesis – making the links

The nature of the writing process may mean that chapters have been written at different stages in the study period; they may have been written when you were unsure of what would precede or follow them. For such reasons you may find that some to the introductory or closing paragraphs in your chapters seem awkward and even inelegant in the way that they are written. To smooth out this roughness, you should review your entire thesis ensuring that there are clear 'backward' and 'forward' links between the chapters as they appear in the final sequence. You can enhance the cohesion of your work by ensuring that you relate your activities, findings, conclusions and recommendations to the literature that you introduced earlier in the work. New literature should not be introduced in the final sections; if new material has been published then you should revisit the earlier literature review content of the work and update it appropriately.

References (Bibliography) (Literature cited) (Works cited)

This section (all the names effectively mean the same thing but depend on the referencing style you follow) gives the details for any articles cited in the text. There will be a precise format for doing this, depending on the rules adopted by your department or discipline. Even if you select a referencing style yourself, you will need to adopt it accurately and consistently. See **Chapter 20** and McMillan and Weyers (2013) for further discussion.

Glossary

This lists all specialist terms or terms that have been used in a way that is unique to the thesis, and so may require definition. The inclusion of such a listing allows the non-expert to understand the content of the thesis without recourse to specialist dictionaries.

Appendices (Supplementary material)

An Appendix (plural: appendices) is a section at the end of piece of academic writing – for example, a thesis. It consists of information which is closely related to the content of the main body of the work. Nevertheless, it is usually material which, while adding further understanding, might clog up the main part of the work with distracting detail which would inhibit the flow of the key issues in the discussion. Appendices are usually listed as Appendix A, B, C etc. or as Appendix 1, 2, 3 etc. The pages are usually numbered with lower case Roman numerals, that is, (i), (ii), (iii) and so on.

Supplementary material may be required in some disciplines, for example where the thesis involves discussion of an artefact. This could be shown via material on a CD/DVD – consult your university regulations or postgraduate office.

When should I stop writing?

Obviously, you need to complete a thesis plan, having all relevant sections and chapters complete. You may then wish to refine your text, perhaps via successive editing 'sweeps' (as discussed in **Chapter 29**). You will then need to receive feedback on this material from your supervisor, discuss this and incorporate any agreed changes. If you are a perfectionist, you may still wish to tinker with the text. Unless you are well ahead of the submission date, this is probably not a good idea. So long as your supervisor is happy with the product, start the submission process.

ACTION POINTS

28.1 Ensure you file your progress reports, notes and early drafts in a well-organised way. These will be very useful sources when you come to write the final version of your thesis, and you should be able to find relevant material easily. Files should carry meaningful names and a version number or date should be dated.

28.2 Ensure your references are well organised from an early stage. This is a very tedious part of writing up if you do not tackle it as you go along. Programs such as Endnote may be helpful in organising and presenting this information in the appropriate manner (**Ch 20**).

28.3 Keep back-up files (including print-outs) at all stages. There are heartbreaking tales of students who lose all their files near to the end of a write-up. Printing out hard copy as you complete chapters is another way of ensuring that you have a working text should electronic disaster strike. This can always be scanned if required.

29

BECOMING AN AUTONOMOUS WRITER

How to take control of the writing process

Thesis writing is a developmental process. At the start, there will be much to learn from your supervisor and other sources, as you come to terms with the art of academic writing and learn about discipline standards and conventions. Finding a personal yet truly scholarly style will take time and effort. Eventually, however, you will emerge from this process as an independent writer capable of high-quality output.

KEY TOPICS

→ Planning towards autonomy

→ Learning from feedback

→ Improving your self-editing skills

→ Developing a personal writing style

→ Striving for the goal of writing autonomy

Unless you move on to author a (largish) book, you will probably never write as lengthy a document as your PhD thesis. It will need to have a consistent style and there needs to be an accuracy and attention to detail that will be very demanding. Most graduating PhD students readily agree that the experience of writing up not only developed their writing skills, it transformed them to new levels.

The ultimate goal associated with this transformation is 'writing autonomy'. That is, knowing what to write, how to structure it, and how to present it *by yourself*, without substantive guidance. This requires meticulous planning, experience in writing, which writing your thesis will certainly give you, and advanced self-editing skills. The path to autonomy is rarely easy. You will make mistakes in the early stages, and will carry on doing so – written language is capable of so many different forms of expression that this is inevitable.

At PhD level, key stages in this continuing process are:

- planning your writing;
- learning from your supervisor's feedback;
- learning how to self-edit your work to the highest of standards;
- developing a personal writing style.

PLANNING TOWARDS AUTONOMY

There are two aspects to planning that are relevant; the first is in relation to the structure of the writing and the second is the scheduling of your writing.

At the outset of your PhD study, you will have had to plan your proposal, your research of the literature and make a myriad of decisions each of which may not in itself have been of major significance. Cumulatively, these decisions will have contributed to your increasing confidence in your mastery of your topic. As you contemplate the task of writing up your thesis, you will need to make further autonomous decisions, initially about planning the whole thesis, and then about planning the individual components and chapters related to them (**Ch 28**). This planning is the key to achieving synergy between your research and writing. It is essentially a solo activity where minor and major decisions are yours alone.

Without the necessary planning, your writing will be without structure and will almost certainly fail to demonstrate real independence of thought. The success of your planning of your writing will become apparent when you receive your supervisor's feedback.

Setting up a timetable for your work will be vital to completing your thesis on time (**Ch 6**). This can only be done once you have decided on the structure, so that aspect needs to be tackled at an early stage. The structure may change as you write, and that is an acceptable and natural part of the writing process. However, without some organisational intention at the start, your writing effort is likely to drift and fail to make both self-imposed and external deadlines.

The process of planning your effort can be divided into three stages:

1 Make a *realistic* estimate of the time available for writing. This should take into account your continuing research effort where relevant, work and teaching commitments, family and social time and 'maintenance' tasks. Sum this over the days, weeks and months until your submission deadline.

2 Using your draft thesis plan, estimate the proportion of time you feel you should devote to each part. Some parts may be already near-final from past work, such as methods or reference lists. Others you will know to be potentially time-consuming or difficult. Allow sufficient time for dealing with feedback, and the presentational aspects discussed in **Chapter 30**, including printing, copying and binding. Allow also some time for slippage in the timetable.

3 Allocate the total time to these elements of the work. This will create a set of mini-deadlines for the completion of each part.

The hard part, of course, is keeping to your timetable – but having one will let you know how well you are progressing and whether you need to step up your work rate or deserve a break.

 Working back from your submission date

Sometimes it is easy to be lulled into a false sense of security by thinking that there is plenty of time until the deadline date for any big task. In the case of the submission date for your thesis, a reality check may be needed and this can be achieved by working *backwards* from that date, factoring in all remaining tasks, such as the time needed to:

■ Finalise your remaining research – how long will it take to obtain the information you still require and to analyse it?

■ Personally edit and proof-read your final version – do you really know how long it will take to implement changes?

■ Obtain final feedback from your supervisor – do you know what their work commitments are?

■ Print and bind the work – do you know how long the printer/binder will take to create a set of copies for the *viva*?

The list could go on and on, but these examples are sufficient to show that there are many steps in the process leading up to final submission and it would be wise to outline list all that apply in your case.

LEARNING FROM FEEDBACK

In progressing from the planning to the production phase of writing, you will be moving to a new level in your relationship with your supervisor as you handle his or her feedback and explain some of your decision-making. Feedback from your supervisor or lecturer may be oral or written: some feedback may be informal, for example, a comment given as you work in the lab, or an observation on your contribution in a seminar. Take every comment seriously, even if stated with humour. Reflect on the potential reasons for positive and negative pointers, and try to learn from them all.

Written feedback may be provided on your thesis drafts and other work, such as progress reports. This may take the form of handwritten comments over your text. Alternatively, your supervisor may use a tool like the 'Track Changes' facility in Microsoft Word. This allows amendments to your work. In addition, he or she may use the 'Comments' facility in Word, to add explanations or ideas.

How often will my supervisor read my draft versions?

This is a thorny issue. Supervisors are busy people; they may be supervising several students. Some supervisors will only survey a single draft and expect you to work from there by yourself; others will be prepared to look at a number of versions. Most supervisors will become irritated if you submit sloppy work or fail to take on board past comments and repeat mistakes.

Different supervisors use different terms to express similar meanings, and because they work quickly, their handwritten comments may sometimes be untidy and may be difficult to interpret. It won't take long to learn how to decipher the handwriting and coding quirks of your supervisor, but you will have to work at it. For example, they may use the standard proof-reading symbols and if unfamiliar with these you may need to find out about them. Table 29.1 provides a list of the more common, but others are available from sources like Ritter (2005). If a particular comment or mark does not make sense to you or you cannot read it, then approach your supervisor for clarification, but be sure to make a note of the explanation as asking twice will not go down well.

Table 29.1 Common proof-reading symbols. Supervisors use a variety of symbols to indicate errors, corrections or suggestions. These can apply to punctuation, spelling, presentation or grammar. The symbols provide a kind of 'shorthand' that acts as a code to help you see how you might be able to amend your text so that it reads correctly and fluently. In this table some of the more commonly used correction marks are shown alongside their meanings. The example text shows how these symbols may be used either in the text or the margin to indicate where a change is recommended.

Correction mark	Meaning	Example
⌐ (np)	(new) paragraph	*Text* *margin*
≢	change CAPITALS to small letters (lower case)	The correction marks that supervisors
⌇	change into **bold** type	use in students' texts are generally Y
≡	change into CAPITALS	made to help identify where there
⌒	close up (delete space)	have been errors of splin or ʌe/ʌg
/ or ⁊ or ⊢	delete	punctuation. They can ~~often~~ (STET)
⋏	insert a word or letter	indicate where there is lack of
Y	insert space	paragraphing or grammatical
.... or (STET)	leave unchanged	accuracy. If you find that work is (np)
Insert punctuation symbol in a circle (P)	punctuation	returned to you with such
		marks correction, then it is ⌐⌐
plag.	plagiarism	worthwhile spending some time
⟶	run on (no new paragraph)	analysing the common errors as ⁊
Sp.	spelling	well as the comments, because this
⌐⌐	transpose text	will help you to improve the
?	what do you mean?	quality of presentation and content
??	text does not seem to make sense	of your work this reviewing can ⊙/≡
✔	good point/correct	have a positive effect on the
✗	error	quality of your writing
		In the margin, the error symbols are separated by a slash (/), as in the third example down.

It is important to put yourself in the correct frame of mind to learn from the views of your supervisor. You may initially feel that feedback is unfair or harsh or that it misunderstands the approach you were trying to take to the topic. A natural reaction might be to dismiss many of the comments. However, you should recognise that your supervisor probably has a much deeper understanding of the topic than you and, of course, greater experience in the conventions of this level of writing, and concede that if you want to do well, then you need to gain a better understanding of what makes a good dissertation or project from the academic's point of view.

IMPROVING YOUR SELF-EDITING SKILLS

Writing is a process. It begins with a plan and it finishes with reviewing, editing and proof-reading. This means that you should review your text critically before submitting it to your supervisor for comment. Looking analytically at your own writing is essential if you want to produce work of the highest quality. These editing skills will allow you to improve the sense, grammar and syntax of your written assignments.

At the start of thesis writing, you will probably need to rely on your supervisor's comments to gain an appreciation of the writing style required in your discipline, but sooner or later you will have to develop your own abilities in this area.

The effort you invest in this final stage will contribute to the quality of your work. Ideally, you should leave a gap of time between completing the writing and beginning the reviewing process, as this allows you to 'distance' yourself from the work and helps you look at it as a new reader would.

Allow plenty of time for self-editing

When planning your writing schedule, ensure that you have allowed adequate time for reviewing and proof-reading. It requires powers of concentration that cannot be rushed and consequently takes a long time. You don't want to spoil all your hard work by skimping on this final stage.

At this stage you are performing the role of editor. This means that you are looking critically at your text for content, relevance and sense, as well as for flaws in layout, grammar, punctuation and spelling.

You should also check for consistency in all aspects, for example, in the use of terminology, in spelling, and in presentational features such as font and point size, layout of paragraphs, and labelling of tables and diagrams.

Clearly, there are a lot of aspects to cover, and some degree of overlap in different parts of the process. In the reviewing process, you should consider several aspects:

- Content – is the substance of your text correct?
- Relevance – is what you have written appropriate?
- Clarity – are your thoughts clearly expressed?
- Style – have you used expressions appropriate for academic writing?
- Coherence – does everything fit together to create a meaningful whole?
- Grammatical correctness – is the language and syntax right?
- Spelling and punctuation – are these correct?
- Presentation – is the text formatted correctly?

You can review some of the key aspects that you should bear in mind in this phase of reviewing by looking at Tables 27.5 and 30.1.

Definitions

Reviewing – appraising critically; that is, examining a task or project to ensure that it meets the requirements and objectives of the task and that the overall sense is conveyed well.

Editing – revising and correcting later drafts of an essay, to arrive at a final version. Usually, this involves the smaller rather than the larger details, such as details of punctuation, spelling, grammar and layout.

Proof-reading – checking a printed copy for errors of any sort.

Ideally, you might consider each of these in a different editing 'sweep' through your draft text. Experienced editors can achieve all of this in one read, but this is probably not possible for most research authors. Instead, we recommend a compromise review process which incorporates a minimum of three sweeps, sequentially looking at different aspects. Table 29.2 illustrates the points that might be covered in each sweep, with an easy-to-use checklist for each review.

Although the editing process may seem tedious and more complex than it might have appeared at first, a text revised in this way will be far more likely to receive a favourable reading than one that is not reviewed, edited and proofed.

Table 29.2 Editing strategies. Initially, it might help you to focus on each of these three broad aspects in a separate 'sweep' of your draft text. As you become more experienced, you will become adept at doing this, and the reviewing/editing/proof-reading process can be done in a single combined sweep.

Sweep 1: Content and relevance; clarity, style and coherence	
Tips for each sweep	Checklist of items to review
• Work on a hard copy using editing symbols to correct errors • Revisit your aim in writing the text in question; check your interpretation if what you have written against the original 'specification' • Read objectively and assess whether the text makes sense • Look for inconsistencies in argument • Confirm that all your facts are correct • Insert additional or overlooked comment or evidence that strengthens the whole • Remove anything that is not relevant or alter the text so that it is clear and unambiguous • Check whether your text is too wordy Reducing text by 10–25 per cent can improve quality considerably • Honestly and critically assess your material to ensure that you have attributed ideas to their sources, that is, check that you have not committed plagiarism (**Ch 20**) • Remodel any expressions that are too informal for the academic context • Eliminate gendered or discriminatory language	❑ Your original intent has been observed ❑ The structure is appropriate ❑ The text shows objectivity ❑ The examples are relevant ❑ All sources are correctly cited ❑ The facts presented are accurate ❑ The rationale of your approach to the topic will be clear to the reader ❑ What you wrote is what you meant to write ❑ The text is fluent, with appropriate use of signpost words ❑ Any informal language has been removed ❑ The style is academic and appropriate for the task ❑ The content and style of each section is consistent ❑ The tense used in each section is suited to the time-frame of your text ❑ The length of the text sections are balanced appropriately
Sweep 2: Grammatical correctness	
Tips for each sweep	Checklist of items to review
• Check titles and subtitles are appropriate to the style of the work and stand out by using bold or underlining (not both) • Consider whether the different parts link together well – if not, introduce signpost words to guide the reader through the text	❑ All sentences are complete ❑ All sentences make sense ❑ Paragraphs have been correctly used ❑ Suggestions made by grammar checker have been accepted/rejected

Continued overleaf

• Check for fluency in sentence and paragraph structure – remodel as required	❏ The text has been checked against your own checklist of recurrent grammatical errors
• Check sentence length – remodel to shorter or longer sentences; sometimes shorter sentences are more effective than longer ones	❏ The text is consistent in adopting British or American English
	❏ Any blatant 'typos' have been corrected by reading for meaning
• Ensure that you have been consistent in spelling conventions, for example following British English rather than American English spelling	❏ The text has been spell-checked and looked at for your 'own' most often misspelled words
• Use the spellchecker but be prepared to double-check in a standard dictionary if you are in doubt or cannot find a spelling within the spellchecker facility	❏ A check has been made for spelling of subject-specific words and words from other languages
• Check for cumbersome constructions – divide or restructure sentence(s); consider whether active or passive is more suitable; consider using vocabulary that might convey your point more eloquently	❏ Punctuation has been checked, if possible, by reading aloud
	❏ Proper names are correctly capitalised
	❏ Overlong sentences have been divided
• Check for use of 'absolute' terms to ensure that you maintain objectivity	

Sweep 3: Presentation

Tips for each sweep	Checklist of items to review
• Check that you have made good use of white space, that is, not crammed the text into too tight a space	❏ The text length is as might be expected for the standard of this level of work
• Check that you have followed standard typing conventions; follow any 'house style' rules stipulated by your department	❏ Overall neatness checked
	❏ The presentational aspects are as required by your department (font, margins, page numbering, etc.)
• Check that all your citations and references consistently follow a recognised method (**Ch 20**), and that all citations in the text are matched by an entry in the reference list and vice versa	❏ The bibliography/reference list is correctly formatted according to the recommended style
• Ensure all pages are numbered	❏ Page numbers have been included (in position stipulated, if given)
• Ensure all necessary preliminary material has been completed	
• Check that labelling of diagrams, charts and other visual material is in sequence and consistently presented	❏ The figures and tables are in appropriate format and are appropriately titled
• Ensure that supporting material is added in sequence as appendices, footnotes, endnotes or as a glossary as applicable	

Technical aids for reviewing

The word processor has made the reviewing and editing task much easier. Here are some tips for using this software effectively:

- Use the word-count facility to check on length.
- Use the 'View' facility to check page breaks and general layout before you print out.
- Don't rely 100 per cent on the spell- and grammar checker.
- Sometimes the grammar checker will announce that you have used the passive voice. This is often a standard academic usage and, therefore, is not an error (**Ch 27**).
- Sometimes supervisors add comments to students' work using 'Track Changes' or 'Insert > Comments' in Microsoft Word software. Depending on the version you are using, feedback information can usually be accepted or rejected by right-clicking on the word or punctuation point that has been marked for alteration.

When checking your work it is usually a good idea to work from a hard copy. Reading through your work laid out on paper will help you identify errors and inconsistencies more readily than might be possible on a computer screen. A paper version is also easier to annotate (although this can also be done using the 'Track Changes' or 'Comments' facility on your word-processor). A printout also allows you to see the whole work in overview, and focus on the way the text 'flows'. If necessary, spread it out on the desk in front of you to gain an idea of the balance between sections.

Map your work to obtain an overview

'Label' each paragraph with a topic heading and list these in a linear way on a separate paper. This will provide you with a 'snapshot' of your text and will allow you to appraise the order, check against the original plan, and adjust the position of parts as you feel necessary.

Professional writers – novelists as well as academics – often report that their initial drafts are frequently much longer than the final version. If you follow their example of writing 'large' and then cutting down the text with intelligent editing, then your text will be crisper. Some of the things that can be easily removed are redundant words ('add up' = 'add') or lengthy expressions ('a lot of' = 'many') which will help to achieve that crispness of expression. At sentence level, you may find that you have written something like:

These changes have caused shortages in almost all commodities in the market that are derived from milk. This means that milk products are in short supply.

Essentially, these two sentences mean the same and so you could eliminate one of them. Which one you decide to cut might depend on the context; equally, it might depend on your word count. Either way, the resulting, shorter, text will send a clearer message to your reader.

Table 29.3 shows how text that is wordy, lacking good sentence structure and which runs all ideas into a single paragraph can be made much more meaningful and easier to assimilate if the text us broken up into shorter sentences where use is made of appropriate discourse markers (**Ch 27**).

DEVELOPING A PERSONAL WRITING STYLE

Most writers have a writing style or 'voice' of their own. For example, you might have a favourite set of vocabulary, use certain collocations

Table 29.3 Comparative illustration of text transformation from first draft to edited text.

First draft text. Highlighted text indicates words, expressions or structures that were clumsy or confusing	Edited text. Underlined text indicates words or expressions that have been adjusted to produce a more concise and precise text. Note also the reduced word count.
Drawing on the findings presented in the last chapter, it was established that previous studies in this research field have tended to be limited in their scope with respect to these two aspects and this means that this is what it is felt has contributed to reducing the impact of their studies which allowed the current research work sufficient diversity in which it would be possible to draw wider ranging conclusions whilst also increasing the impact which this research may have in the construction industry. **[85 words]**	The findings presented in the last chapter indicated that previous studies in this research field were limited in scope relating to the two latter aspects. This shortcoming contributed to reducing the impact of the studies. Consequently, the current research sought to provide sufficient diversity and to allow wider ranging conclusions with greater potential impact on the construction industry. **[58 words]**

(**Ch 27**) more frequently than others and favour longer complex sentences over shorter, simpler ones. This might be influenced by what you have read in the past, or a method of teaching writing in school. It is what would make your own writing recognisable to another person.

As stressed in **Chapters 26** and **27**, the writing style you may have carried over from school must progressively move towards standard academic style. This process may have started in your undergraduate days, but the results will need to approach perfection for thesis writing. This does not mean that you will or should lose all of your idiosyncrasies, more that you must observe all the conventions expected within your chosen forms of expression.

Aspects of style tend to come to the fore when expressing your own thoughts and ideas, rather than describing those of others, where standard constructions are adopted. As you gain experience, your own position/viewpoint will become more evident in the way you write. As you gain confidence, so your writing will become more fluent and even assertive.

Don't be too consistent in your writing style

As you develop your writing skills, you will need to learn how to 'play' with language. This involves experimenting with each choice of word, each phrase, the order of words, the construction of sentences and the sequence within paragraphs. The ability to manipulate writing in this way is important for a number of reasons:

- it allows you to exploit the flexibility of the English language to express your meaning as clearly and as accurately as possible;
- it demonstrates your ability to group ideas in a logical way;
- it ensures that you maintain the reader's attention and interest.

STRIVING FOR THE GOAL OF WRITING AUTONOMY

There will be times during the completion of your thesis where you will wonder whether you will ever master the writing techniques required. It is often very difficult to articulate complex thoughts and ideas, especially when these are new. Sometimes when you have used words poorly, it will be highly embarrassing when your supervisor points out an elementary error. However, take heart. Every PhD student who ever submitted a thesis has felt the same at times. Your aim should be to learn from your mistakes and to be proactive in learning more about language and methods of concise, clear expression.

The goal of writing autonomy is one to aim for, but perfection is not a prize that many achieve. Even noted writers will go through many drafts before finalising their text and even then would probably find something to change given another opportunity. What is realistic is to develop the skill of self-criticism and self-editing to such a level that you can see in your own writing that it needs to be altered to refine meaning. In the longer term, learning how to edit your work properly will help you to develop a skill of critical analysis that will stand you in good stead throughout your career. However, once you have a version that meets with your own and your supervisor's approval, don't be tempted to keep tinkering with it; a point has to come when you must accept that the manuscript is about as near-perfect as you can make it.

It is in the nature of language that the same ideas can be expressed in many different ways. Some may be suitable for your purpose and some not. Having created a logical structure for your writing (**Chs 26–28**), your task is to think through these options for each and every paragraph and sentence that you write, and to choose appropriate sentence and word sequences.

Finally, always remember that your thesis is exactly that: *your* thesis. You must take total responsibility for everything in it, and be prepared to defend it under close questioning. That final stage of the PhD process is the point where you will realise true autonomy in your research.

ACTION POINTS

29.1 Decide what to do about feedback comments you frequently receive. For instance, does your supervisor always comment about your spelling or grammar; or suggest you should use more examples; or ask for more citations to be included? If so, look at relevant reference books to learn how to adjust appropriately, or seek assistance from the Academic Support Service in your institution for support in language and writing skills.

29.2 Practise using the standard proof-reading marks. When editing your own work, learn how to use some of these symbols as this will help you speed up the proof-reading process.

29.3 Try condensing a piece of your text. This is an acknowledged way of improving your work. Look at your text for irrelevant points, wordy phrases, repetitions and excessive examples; if you can reduce its original length by 10–25 per cent, you will probably find that you have created a much tighter, easier-to-read piece of writing.

30

THESIS PRESENTATION

How to submit your work in the appropriate manner

Your thesis must be presented according to the appropriate academic conventions and specific university rules. This chapter explains how to create a polished submission that follows the established standards of academic writing in your discipline.

KEY TOPICS

→ Following institutional guidance for the presentation of theses

→ Layout of text

→ Incorporating figures and tables

→ Formatting, printing and binding

The quality of your thesis will be determined by a combination of factors, but principally:

- activities that take place before you write, such as researching your sources, conducting experiments or analysing the literature;

- the way you express your ideas in writing.

Your examiners (**Ch 31**) will be expected to verify that it has been submitted according to the local rules. Moreover, directly or indirectly, the presentation of your thesis will make a statement about the overall care you have taken in conducting your analysis and preparing the content, and might therefore influence your examiners. This chapter provides reminders of what may seem to be the 'cosmetic' details of layout and visual elements, but which, in fact, reflect the professionalism you should attach to all aspects of your work.

Good presentation involves accuracy, consistency and attention to detail. For this reason it is often associated with editing and proofreading (**Ch 29**).

Why does good presentation matter?

- It forms an element of the assessment.
- It helps the marker or examiner understand what you have written.
- It shows you can adopt professional standards in your work.
- If you have taken care with meticulous presentation, then this suggests that the work it reports will have been done with equal attention to detail.
- It demonstrates you have acquired important skills that will transfer to other subjects and, later, employment.

FOLLOWING INSTITUTIONAL GUIDANCE FOR THE PRESENTATION OF THESES

Acceptable thesis structures depend on discipline and subject (**Ch 28**). You should research this carefully before you start to write up, by consulting the relevant postgraduate degree regulations. Institutions provide information about thesis submission and presentation – sometimes this is very prescriptive and relates to the appearance and layout, sometimes only minimal direction is provided.

You may have to search for the information on your university's website, through the University Library, the Registry, the Media or Printing Services Department or the School or Faculty. If you have difficulty in locating these guidelines, then a good starting point would be your university's Postgraduate Office. Specifications often vary within an institution, so an alternative is to check with your Faculty, School or Department Office.

Some institutions use the British Standard BS4821:1990 as the point of reference for their thesis requirements but note that this predates many functions and applications now available on personal computers.

Specifications now generally include:

- details on submission process, binding formats and number of copies to be provided;
- inclusion of certain introductory elements, namely, title page (title, author, year of presentation), abstract, declaration as to originality of the document (both student and supervisor), acknowledgements, and table of contents (**Ch 28**);

- length of theses (these vary depending on the level of degree for which the thesis is submitted) but usually range from 75,000 to 100,000 words (variously including or excluding appendices, footnotes and bibliography);
- page and margin sizes; page numbering; justification and indentation;
- font, point size and line spacing (usually 1.5 or double line);
- numbering of chapters, headings and sub-headings;
- layout of diagrams, illustrations and other visuals including photographs as well as inclusion of electronic data or other realia;
- inclusion of glossaries, footnotes, endnotes and reference list or bibliography (referencing style may be prescribed by the institution or may be dictated by professional standards).

Obviously, any guidance regarding format has to be followed precisely as part of the regulatory system that applies to postgraduate degrees.

LAYOUT OF TEXT

Theses are normally word-processed. This gives a professional result and also makes the drafting and editing phases easier. Some regulations require printing on only one side of the paper, others (as an eco-friendly measure) wish printing on both sides.

There are a number of conventions regarding the presentation of academic writing. These are discussed below and some important aspects are summarised in checklist form in Table 30.1.

Font

There are two main choices: serif types, with extra strokes at the end of the main strokes of each letter, and sans serif types, without these strokes (see Figure 30.1). The type to use is usually left to personal preference.

Serif font
Times roman 11 pt
Times roman 12 pt
Times roman 14 pt

Sans serif font
Arial 11 pt
Arial 12 pt
Arial 14 pt

Figure 30.1 Examples of the main types of font at different point sizes.

Table 30.1 Checklist for conventions in the presentation of academic writing.

❏ In some disciplines the abbreviations i.e. and e.g. are acceptable in academic text; in others these are not used; etc. should never be used in academic text

❏ &, the ampersand, is not commonly used in text, although it is used routinely in certain referencing styles

❏ Where abbreviations are used to express units, for example, SI units, then this is acceptable

❏ Subject-specific dictionaries will provide most common abbreviations used in a particular field

Acronyms

❏ Do not use acronyms in the title of a paper or thesis

❏ Provide an alphabetical list of abbreviations and acronyms at the beginning of technical reports and manuals

❏ Define acronyms the first time that they appear in the text

❏ Only capitalise definitions of acronyms if they are proper nouns

❏ Form plurals of acronyms only by adding -s, as in QUANGOs – do not add an apostrophe

❏ Some acronyms become 'words' in their own right: NATO (North Atlantic Treaty Organisation)

Fonts and point size

❏ The norms are either Times New Roman or Arial

❏ The point size is usually 12 point

❏ Larger point size is usually selected for chapter headings and sub-headings

❏ The same font and selected point sizes should be used consistently throughout the work

❏ Latin words such as *et al.* (and others) and *in vitro,* should be printed in italics

❏ If emphasis is required – usually rarely in academic writing – then use only one feature: either bold or italics or underlining, but not any combination of these

Headings and sub-headings

Conventions and preferences differ. Check with your department or supervisor about presentation 'rules' that will apply to your thesis. In the absence of any other instruction, the following approach may be followed:

❏ Use a capital only at the first letter of a title and at proper nouns within the title

❏ Full stops are not necessary in titles

❏ If a strap line, introduced by a colon, is used after the title, place the words following in lower case unless they are proper names (initial capital) or acronyms

❏ Sub-headings, if used/permitted, need to be laid out consistently using the same font and point size throughout

Continued overleaf

Lists
❑ Each point on bulleted lists should begin with a capital letter provided that there is no preceding 'sentence stem' introducing the list (usually ending with a colon)

Punctuation
❑ If in doubt, add punctuation where you would normally pause, if you were to read your work aloud
❑ For bullet points, the academic conventions vary. (a) One commonly used convention in some disciplines requires no full stops at the end of each bullet (particularly if the bullet consists of only a few words). Where the bullet extends into more than one sentence, then the last sentence and any intervening ones are finished by full stops. (b) In other areas, the convention adopted is to use a full stop at the end if the bullet point is a complete sentence and a semi-colon if the bullet is incomplete. (c) Another option commonly used is one in which a phrase or sentence 'stem' (followed by a full colon) introduces the bulleted list. The bullets that follow each 'complete' the introductory stem as a sentence. Thus, the list of bullets creates an extended sentence in which each bullet is an element. In such cases a semi-colon is used at the end of each bullet point and a full-stop after the last bullet.
❑ Whichever citation system you use, ensure that the punctuation format is followed consistently

Spelling
❑ In some disciplines, for example, chemistry, the internationally recognised convention is to use American spelling for words such as, sulfur, analyze, organization
❑ Spell-checking is not a guarantee of error-free spelling; ensure that you check your work by reading it through to avoid errors such as: from/form – both are perfectly good words but if you mean one and not the other, the spell-checker would not identify the error

A serif font is said to be easier to read. The point size (pt) of the font is more likely to be specified, which will probably be 11 or 12 point for ease of reading. You should avoid using elaborate font types as generally they will not help the reader to assimilate what you have written. For the same reason, you should not use too many forms of emphasis. Choose italics or bold and stick with one only. Symbols are often used in academic work and in Microsoft Word can be added using the 'Insert > Symbol' menu.

Margins

A typical convention is for left-hand margins to be 4 cm and the right-hand margins 2.5 cm. This allows space for any examiner's comments and ensures that the text can be read if a left-hand binding is used.

Line spacing

Text that is spaced at least at 1.5–2 lines apart is easier to read. Some examiners like to add pencil comments as they read the text and this leaves them space to do so. The exception is where you wish to use long quotations. These should be indented and typed in single-line spacing in most citation styles but not all (see McMillan and Weyers, 2013).

Paragraphs

The key thing to remember about layout is to make good use of the 'white space'. This means that you should lay out your paragraphs clearly and consistently. Some people prefer the indentation method, where the paragraph begins on the fourth character space from the left-hand margin (Figure 30.2(a)). Others prefer the blocked paragraph style, that is, where all paragraphs begin on the left-hand margin, but are separated by a double-line space (Figure 30.2(b)). The space between paragraphs should be roughly equivalent to a missing line.

In Microsoft Word these aspects can be controlled using the 'Format > Paragraph' menu.

Sub-headings

In some disciplines use of sub-headings is acceptable or even favoured, though in others these 'signpost' strategies are discouraged. It is best to consult your supervisor about this if you are uncertain. Sub-headings are usually in bold.

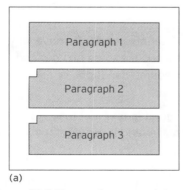
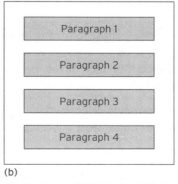

(a)   (b)

Figure 30.2 Types of paragraph layout. (a) Indented and (b) blocked. Note that in the indented model, by convention, the first paragraph in any section is not indented.

Punctuation

Standard punctuation applies to all types of academic writing. One decision you may wish to make is about spaces between sentences – whether to use one or two. This is generally a matter of personal preference. Take special care to ensure the punctuation of the reference list follows the appropriate convention and is consistent (**Ch 20**).

Word count

You may be asked to work to a word count and this can be checked using standard functions on your word-processor. If you greatly exceed this limit, this will almost certainly impact on your presentation as you will confront the reader with too much information and will probably not be writing in the expected concise fashion (**Chs 26** and **27**).

Citations and references

Providing citations and a reference list is standard practice (**Ch 20**). You must be consistent in the referencing style you adopt, and some disciplines impose strict subject-specific conventions. If in doubt, consult your course handbook, institutional regulations or library guidelines.

Quotations and formulae

Quotations can be integrated into the text when short, but are usually presented as a 'special' type of paragraph when long. In either case, the source and date of publication are provided after the quotation. **Chapter 20** provides detailed guidance on the presentation of quotations.

Some disciplines, for example, English Literature and Law, have very specific rules for the way in which quotations are to be laid out and referenced. In such cases, consult your course handbook or ask for guidance from a tutor.

Short formulae or equations can be included in text, but they are probably better presented on a separate line and indented, thus

$$\alpha + 4\beta/\eta^2\pi = 0 \qquad\qquad\qquad \text{(Eqn. 8.7)}$$

Where a large number of formulae are included, they can be numbered for ease of cross-reference, as shown in this example.

Quoting numbers in text

Adopt the following rules:

- In general writing, spell out numbers from one to ten and use figures for 11 and above; in formal writing, spell out numbers from one to a hundred and use figures beyond this.

- Spell out high numbers that can be written in two words ('six hundred'). With a number like 4,200,000, you also have the choice of writing '4.2 million'.

- Always use figures for dates, times, currency or to give technical details ('5-amp fuse').

- Always spell out numbers that begin sentences, indefinite numbers ('hundreds of soldiers') or fractions ('seven-eighths').

- Hyphenate numbers and fractions appropriately ('twenty-five').

INCORPORATING FIGURES AND TABLES

In many disciplines, you will be expected to support your discussion with visual material or data, and it is important that you do so in a fashion that best helps the reader to assimilate the information. You must also follow any specific presentational rules that apply in your subject area.

Inserting figures in text

Integrated suites of office-type software allow you to insert the graphs you produced using the spreadsheet program into text produced with the word-processing program. The two programs can even be linked so that changes on the spreadsheet data automatically appear in the graph within the word-processed file. Consult the manual or 'Help' facility to find out how to do this. In Microsoft Word, digital photographs can be inserted using the 'Insert > Picture > From File' command.

Figures

The academic convention is to include a wide range of visual material under the term 'Figure' ('Fig.' for short). This includes graphs, diagrams, charts, sketches, pictures and photographs, although in some disciplines and contexts the latter may be referred to as 'plates'.

The following set of guidelines should be adopted when including figures:

- All figures should be referred to in the text. There is a range of 'standard' formulations (collocations, **Ch 27**) for doing this, such as 'Figure 4 shows that...'; or '... results for one treatment were higher than for the other (see Fig. 2)'. Find what is appropriate from the literature or texts in your subject area.

- Figures should be numbered in the order they are referred to in the text. If you are including the figures within the main body of text (usually more convenient for the reader) then they should appear at the next suitable position in the text after the first time of mention. At the very least this will be after the paragraph that includes the first citation, but more normally will be at the top of the following page.

- Figures should be positioned at the top or bottom of a page, rather than sandwiched between blocks of text. This looks neater and makes the text easier to read.

- Each figure must have a legend, which will include the figure number, a title and some text (often a key to the symbols and line styles used). The convention is for figure legends to appear below each figure. Your aim should be to make each figure self-contained. That is, a reader who knows the general subject area should be able to work out what your figure shows, without reference to other material.

- Figure presentation should follow normal academic conventions. For example, with line graphs, the norm is to put the controlled variable or category of measurement on the x-axis (horizontal axis) and the measured variable on the y-axis (vertical axis). Take great care to ensure that the quantity plotted and its units are provided for all axes. (**Ch 21**)

Choosing the right type of figure to display information is an art in itself (**Ch 21**). Although there are technical reasons why some forms of data should be presented in particular ways (for example, proportional data in a pie chart rather than a line chart), your main focus should always be on selecting a method that will best help the reader assimilate the information presented (**Ch 21**). The 'Chart Wizard' in the Microsoft Office Excel spreadsheet program is a possible starting point for exploring the range of possibilities.

When presenting individual figures, clarity should be your main aim – ensuring, for example, that the different slices of a pie chart or the

Don't automatically accept the graphical output from spreadsheets and other programs

These are not always in the 'correct' style. For example, the default output for many charts produced by the Microsoft Office Excel spreadsheet includes a grey background and horizontal gridlines, neither of which is generally used in academia. It is not difficult to alter these parts of the chart, however, and you should learn how to do this from manuals or the 'Help' facility.

lines and symbols in a graph are clearly distinguishable from one another. Consistency is also important, so you should use the same line or shading for the same entity in all your figures (for example, hollow symbols for 'controls'). The widespread availability of colour printers should help with this, but some departments may insist on the use of black and white, since this was the convention when colour printing was prohibitively expensive. If you are using colour, keep it 'tasteful' and remember that certain colour combinations are not easily differentiated by some readers.

Tables

These are used to summarise large amounts of information, especially where a reader might be interested in some of the detail of the data (Ch 21). Tables are especially useful for qualitative information but numerical data can also be presented, especially if they relate to a discontinuous qualitative variable (for example, the population sizes and occupation breakdown of various geographical regions).

Tables generally include a number of columns (vertical) and rows (horizontal). By analogy with figures, the convention is to put the controlled or measured variable on the column headers (horizontal) and to place the measured variable or categories of measurement in the rows (vertical). Do not forget to include the units of the information listed if this is relevant.

The rules for presenting tables are very similar to those for figures, with the important exception that a table legend should appear above the table. It is quite common to give exceptions and other information as footnotes to tables.

Figure or table?

In certain cases it may be possible to present the same data set as a figure or as a table. The first rule in such cases is never do both – choose the method that best suits your data and the target reader. An important criterion is to decide which will best help the reader assimilate the information. If the take-home message is best shown visually, then a figure might be preferable; whereas, if details and numerical accuracy are important, then a table might be more suitable.

FORMATTING, PRINTING AND BINDING

There will come a time when you consider your thesis writing is ready for the final stages of presentation. This involves a number of checks where attention to detail is essential:

- Final inspection for consistency. This will depend on the nature of the research, but could involve spelling checks, consistency in punctuation, explanation of abbreviations at first use, fonts for headings, and so on.
- Formatting. You will need to check each page carefully and in sequence to see that spacing conventions have been obeyed and that there are no untidy 'widows' and 'orphans' – paragraphs where splits between pages result in one or few lines on either side. Any tables or figures should be in the correct position and orientation.
- Numbering. You will need to ensure that all pages are numbered correctly and in true sequence, as well as the figures, tables and other numbered elements, such as case studies.
- Contents page. You can only complete this once the final page numbering is known. You will also then be able to complete the lists of figures and tables with page numbering.
- References. You need to run a final check to ensure (a) that all citations in the text have a corresponding entry in the reference list and (b) that all entries in the reference list are actually cited. Checking the formatting of references is a very tedious task, but essential.

When these checks are complete, you will be ready for printing. This should be carried out using a good (laser) printer using good quality

Take pride and pleasure from your work

By the time that you reach this final stage you will have spent many, many hours on producing the final thesis. What you are handling now will be the product of those hours and the culmination of study and thinking about a complex research issue. Even though your energy reserves may be low, keep your standards up to ensure that your submission is of the best possible quality. At this time, you should take huge pride in what you have done – the breadth of the research, the triumph over problems and the sense that you have done the job and done it well.

paper. You will need several copies – one for yourself, one for your supervisor, and others for the examiners (and possibly for the library). Although there is an expense attached, this is probably best carried by a specialist photocopy or printing house. They can also advise on temporary binding options. You should not contemplate a final binding at this stage in case there are changes to be made after the *viva* exam (**Ch 31**).

The postgraduate office (or equivalent) will specify how to submit. Normally there is a process whereby you advise them of your 'intention to submit', which allows them to carry out the necessary administrative processes to set up your *viva*.

Following your *viva*, you may have corrections to make, and after these have been 'signed off' (often by your supervisor), you can proceed to the final thesis binding. There are binderies in most large cities and some of the larger universities.

ACTION POINTS

30.1 Prepare well for printing out your final version. Many students opt to print out their final thesis copies using their own word processor and printer. Should you choose to do this rather than use the services of a professional printing company, be sure that, before you begin, you have sufficient paper of the same (high) quality and ink to allow you to complete the necessary processes. Finding that your supplies run out part way through the process could involve you in significant delays and even make you miss the submission deadline.

30.2 Look at a recently submitted thesis to gauge the overall standard or presentation expected. Ask a past student (perhaps someone in your supervisor's research group) whether you can look at their thesis, or ask your supervisor whether he or she can show you a past example that was rated highly. Examine this carefully for elements of presentation mentioned in this chapter.

30.3 Make good use of the 'dead time' between submission and your *viva voce* exam. By all means take a well-deserved break, but don't rest on your laurels entirely. You could use this some of this time productively by preparing for the *viva* (Ch 31) and checking out recent additions to the literature in your field.

EXAMINATION AND BEYOND

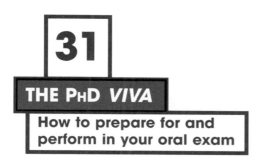

31

THE PhD VIVA

How to prepare for and perform in your oral exam

The *viva voce* exam requires preparation as much as any other exam. This chapter informs you about the aims and conduct of oral exams, so you can be ready to make the most of the experience.

KEY TOPICS

→ What is the purpose of the *viva voce*?

→ The format of the *viva voce* exam

→ Criteria on which the *viva voce* is judged

→ Preparing for the *viva voce* exam

→ Conduct during the exam

→ The outcome of the *viva voce* exam

For some postgraduate students, the *viva voce* is an unknown quantity; for others it is a subject that has been much discussed with fellow postgraduates to the point of confusion. It can be one of the least understood (or perhaps the most misunderstood) phases of the doctoral process. At the outset, it must be noted that each *viva* is unique to the topic and to the personalities involved. However, it can be generally acknowledged that it is a compulsory part of your examination and one where certain regulations apply to the conduct and outcomes.

What does *viva voce* mean?

The term is Latin, meaning 'by live voice'. The intention is an interactive face-to-face discussion about your research, as presented in your thesis.

WHAT IS THE PURPOSE OF THE *VIVA VOCE?*

In the preparation and submission of the thesis you effectively complete the written criteria for the examination of your postgraduate programme. The *viva voce* exam serves two main purposes:

- a formal platform to assess the level of your theory, technical expertise, and the effectiveness of your understanding of communication skills;

- a test of quality assurance – to determine how and why you approached your project the way you did, and whether your work is original.

With respect to the latter, you are expected to defend and justify the quality of your thesis, which is why some refer to the *viva voce* exam as the 'defence' of a thesis.

Understandably, many students are apprehensive about their *viva* for any of a variety of reasons – for example, it is the last phase of the process and the huge investment of time, money and effort may result in failure; they may be daunted by the reputation of the external examiner and fear that they will not be able to meet exacting questions; they may simply be overawed by the occasion. To counter this apprehension, several points should be considered:

- Fear of failure is a natural human feeling, but very few PhD students actually fail their *viva* and you should also take confidence from the fact that you probably know as much as anyone about your subject. An 'I can do this' attitude will serve you well in the *viva* itself, so trying to master that mental attitude should be an important part of your preparation.

- The external examiner, of course, was once in your position, nervously facing the *viva.* While he or she has a duty to ask challenging questions, they will also have a degree of empathy with your position and recognise that helping you feel at ease is part of their role. Nerves are perfectly natural and should be regarded positively as the body's way of putting itself on alert for a challenge ahead.

- Being intimidated by the *viva* process is a natural reaction, especially since you will not have been in an examination situation for some years. As noted above, by this stage you will possibly more of an expert in this particular topic than those examining your thesis.

For this reason, you should think of this as an opportunity to share your understanding with fellow colleagues and regard it more as a conversation than a confrontation. Not only will this attitude help to reduce your tension, it will also help the examiners to help you to show yourself at your best.

Knowing what to expect, as explained in this chapter, coupled with good preparation, will put you in a position to learn from and even enjoy the occasion.

Find out about your examiner

Once you know who your external examiner is going to be, look into his or her profile online, using appropriate web searches. Seeing a smiling face in a publicity photograph might help to convince you that he or she is no ogre. Knowing more about your external's research interests, teaching and other information will also set you mind at ease and may help with your preparation for questions.

THE FORMAT OF THE *VIVA VOCE* EXAM

You will normally be examined during the *viva voce* by a panel of two or three people. This is your *viva* committee and will generally consist of an external examiner, internal examiner and the convenor. The external examiner is the most important person and will co-ordinate and lead proceedings. Most of the questions posed to you will probably be directed from this person and it is therefore important that you familiarise yourself before the *viva* on the area of expertise of your external examiner.

You will probably already be familiar with your internal examiner since he/she may well conduct their research within your department. This person will also question you, though normally the internal's role is primarily regulatory, to ensure that the examination is run fairly and that proceedings are carried out according to your university's guidelines. They may interject at certain stages during the examination.

The convenor's role will probably be carried out by another academic from a non-related area in the department or institution. He or she will help identify and call together the examiners at a time which is suitable for all parties. Once this has been accomplished the convenor's task is effectively complete although he or she may chair the event. Your supervisor may or may not sit in on the examination, though their role will be essentially passive if they do, and may just involve note-taking. They rarely take an active role in defending the student's thesis or questioning, but may be drawn in by the external in the later stages of discussion.

CRITERIA ON WHICH THE *VIVA VOCE* IS JUDGED

Formal criteria are laid out by each university on which the assessment of the *viva voce* is based. Your examiners will be made aware of these as part of their preparation for the exam. A good examiner will focus the proceedings appropriately in order to make informed decisions on your performance in each of these areas. The precise criteria differ according to university, but the emphasis will be on:

- the requirement for novelty – ascertaining your unique contribution to the field;
- the need for reliability – confirming that you are ethical and honest;
- demonstrable ownership of the work – that you have the ability to discuss the thesis in detail.

Some encapsulate this in stating that the thesis, or large parts of it, should be of 'publishable quality' (**Ch 32**).

PREPARING FOR THE *VIVA VOCE* EXAM

Good preparation for the *viva voce* is as important as it is for a written exam. However, many research students often find the event hard to picture. How do you prepare for this type of exam? What do you need to revise? These kinds of questions regularly crop up.

If you have got this far, it is highly likely that you have been very successful at written examinations in the past. You need to determine a systematic strategy of revision, similar, or adapted from that you may have incorporated into your revision for previous exams. Presented here are the most important points to bear in mind.

- Firstly, and most importantly, make sure you know your thesis. Although you wrote it, you will almost certainly need to refresh yourself on some of the finer points by the time the examination approaches. Read through it carefully, and make notes and a list of wider reading points you would like to check up on, or research in more depth.

- Research your examiners. Be familiar with some of their more recent publications or reviews. This might help you to predict likely lines of enquiry.

- Think of potential questions. As you read your thesis, imagine yourself in the *viva* and envisage the questions that may crop up, based on the expertise of your internal and external examiners. Table 31.1 provides some representative oral exam questions that may assist with your preparation.

- Think about your previous experiences of similar panel interview situations. Regard these as mini-*viva*s. You will almost certainly have experienced several of these over the last few years in your thesis committee meetings. Be self-analytical: how did you fare? What were your weaknesses? How could you improve?

- Examine your work retrospectively. If you had your time over, how would you change/refine/improve your approach or methods? A good researcher should be able to identify limitations. Expect to be asked about these and you should be frank about them, rather than defensive.

- Know about the technical stuff. As well as showing an understanding your research, it is also likely that you will be questioned on technical details as well as your research methodology. For example, if you used a complex piece of equipment, make sure you know how it works and why you used it.

Explore the ethical dimensions of your research study

The external examiner may wish to discuss this aspect with you. He or she will be looking not only for an appreciation of issues affecting the study itself, but also an awareness of ethics within the wider discipline context.

- Prepare to give spoken answers. Create a list of questions and then orally answer them. Alternatively, get a friend to ask you questions, perhaps based on Table 31.1. These people need not be experts in the field, because often the simplest questions are most difficult to answer – for example, 'how would you describe in a few

Table 31.1 Some representative oral exam questions. Of course, it is impossible to predict the exact questions, as most will be related to detailed content. This listing provides some typical question scenarios where you can provide the detail according to your project. Of course, not all the questions will be applicable to your study, nor will the format always be question and answer.

Rationale	Typical questions
Opening gambits – designed to put you at ease and provide background information for the examiner	• Have you enjoyed your PhD study? • What has been the best bit of the PhD for you? • Why did you choose this field of study? • Why did you choose this approach?
Context – finding out where your research fits into the field	• How would you summarise progress in this research area prior to your study? • Who are the most important researchers in this area in your opinion, and why? • Who were your main influences?
Thesis organisation – understanding the plan behind your thesis	• Can you outline the structure of your thesis for me? • Why did you organise your thesis this way?
Methodology – revealing what you understand about the techniques you used	• Why did you adopt this particular methodology? • What alternative methodologies did you consider? • Why did you discount them? • How did you develop this method? • What are the main weaknesses/limitations of your methods?
Technical details – an exploration of the methods or approach you have used (for sciences mainly)	• How does this instrument work? • Can you talk me through this procedure? • Can you tell me about the standardisation tests you carried out? • Why did you choose these treatments? • Why did you include this control? • What difficulties, if any, did you encounter in gathering data?
Results or position – finding out how you arrived at your results or viewpoint	• Can you sum up your main findings in a few sentences? • What is new or original about your work? • Why did you arrive at this viewpoint? • Can you explain what's involved in this statistical analysis? • Can you tell me about the errors associated with this result?

Interpretation – exploring your analysis	• Can you explain this result? • Why did you conclude this? • What might you have done differently?
Meaning and impact – discussing the significance of your work	• Why do you feel this is a consequence of your findings? • How does your work contribute to the field? • What do you think is the impact of your work? • What plans do you have for publishing your work?

Future development –
finding out what could
happen next
	• What do your results mean in the wider context?
	• If you had another year of research, what would
	  you do?
	• What would you recommend as further steps in this
	  research?

Personal focus –
reflecting on the
experience
	• What skills do you think you take away from this
	  PhD study?
	• What do you think you've learnt about academic
	  research?
	• What do you know now that you wish you had
	  known at the outset?
	• What are you going to do next?

sentences what you achieved in your project'. It is likely that you will face a similar opening gambit near the beginning of your exam. You don't want to produce a rambling response which goes off at tangents. Practise so you can keep it concise and succinct.

- Be aware of where and how you think the research could be developed in the future. What are the wider implications of your work for the field? This is a common question near the end of an oral exam.

- Stay calm and focused. You will probably feel apprehensive before the exam. This is normal and nerves are often a very positive thing enabling you to be alert and focused at the right time. However, you don't want anxiety levels to reach a point where they adversely affect your performance. Use techniques that have worked in the past to keep you composed.

- Prepare a timetable of revision incorporating ideas from these points. Stick to a schedule in the run-up to the exam. Don't cram the night before; get plenty of sleep so that you feel fresh and ready for the event.

Be prepared to expand on answers to 'closed' questions

Some *viva voce* questions will be 'closed' – that is, inviting a 'yes' or 'no' answer (for example, 'can you tell me about x?'). In this situation you should elaborate your answer with more detail or reasoning.

CONDUCT DURING THE EXAM

Most research students feel apprehensive before their *viva voce* exam. Some students find it useful a day or so before the event, to visit the room in which the thesis committee will meet, so rehearsing the occasion as mental preparation. Once you arrive at the real exam make sure you have considered these important points:

- Make sure you arrive promptly and wear reasonably smart clothing. It may be regarded as disrespectful to the examiner and the general situation to turn up late in jeans and a T-shirt.

- When answering questions, take your time and speak clearly. Pause before responding and use this as a strategy to think about what you have been asked and gather your thoughts to form a concise answer.

- Use a logical structure for your responses. Start with the basics and then you can develop the deeper aspects.

- Don't give long, rambling answers. Try to produce a clear, crisp response and then stop speaking when you have finished.

- If you do not know the answer to a question, then say so. Your examiners will quickly pick up your lack of knowledge, if you try to give a waffled or irrelevant answer. If you are unsure what the examiner meant by the question, ask them to clarify or repeat the question.

- Give balanced answers and discuss the appropriate evidence for and against your viewpoint, explaining why you think the way you do.

- Be prepared to hold your ground, but don't argue with your examiner if your ideas are not in agreement. It is reasonable to accept that there might be an alternative point of view or interpretation while also defending your ideas, detailing the supporting evidence.

- Most of all, project your enthusiasm for your project and be positive.

Arrive at the *viva* with your own list of errata

The external examiner will have closely read your thesis, and will probably have spotted a number of minor errors (errata). Some examiners will simply present a paper listing these errors for correction before thesis binding, but, on occasion, they may wish to discuss particular points in detail. It is a good idea to come to the exam with your own list of errors. This shows that you have been self-critical and are aware of the technical requirements of thesis writing.

THE OUTCOME OF THE *VIVA VOCE* EXAM

A *viva voce* exam generally lasts for one to three hours, but may extend up to five. The length is not necessarily an indication of how well or how badly the proceedings are going – it may be that you have an extremely thorough external examiner, or that you simply have a lot of interesting material to talk about.

Once the exam is brought to a close you will generally be asked to leave the room while your internal and external examiners agree on a decision regarding the outcome of the combined thesis and *viva*. You will be invited back after five or ten minutes and informed immediately of this decision. Typically, the recommendation arising from the thesis examining committee will fall into one of six categories.

1 The thesis is accepted for the degree.

2 The thesis is accepted subject to: (a) minor corrections being made (time limitations may apply) and/or (b) the thesis being bound satisfactorily.

3 The thesis is not accepted in its present form, but the candidate is given the opportunity to re-submit a revised form.

4 The thesis does not meet the requirements of a PhD, but does warrant consideration for Master's level degree. No re-examination required following the appropriate amendments.

5 The thesis warrants consideration for a Master's degree, but will also require re-examination after amending.

6 The thesis is rejected with no right for revision or re-submission.

Your examiners will provide you with instructions on what the next steps will need to involve. For example, category 2 above is probably the most common outcome, so you may be required to make minor corrections, which will need to be verified subsequently by the internal examiner. Once the standard is met for submission to the university, you will be required to produce several hard bound copies of the thesis, and, increasingly, an electronic copy on DVD, which are delivered to the postgraduate office.

The final remaining step will be the administrative forms for graduation, and, we trust, organising a suitable celebration with friends, family and staff.

ACTION POINTS

31.1 Speak to a recently successful PhD student. Ask them about their *viva voce* experience, the sorts of questions asked by the external examiner and how they might have prepared differently, given a second chance. Remember, however, that external examiners differ in approach.

31.2 Practise summarising your key findings. You should be able to state, in relatively few words, what advances you feel you have made and the context in which they sit. You should also think through any deficiencies in your work and how you might remedy these, given time and resources.

31.3 Set up a mock PhD *viva*. Your supervisor may suggest having a mock *viva,* but, if not, ask them or another academic working in your area to spend a while letting you practise speaking about your work by answering typical questions, such as those in Table 31.1. Their feedback may provide vital pointers for the real examination.

32

PUBLISHING YOUR RESEARCH

How to write and submit a successful paper

In some ways the high point of research activity is publication of your results or ideas in the academic literature. This ensures your thoughts are a matter of record, establishes your precedence and communicates your work to others. Having your thesis work published also ensures that you have met relevant discipline standards.

KEY TOPICS

→ Is your work publishable?

→ Choosing a journal

→ Writing and submitting a paper

→ What happens to my paper after submission?

For a large part of your time as a postgraduate, your focus will be on completing your thesis. However, some might regard the pinnacle of postgraduate research as the publication of your work, rather than its production as a thesis. Certainly, producing work of publishable quality is one of the recognised benchmarks for the PhD degree. The best way to ensure that you meet that criterion is to submit, and have accepted, a journal article, book chapter or abstract. There will be few prouder moments in your research career than when you see your first publication in print.

IS YOUR WORK PUBLISHABLE?

There is no point in submitting research that will be rejected at the first hurdle. Your supervisor will be the best source of advice on the 'publishability' of your work. The criteria for this differ among disciplines and journals, but essentially, to be of an appropriate standard to be published, the work should be 'new, true and meaningful'.

Before starting to write, you will need to review your work critically under these headings (see also **Ch 31**):

- 'New' means a variety of things including being original, adopting a novel approach and adding to the sum of knowledge and understanding.

- 'True' encompasses elements of reliability, in other words, satisfying the scholarly standards of your discipline in terms of, for example, sources cited, methods used, or statistical analysis of results.

- 'Meaningful' means having impact within your field. It is not enough to satisfy the first two measures above without meeting this one. This carries connotations of newsworthiness, timeliness and added-value.

Another way to look at this topic is to review methods of persuasion (**Ch 18**). The advice given there can be adapted to the way in which you 'sell' your paper in the introductory section. If you can do this convincingly, you will be half-way to acceptance.

Write out a three-sentence description of your paper

This outline should encapsulate how you might persuade a potential reader to explore the detail of your work. If, when you have done this, you feel you have something to say, then continue with the draft. If not, review your possible contribution with your supervisor.

The material included in a paper will generally be a subset of the total work done during a project, so it must be carefully selected for relevance to a clear central position or hypothesis – if the authors will not prune, the referees and editors of the journal certainly will.

CHOOSING A JOURNAL

You should try to publish in an appropriate journal for the subject of your paper, and preferably one with a high reputation for its content. Newer journals (for example, some online publications) often struggle to establish their status immediately.

Having reviewed the literature in your subject for your thesis proposal, mid-term progress reviews and Introduction, you will have a good overview of the main journals in your area and will be able to characterise them in terms of content of papers and style. If not, perhaps your supervisor will be able to make some suggestions. Otherwise, consult your subject librarian, and ask them to list the premier titles in your area, so that you can look at these. Matters of content and style change over time, as the subject evolves and editorial teams come and go, so ensure that you are looking at current volumes of any title.

Impact factors for journals

The impact factor is a method is assessing the importance of a journal within an academic discipline. It is based on the average number of citations for articles in that journal over a specific time period. Although each paper must be judged on its own merits and not just in the short term, the fact that a publication is accepted for a high-impact journal is often taken as an indicator of its potential importance. Institutional research funding may rest on such metrics. Therefore, both you and your supervisor should be aiming for publication in journals of the highest possible impact factor. Journal impact factors can be found at the Thompson Reuters *Web of Knowledge* if your institution has signed up to this database.

Other factors that might be taken into account include:

- your supervisor's track record of publication in the journal;
- whether there is a continuing 'theme' of publication on your specific topic;
- whether you or your supervisor are members of a journal's sponsoring academic society;
- the number and geographical distribution of potential readers.

It will probably be evident which candidate journals are realistic options. Once you have such a short-list, you should review each journal's criteria for submission. These will be published in the 'Instructions to Authors' rubric that is included from time to time in the published editions or on the publisher's website. This may help you to narrow down the choice yet further. You should note that some journals require the submission of an outline of the proposed paper which is then vetted for its suitability in terms of content and relevance to the journal before the author is invited to submit a full paper.

Concurrent submissions

The convention is that authors can only submit a paper to one journal at a time and you may be required to sign a declaration stating that is the case. This is because issues of copyright are involved.

WRITING AND SUBMITTING A PAPER

The choice of journal always dictates the format of a paper since authors must follow to the letter the journal's 'Instructions to Authors'. If you seek out a recent article covering a similar area to yours, you can work using this as a model. Ideally, it will be a well-written example.

Matters to look at closely are:

- overall structure and subdivisions of typical papers (there may be different forms covering, for example, short communications, papers or reviews);
- the relative extents of the different components (some journals prefer very short introductions, for example);
- the language style used (what specialised language is used);
- brevity (whether very short introduction, description and discussion is encouraged, or whether there is the opportunity to expand on your theme);
- the style used for citations and references (see **Ch 20**);
- the numbers of references and the way citations are used (some journals and editors expect all substantive statements to be backed up);
- styles used for figures and tables;
- the recommended total extent in words or pages (this will limit what you can include).

If your submitted paper mimics the expected standards and style of your chosen journal, then this will help referees and editors visualise it in print in the journal and make their task of reviewing and editing easier. In short, it will put them on your side.

In the non-sciences, if a PhD student submits to a journal, it is quite likely to be a single-author paper in their own name. Nevertheless, you should always keep your supervisor informed and ask him or her to look over drafts. In the sciences, multi-author publications are normal, and there are often local conventions about the order of authorship that will appear in the final printed version.

Deciding on authorship

In the case of multi-author papers, a contentious issue is often who should appear as an author and in what order they should be cited. It is important to decide this at an early stage. Where authors make an equal contribution, an alphabetical order of names may be used. Otherwise, each author should have made a substantial contribution to the paper and should be prepared to defend it in public. Ideally, the order of appearance will reflect the amount of work done rather than seniority. This may not happen in practice.

The actual process of writing will include outlining and reviewing as discussed elsewhere in this book. The final version must be as clearly written and as error-free as possible, so it may be a good idea to allow an independent academic to look over it with a critical eye. Any figures must be finished to an appropriate standard and this may involve preparing photographs or digital images of them.

WHAT HAPPENS TO MY PAPER AFTER SUBMISSION?

When you have completed your paper, you will need to submit copies to the editor of the chosen journal with a simple covering letter or email. He or she will decide whether the article is worth considering seriously. If not, it will be returned, perhaps with some suggestions as to how it might be improved.

If your paper is to be considered for publication, it will first be distributed to two or more referees (usually anonymous, but not always) who will have some expertise in the field of the topic area. Their role is to check the paper to ensure that it is novel, factually correct (if applicable) and that its length is justified. They may be asked to 'grade' the submission as to its suitability for publication, often using journal-specific criteria, and to list any corrections or modifications they would like to see. A delay of one to two months can arise while the manuscript goes through this refereeing process.

The process of evaluation and review of manuscripts is known as peer review.

Once the referees' comments are returned to the editor, either the editor or an editorial committee will consider whether the paper should be published in the light of the comments. Either the paper will be rejected with an explanation based on the journal's publication criteria or the referee's report. Even if the paper is accepted, it is normal for this to be conditional on the author(s) amending, cutting or otherwise altering the material.

The editor will send on the referees' comments to the authors, who will then have a chance to respond. The editor will decide on the basis of the comments and replies to them whether the paper should be published. Sometimes quite heated correspondence can result if the authors and referees disagree.

Take a positive view when reading referees' comments

You will have a vested interest in your work and may not see it as dispassionately as the referees. As a result, you may feel their comments are unfair, involve a mis-reading of your intent, or are wrong in academic terms. Unless the editor's decision is outright rejection, there will be a possibility to answer their points and resubmit on the basis of adjustments. This should be done in a positive fashion, and is perhaps best approached from the viewpoint that is a misunderstanding has occurred, then this may be due to the way you have explained things, rather than bone-headedness on the part of the referee.

If a paper is accepted, it will be sent to the typesetters. The next the authors may see of it is the proofs (first printed version in style of journal), which have to be corrected carefully for errors and returned. Eventually, the paper will appear in print, but a delay of six months following acceptance is not unusual. Nowadays, many papers are also available electronically, via the Web, in pdf format.

ACTION POINTS

32.1 As you read the literature in your area, evaluate the journals in which the articles and reviews are published. Which ones do you admire or feel would suit your form of writing and research interests? Which might contribute most to your CV?

32.2 Review your current work for the potential for publication. As discussed in **Chapter 28**, this also is one way of deciding on a thesis structure. Thinking and writing in the manner expected for publication can also help to improve the standard of your general thesis writing.

32.3 Think about different potential approaches to publication. This chapter has focused on journal articles, but, for example, you might be able to publish parts of your Introduction as a review. If unsure of the value of your work, you might consider gaining feedback on it by first presenting it as a spoken presentation **(Ch 14)**, gauging the reaction to it, and then moving on to submission of a manuscript. In the arts, some theses are published in their entirety. This might require prior discussion with a publisher. If your university has an in-house imprint, this may be a possible avenue.

33

How to make appropriate use of your qualification

During the tenure of your PhD studentship, your outlook on life and skill-set will almost certainly have changed. This may be reflected in new ambitions for your career. This chapter focuses on the decisions you need to make related to this, and how to present yourself to good effect when applying for jobs.

KEY TOPICS
→ Career planning
→ Applying for jobs

Towards the end of your PhD period, your primary focus will have been on writing up, but at the back of your mind will have been the question 'where do I go from here?' To a certain extent, the answer to this question depends on why you signed up for the qualification in the first place:

- If it were envisaged as a projected first step on a career pathway as a researcher, then you might now be looking for postdoctoral posts or even junior lectureships.

- If it were to 'expand you mind' or make a contribution to your subject, then you may be completely open about future directions – in this case you will be hoping to put the skills you have gained to good use, but will to consider a wide range of opportunities.

The experience of carrying out a PhD is often transformative, so you may have completely changed your intended direction – you may have been turned on or off a subject, or become more or less keen on research as an occupation, or you may have uncovered new skills and interests from your experiences. For example:

- You may have decided that you prefer research over teaching and may therefore wish to work within a research institute environment.

- You may have found a burning desire to work as a postdoc in a particular researcher's group.

- The self-understanding and confidence gained when teaching as a postgraduate may have convinced you to pursue a career in that direction.

- You may have learnt how to use a research instrument, piece of software or investigative approach that is in demand as an occupational skill.

- You may have enjoyed the experiences of thesis writing so much that you feel you would like to work in writing or journalism as a profession.

CAREER PLANNING

The term 'career planning' may have appeared from time to time during both your undergraduate and postgraduate days. It encompasses:

- being aware of the opportunities for someone with your qualification;
- deciding on a potential career trajectory that suits you as a person;
- finding suitable vacancies;
- making appropriate decisions related to applications.

If you do apply for a vacancy, then you will need to:

- present yourself in the best possible way to potential employers;
- perform well in interview.

If you have been carrying out personal development planning or a similar exercise (**Ch 5**), you will probably be in a good position to move forward from here as you will probably have devoted time and effort to think about it.

As soon as you are ready, approach your university's careers service. They have a duty to support postgraduates as well as undergraduates.

Even if you feel that the sorts of position you will be applying for are limited, and you feel you know where to find out about them, the staff of the careers service will be willing not only to assist in this, but also to help you to present yourself in the best possible way, including help with CVs and interview technique.

If you are less certain about your future, careers advisors are experienced in asking the right questions so they can present you with options to consider. The careers service will also offer a series of seminars and workshops than might be useful.

 Vitae

A good source of independent advice is the Vitae website (*http://www.vitae.ac.uk/*). This organisation exists to champion 'the personal, professional and career development of doctoral researchers and research staff in higher education institutions and research institutes' (**Ch 5**). Its excellent website includes sections on:

- managing your career;
- working in higher education;
- career opportunities outside higher education;
- research versus non-research careers;
- working overseas;
- employment by discipline.

APPLYING FOR JOBS

Updating your CV

Your *curriculum vitae* (CV) is, of course, your primary mechanism for assisting a possible employer to find out who you are and what qualifications, experience, skills and qualities you have to offer. It is important to realise that your CV may be one of many that a potential employer will scan, and that you may only have a few seconds of their attention to make a favourable impression. The quality of this document and of the accompanying application letter and personal statement are vital for successful job-hunting. Typically, a recruiter will use the following criteria to evaluate your CV:

- Good presentation. They'll want to see clear layout that makes it easy to find the information they want to see and possibly signs that you can express yourself fluently and have some design flair.

- Lack of obvious mistakes. Employers will not think highly of CVs

Initial impressions count

The presentation of your CV is the first thing a potential employer notices. Aspects such as quality of paper and print are important, but the document's design and the clarity of wording will be the most important factors. As these will be taken as an indication of your character, you should think about them very carefully.

containing spelling errors or grammatical mistakes. They'll think you may bring such sloppiness to their job.

- Professional qualifications and expertise. Specialist recruiters will be looking for key information about your field of expertise and this can take the form of a very brief outline of your doctoral topic. You may need to rework this for different applications so that your application is relevant to specific posts.

- Fitness for the post. They'll expect to see from the content that you would be a good fit to the job description. They'll need sufficient detail to determine this, but at the same time not too many facts of doubtful relevance that might waste their time and call into doubt your ability to evaluate and filter information.

- Honesty. They will demand full information and frankness about personal qualities and skills. If there is an obvious mismatch between your CV claims and your references, university transcript or interview performance, this will count severely against you.

- Character. They will want to see evidence that you would make an interesting and stimulating colleague. They will not want to see yet another clichéd CV produced by one of the common templates.

- Added value. They'll hope that you have qualities and skills additional to the ones in the job description. Since there may be many applicants with similar qualifications, this may mark you out from the crowd.

- Evidence and examples. They will want some means of confirming that the claims you make are valid. This may come from your referees or university transcript, but you should also mention reports, talks or other things you have done. They may ask you about these at interview.

- Completeness. They will expect your CV to be right up-to-date. Also they'll look for periods where you do not appear to have been doing anything – and ask you about these at interview.

Seven basic elements of a typical UK-style CV are described in Table 33.1. Most CVs will include all of these sections, but you may choose to use different titles for the headings and to include appropriate amounts of information, as suits the job specification. Of course, because you are a unique person, the precise details will be your own.

Your CV should be brief and to the point and appropriately balanced. Aim for about two to three A4 pages and emphasise sections using headings. Sometimes you will be expected to fill in a form instead of supplying a CV. This aids the initial screening of applicants and is common where an employer regularly takes on large numbers of starters. Where a format is specified by an employer, make sure you comply with it.

Online and hard copy application forms

Employers are increasingly making use of automated packages to harvest applications. It is very easy to click the 'send' button and immediately forget what you entered on the electronic form or even what the job was. Similarly, hard copy forms may be sent off without any record of what you wrote. To avoid embarrassment, keep a record of applications you make and what you entered on the form. Electronic versions can be recorded by using the keyboard *Print Screen* function or you can prepare and file these using a word processor. Should you be fortunate and find that your application is taken further, then you will be able to review what you wrote on your applications so that you follow through consistently with this at interview.

When using your CV to make an application for a job, it is vital that you tailor it to the job specification, so that you bring out the match with your qualifications, experience, skills and personality. You will often find a brief job description within the job advert or associated web-based material, or this may be provided as part of an application pack. For each position you should carry out a mapping exercise between the key elements of the job description and your own. This should take into account the following:

● The minimum qualifications and skills required. If you don't have these, it will probably not be worth applying.

● The specific experience, competences and qualities required. Importantly, present evidence that shows that you have these.

Table 33.1 Elements of a typical CV.

Element, with alternative headings	Usual contents
1 Personal details Name and contact details	Your full name, date of birth, contact address(es), contact phone/mobile numbers and email address. You don't have to include your sex, but may wish to, especially if your name could apply to a man or a woman.
2 Profile Career aim; Career objective; Personal profile	A summary of your career plans. Aspects of your goals and aspirations that you would like the employer to focus on. Your key attributes/strengths in the context of the post.
3 Education Qualifications; Education and qualifications	The qualifications you have already achieved including those that may be pending. Most people put current qualifications first, and then work backwards. State educational institutions, years of attendance and the academic year in which each qualification or set of qualifications was gained. Include more detail if it is relevant, e.g. aspects of a subject covered in courses. Give the title of your PhD, even if provisional.
4 Work experience Employment	Details of past and current work (both paid and voluntary). Include dates, employer's name and job title. You may also wish to add major duties if these are not obvious from the job title. Also include contributions to collegiate and departmental work as these community contributions can involve a variety of relevant skills. These work experiences should be arranged in reverse time sequence – from present to past.
5 Skills and personal qualities Skills and achievements; Skills and competences	An indication of the match between your abilities and the job description. You may wish to refer to examples and evidence here.
6 Interests and activities Interests; Leisure activities	This is a chance to show your character, and perhaps to indicate that you would make an interesting and enthusiastic colleague. Employers will use this section to build a picture of you as a person; however, they may be put off someone who appears quirky or bizarre. Also if this section is over-emphasised, they may assume that you have placed greater emphasis on your social life than on your studies. Choose interests which display potentially valuable aspects of your character, e.g. sports activities that indicate you are a good team member.
7 Referees References	This is where you provide the names and contact details for those who have agreed to provide a reference for you. At least one of these should be an academic referee.

- Anything beneficial you might add if you were appointed to the job, such as an IT or technical qualification gained in a particular module.

- Anything not stated in the job description, but implied, such as the ability to write or edit copy.

Tips for CV presentation

There are no hard and fast rules, but the following may help:

- Don't try to cram too much into your CV – the reader can only absorb the key points. They can always ask you more if they select you for interview.

- Avoid long paragraphs in favour of bullet points, as these are assimilated more readily.

- Use 'white space' to spread out the information so it is easy to read and the design is pleasing to the eye and is more readable.

- Use a single font throughout and avoid over-use of emphasis such as capital letters, italics and bold.

- Limited use of colour can look attractive, for instance in headings, and might mark your CV out from the rest. Do not overdo this, however, or it will lessen the impact and give an unfocused feel. Remember that colours will appear in greyscale or may even disappear if your CV is photocopied for interview panel members and may in fact dull down your document rather than brighten it.

Application letters

Your letter of application provides an additional chance to impress a potential employer. As with your CV, it should be well-presented and error-free. Use the normal format and style that you would for a formal business letter.

The content should include the following:

- both the name of the position you are applying for and any reference number that is given;

- the key qualifications, skills and qualities you feel you can offer;

- if possible, specific links between your CV and the job description;

- reference to your commitment and enthusiasm for the job;

- your career objectives and what you hope to gain from the job; and

- your contact details.

Personal statements

For some posts, you will be asked to provide a personal statement, which is a chance to expand on some of the points noted above for a standard application letter. As with your CV and covering letter, a personal statement should be closely linked to the job for which you are applying. This is your chance to stand out from other, similarly qualified, candidates.

If a format or content is suggested, then follow this carefully, and in particular, cover as directly as possible any areas that are specified.

Keep to any word limit that is given. Even if no limit is stated, write concisely and present things so that they can be easily assimilated, for example by using short paragraphs, headings and/or or bullet points.

Selecting referees

When you apply for any job, you will be expected to nominate at least two referees – people who know you and can comment on your character and suitability for the position. In choosing referees, select people who genuinely know you, and who can comment on different aspects of your CV. Typically, a postgraduate would pick one referee who knows about their undergraduate academic history, and one who can comment on their current PhD work (usually the supervisor).

You should contact your referees in advance to ask politely whether they would be willing to provide you with a reference; and at that time you could tell them about the specific position(s) you have applied for, or give them details of the sort of jobs you intend applying for. It is in your interest to provide your referees with an up-to-date CV as this will help them provide an effective reference. It is also good manners to let them know whether your application(s) were successful.

Preparing for interview

Being short-listed for a post is an achievement, but many people find the subsequent interview stage even more of a challenge. As well as the fact that you will be expected to answer difficult and unseen questions, you will be nervous because your chances of getting a coveted post may depend on your performance. There are various ways in which you can prepare before an interview.

- Carry out some research on the company and organisation, and the key figures on the interview panel, if you know who they are.

- Look again at the job description and how you can demonstrate the ability to carry out the duties of the post.

- If the post is professional or technical, revise relevant theory, techniques, practice and law. Anticipate, as best you can, how your area of expertise might relate to the recruiting organisation.

- Note questions you may have about the organisation and post.

- Ensure you can answer some of the more common interview questions, and where these appear tricky, evolve strategies for providing a positive slant to your answer.

- Think carefully about appropriate dress for the interview.

At the interview itself, focus on the following:

- When you are introduced to the panel, make eye contact with each member and smile at them.

- Where appropriate, give a firm, confident handshake.

- Adopt confident and relaxed body language and try not to fidget.

- Give informative answers of appropriate length – neither too short, nor too long; neither too shallow, nor too detailed.

- Speak clearly and to the person who asked the question, making occasional eye contact around the panel.

- Try to be positive about all questions and take all opportunities you can to mention relevant experiences.

- Be genuine, truthful and never waffle.

- Remember that the interview is a two-way process: be ready for the end of the interview, when applicants are traditionally asked whether they would like to ask any questions.

Good luck!

What will they ask me?

Here are some traditional interview questions – note that these may be wrapped in subtly different phrasing, or specifically related to the organisation and job description:

- What attracted you to this post?
- What makes you think you are the right person for this job?
- How did your degree and/or work experience prepare you for the challenges of this job?
- Please tell me about your experience doing X…
- Tell me about your interest in [a hobby or pastime]…
- What are your strengths?
- What are your weaknesses?
- What would you do if you held this post and the following scenario occurred…?
- How do you see your career here evolving?
- Could you tell me about…? [Techniques, procedures or legislation related to the role.]
- When would you be able to take up the post, if offered it?
- Seemingly 'off-the-wall' questions, such as 'Do you keep a tidy or an untidy desk?'
- Would you accept the post if offered and, if so, what salary are you looking for?
- Do you have any questions for us?

ACTION POINTS

33.1 Visit and explore on the Vitae website (*http://www.vitae.ac.uk*). This site is an extremely valuable resource and specifically targeted at doctoral students. It is managed by CRAC, the Careers Research and Advisory Centre.

33.2 Update your CV. Take full account of all the skills you have developed during your PhD including technical, teaching, teamwork, organisational and other competences.

33.3 Discuss your draft CV and careers prospects with a university careers advisor. They will be pleased to comment on its structure and content, and will be able to give advice about ways you might develop it in relation to your career goals and subject area.

LIST OF REFERENCES

Belbin®, 2012. *Team roles.* Available at: http://www.belbin.com/ [Accessed 1 August 2012].

Bloom, B. S., Englehart, M. D., Furst, E. J., Holl, W. H. and Krathwohl, D. R., 1956. *Taxonomy of educational objectives: cognitive domain.* New York: McKay.

Careers Research and Advisory Centre, 2010. *Researcher development statement.* Available at: http://www.vitae.ac.uk/CMS/files/upload/Researcher%20development%20statement.pdf [Accessed 23 July 2012].

Careers Research and Advisory Centre, 2012. *Planning your training.* Available at: http://www.vitae.ac.uk/researchers/1607/Planning-your-training.html [Accessed 23 July 2012].

CILIP, 2012. Chartered Institute of Library and Information Professionals: Information literacy: definition. Available at: http://www.cilip.org.uk/get-involved/advocacy/information-literacy/Pages/definition.aspx [Accessed 23 July 2012].

Cohen L., Manion, L. and Morrison, K., 2007. *Research methods in education*, 6th ed. London: Routledge-Falmer.

Crozier, J. and Gilmour, L., 2006. *Collin's A–Z thesaurus*, 2nd ed. London: Harper Collins.

Denzin, N. and Lincoln Y., eds., 2005. *The Sage handbook of qualitative research*, 3rd ed. London: Sage.

Krueger, R. A. and Casey, M. A., 2000. *Focus groups: a practical guide for applied research*, 3rd ed. Thousand Oaks, California: Sage Publications.

Leech, G., Conrad, S., Cruickshank, B. and Ivanic, R., 2001. *An A–Z of English grammar and usage*, 2nd ed. Harlow: Pearson Longman.

McMillan, K. M. and Weyers, J. D. B., 2012. *The study skills book*, 3rd ed. Harlow: Pearson Education.

McMillan, K. M. and Weyers, J. D. B., 2013. *How to cite, reference and avoid plagiarism at university.* Harlow: Pearson Education.

Ritter, R. M., 2005. *New Hart's rules: the handbook of style for writers and editors.* Oxford: Oxford University Press.

Robson, C., 2011. *Real world research*, 3rd ed. New York: John Wiley.

Sana, L., 2000. *Textbook of research ethics: theory and practice.* New York: Kluwer Academic.

SCONUL, 2011. Society of College, National and University Libraries: The Seven Pillars of Information Literacy model. Available at: http://www.sconul.ac.uk/groups/information_literacy/sp/moel.htiml [Accessed 23 July 2012].

Shamoo, A. E. and Resnik, D. B., 2009. *Responsible conduct of research*, 2nd ed. Oxford: Oxford University Press.

Stevenson, A., ed., 2007. *Shorter Oxford English dictionary*, 6th ed. Oxford: Oxford University Press.

Strauss, A. and Corbin, J., 2007. *Basics of qualitative research: techniques and procedures for developing grounded theory*, 3rd ed. London: Sage.

UK Research Councils, 2001. *Joint statement of the training requirements for research students*. Available at: http://www.vitae.ac.uk/cms/files/RCUK-Joint-Skills-Statement-2001.pdf [Accessed 23 July 2012].